The Essentials of Social Finance

The Essentials of Social Finance provides an interesting, accessible overview of this fascinating ecosystem, blending insights from finance and social entrepreneurship. It highlights the key challenges facing social finance, while also showcasing its vast opportunities.

Topics covered include microfinance, venture philanthropy, social impact bonds, crowdfunding, and impact measurement. Case studies are peppered throughout, and a balance of US, European, Asian, and Islamic perspectives are included. Each chapter contains learning objectives, discussion questions, and a list of key terms. There is also an appendix explaining key financial concepts for readers without a background in the subject, as well as downloadable PowerPoint slides to accompany each chapter.

This will be a valuable text for students of finance, investment, social entrepreneurship, social innovation, and related areas. It will also be useful to researchers, professionals, and policy-makers interested in social finance.

Andreas Andrikopoulos is Associate Professor of Finance at the University of the Aegean, Greece.

The Essentials of Social Finance

Andreas Andrikopoulos
Translated by *Annie Triantafillou*

Routledge
Taylor & Francis Group

LONDON AND NEW YORK

First published in English 2022
by Routledge
4 Park Square, Milton Park, Abingdon, Oxon OX14 4RN

and by Routledge
605 Third Avenue, New York, NY 10158

Routledge is an imprint of the Taylor & Francis Group, an informa business

© 2022 Andreas Andrikopoulos and Propobos

Translated by Annie Triantafillou

Originally published in Greek as 'Κοινωνική Χρηματοοικονομική' by Propobos Publications.

British Library Cataloguing-in-Publication Data
A catalogue record for this book is available from the British Library

Library of Congress Cataloging-in-Publication Data
Names: Andrikopoulos, Andreas, author. | Triantafillou, Annie, translator.
Title: Social finance / Andreas Andrikopoulos ; [translated by Annie Triantafillou].
Other titles: Koinōnikē chrēmatooikonomikē. English
Description: Milton Park, Abingdon, Oxon ; New York, NY : Routledge, 2021. | Includes bibliographical references and index.
Identifiers: LCCN 2021027726 (print) | LCCN 2021027727 (ebook) | ISBN 9781032136622 (hardback) | ISBN 9781032136608 (paperback) | ISBN 9781003230366 (ebook)
Subjects: LCSH: Finance—Social aspects. | Investments—Social aspects. | Community development—Finance.
Classification: LCC HG101 .A5413 2021 (print) | LCC HG101 (ebook) | DDC 332—dc23
LC record available at https://lccn.loc.gov/2021027726
LC ebook record available at https://lccn.loc.gov/2021027727

ISBN: 978-1-032-13662-2 (hbk)
ISBN: 978-1-032-13660-8 (pbk)
ISBN: 978-1-003-23036-6 (ebk)

DOI: 10.4324/9781003230366

Typeset in Bembo
by Apex CoVantage, LLC

Access the Support Materials: www.routledge.com/9781032136608

Contents

Contents

Part I

Social entrepreneurship and social finance

1

Social entrepreneurship

After reading this chapter, you will be able to:

1 Identify the role of the social entrepreneur in the social enterprise
2 Distinguish between the different types of social enterprises
3 Recognize the various components of the business plan of a social enterprise
4 Evaluate the contribution of social economy and social entrepreneurship to welfare and economic growth
5 Explain the importance of impact measurement for social entrepreneurship

INTRODUCTION

Entrepreneurship denotes the undertaking of risk for the purposes of identifying, creating, and deploying opportunities to design innovative products and services. **Innovation** in the context of entrepreneurship signifies the attainment of sustainable competitive advantage that secures profitability by way of managing change and satisfying customer needs in a manner that is superior to that of other enterprises. The basic pillar of entrepreneurship is the **enterprise**, the primary unit of production of goods and services, with the entrepreneur in the role of a catalyst, bringing together and organizing capital and labor, planning the production process, and establishing the strategic orientation of the production unit.

DOI: 10.4324/9781003230366-2

An enterprise does not stand in an economic, social, or political void. It constitutes a node in the nexus of production relationships and a distinct point in the historical trajectory of the society in which it operates. The significance of an enterprise for the economy stems from its interrelation with other nodes of the production nexus, such as the entrepreneur, the employees of the enterprise, the investors who provide it with capital, its suppliers, customers, and rivals, as well as the state.[1]

Social entrepreneurship is part of the broader field of entrepreneurship. As such, it retains some of its basic traits, although it is different in terms of organization, operation and purpose.[2] Social entrepreneurship denotes

> Social entrepreneurship denotes risk-taking, as well as creation and deployment of opportunities for the purposes of generating social value.

risk-taking, as well as creation and deployment of opportunities for the purposes of generating **social value**. Social value denotes the promotion of social welfare through innovative production of **public goods** (Box 1.1 defines and explains the notion of public goods).[3] While profitability and social impact are complementary objectives of the social enterprise, social impact has priority (reversal of this priority is often called **mission drift** for social enterprises).[4]

Box 1.1 Public goods

Public goods are defined in economics as goods that are characterized by non-rivalry and non-excludability. Specifically:

Non-rivalrous are those goods that can be consumed by many consumers simultaneously, as their consumption does not affect availability of supply.[5] Public libraries, motorways, orphanages, policing of public places, and the like constitute examples of non-rivalrous goods. The use of a motorway by a driver would not exclude other drivers from using the motorway at the same time. Similarly, local police safeguard civilians who reside in a certain area, as well as anyone who moves to that area.

Non-excludable goods are those goods that are available to all, meaning that no one can be excluded from their consumption. Public schools, hospitals, parks, athletic grounds, and the like constitute examples of non-excludable goods. For example, primary schooling is compulsory for all children above the age of 6; playgrounds are open to all civilians (nobody is excluded based on their income for example).

In accordance with the definition of public goods, it is worth making the following observations:

1   Public goods are not free of charge, in the sense that even if they do not involve a direct charge to the user, they use up society's resources. Residents of a certain area, for example, may not be charged for using the playground, but construction of the playground involves costs (e.g., use of land, construction materials, the services of an engineer, a subcontractor, and the members of the local city council). Maintenance costs also need to be taken into account.

2 No good is fully public (i.e., non-rivalrous and non-excludable). For example, the capacity of a local police station to provide protection to the residents of a certain area is constrained by the increase in the local population above a certain level. Similarly, it is possible that the public nursery school in a certain area does not have the capacity to serve all the children who reside in that area, excluding some children from the service based on their parents' income. Other examples include exclusion of drivers who do not pay tolls from using parts of the national motorway network or restriction of access to the city center based on the last digit of car number plates.

3 Most goods and services have some public goods characteristics, in the sense that they may incur benefits and costs to parties that are not directly involved in their production and/or consumption. For example, the screening of a film in an open-air cinema makes it occasionally possible to somebody living in a close-by block of flats to watch the film from their balcony without paying a price. By contrast, a film screening may disturb a neighbor who is not involved in the transaction between the party that screens the film and the party that pays a ticket to watch it. Similarly, in an agricultural area, the cleaning of a backyard of dry weeds does not only affect those involved in the transaction, namely the owner of the backyard and the worker who cleans it up; it also affects other neighbors who, incidentally and without contributing to the costs, happen to be protected from the danger of fire or snakes. In the same line of reasoning, a book transaction does not just involve the publisher, the author, and the reader. It affects the residents of the area where the paper factory is located and could also affect society at large by influencing the lives of people who neither produce nor read the book (for example, the book of the New Testament does not only affect those who produce, sell, or read it; it has a broader impact upon society).

For example, Thistle Farms is a social enterprise established by Becca Stevens in 1997.[6] Its mission is protection and empowerment of women who have been victims of sexual abuse, trafficking, or have escaped drug addiction. Thistle Farms provides these women with accommodation, training, employment, as well as remuneration for their work, which is mainly in the production of deodorants, cosmetics, and jewelry. The enterprise maintains its social mandate, even though it makes its products available in the market at prices that make the business financially sustainable. Auticon is another case of social enterprise. It was founded by Dirk Müller–Remus in 2011 in Berlin, inspired by an Asperger's syndrome diagnosis for his son. It provides software development, quality assurance, and data analytics services to a wide range of companies. All its information technology consultants are on the autism spectrum. It expanded to UK in 2016 and now is also active in France, Switzerland, USA, Italy, Canada, and Australia. Its investors include Ananda Social Venture Fund, Virgin Group, and Esmée Fairbairn Foundation.[7] While Auticon pursues profit and growth, the social inclusion of people on the autism spectrum is a fundamental component of its identity. Box 1.2 presents the case of LivelyHoods, a social enterprise that is active in Kenya.

Box 1.2 LivelyHoods

LivelyHoods addresses social and environmental problems in Kenyan urban slums.[8] It was founded in 2011 by Tania Laden and Maria Springer as a US-based non-profit organization and a Kenyan social enterprise. In Kenyan slums approximately 70% of youth is unemployed, with employment being more difficult for women. Moreover, most households burn biomass for cooking which is emitting toxic fumes that are responsible for the death of many Kenyans. Environmental problems are aggravated by deforestation, as 83% of forests in Kenya have been depleted over the past 50 years. LivelyHoods' response is to employ and train young Kenyans who sell environment-friendly products in the slums. Thus, on the one hand young Kenyans find employment and training sales and business and, on the other hand, living conditions are improved with the use of solar products (lamps, mainly), clean-energy cookstoves, and household appliances that save energy (hence costs), protect the environment and health in Kenyan slums. Sixty-one percent of LivelyHoods staff are female and since 2011 LivelyHoods has created almost 2,000 jobs, trained more than 4,000 Kenyan youth, has generated savings in fuel worth more than 22 million US dollars and has saved more than 700,000 trees. Perhaps the most important achievement, in terms of fighting poverty and sustaining social cohesion, is that 50% of the salesforce goes on to start their own businesses, and the likelihood of poverty for the trained salesforce drops by almost 90% for the first year after training. LivelyHoods has received many awards and its funding partners include organizations such as USAID, EEP Africa, the Rockefeller Foundation, the Global Alliance for Clean Cookstoves, and the Osprey Foundation.

Social entrepreneurship focuses on addressing economic and social inequalities by providing food, accommodation, medical care, and education to those in need, as well as by protecting the environment and providing international aid in cases of natural disasters, epidemics, or wars.[9] Given that such provisions also constitute public policy areas, it can be argued that social entrepreneurship has a complementary – or substitute – role in relation to analogous efforts on the part of the state. For example, a social enterprise whose mission is rehabilitation of people addicted to narcotic substances operates in a field of action that is partly complementary and partly substitutive to the respective public rehabilitation center. The unique positioning of the social enterprise amid the private and the public sectors – in the same terrain where the **civil society**[10] is positioned – brings out the role of the **social entrepreneur**, a role between the conventional entrepreneur, who seeks profit, and the public official, who engages in the production of public goods on behalf of the government (Figure 1.1). For the purposes of

> Social entrepreneurship focuses on addressing economic and social inequalities by providing food, accommodation, medical care, and education to those in need, as well as by protecting the environment and providing international aid in cases of natural disasters, epidemics, or wars.

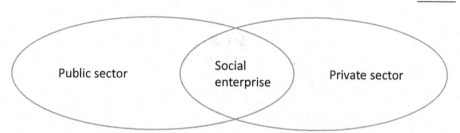

Figure 1.1 Social enterprise, the private sector, and the public sector

this book, conventional enterprises are defined as for-profit businesses that do not have a social mandate.

Being involved in the production of public goods, social entrepreneurs are situated between the private and the public sectors. Their positioning also determines the key challenge they face, namely the production of public goods on the one hand and the pursuit of financial viability on the other. Viability of the production process by the individual firm depends on fluctuations of demand for the products it produces, as well as on fluctuations of supply of labor, capital, and other resources that are necessary for the production process. This is in sharp contrast to the case of production of public goods by the state, which is far more stable (albeit still subject to the rules of fiscal sustainability). For example, a social enterprise that sells confectioneries produced by socio-psychologically challenged workers employed in the enterprise must nevertheless attend to profitability considerations, as well as meet its financial obligations towards its creditors, employees, and associates, while managing to serve its customers in a satisfactory manner.

Social entrepreneurship covers a wide range of initiatives and social interventions. However, the main common characteristic of all social enterprises is that their purpose extends beyond the pursuit of profit.[11] To qualify as social enterprises, businesses need to aim at making a positive **social impact** in a way that is not only distinct from their profitability, but also occasionally against it (Figure 1.2). However, not every pursuit of social impact counts as social entrepreneurship (for example, the action taken by a tobacco company to inform youngsters about the harmful impact of smoking does not render it a social enterprise).

Social entrepreneurship is also related to **social innovation**. Social innovation often emerges in the form of a partnership between the public sector, the private sector, and the civil society[12] and often extends beyond the boundaries of social entrepreneurship to addressing social problems with new effective and sustainable structures. For example, collaboration between banks, the public sector, volunteers, and private organizations offering social services constituted innovation in the case of reintegration of former prisoners in the community in the city of Peterborough, UK. Social innovation in this case was the change in policy against crime per se, which went beyond the boundaries of social entrepreneurship action for each of the participants.

Social entrepreneurship is associated with activities that are not atypical of recent economic history. The cooperative movement of Robert Owen in the 19th century

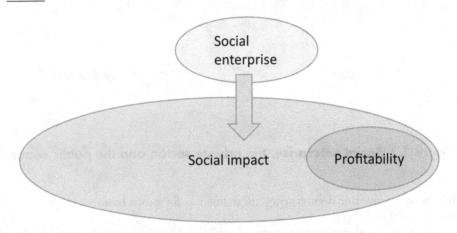

Figure 1.2 Objectives of the social enterprise

constitutes one case in point in the modern trajectory of **social economy**. **Co-operative banking** and entrepreneurship emerging over the past three centuries, along with the forms of cooperative enterprise that occurred following the initiatives of Jean-Baptiste André Godin in 19th-century France, also qualify as social entrepreneurship. Recently, **microfinance** in emerging economies brought into light the ways in which banking activities may combine profit with financial support for very poor people who would otherwise be excluded from conventional money and capital markets, incorporating the specific priorities and structures of local communities. The awarding of the Peace Nobel Prize to Muhammad Yunus for his pioneering work with Grameen Bank in Bangladesh highlights both the economic significance and the distinctive political weight of social entrepreneurship and social finance (see Chapter 5 for a discussion on particular characteristics of microfinance).

SOCIAL ECONOMY AND SOCIAL ENTERPRISE

By and large, the term **social economy** designates the coupling of the private with the public sector in production processes. Thus, the social economy is about involvement of private entities, whose mandate is enhancement of social welfare or preservation of the environment, in the production of public goods (mitigation of social exclusion and extreme poverty are characteristic examples of social-economy objectives). In cases where it may not be possible for the public sector to respond to such challenges in an effective manner through social policy, the private sector may provide these activities in the typical profit-seeking mode. Social economy is often called the **third sector** or **social sector** of the economy and extends beyond social enterprises to incorporate a wide range of civil-society organizations that enjoy the advantages associated with the flexibility of the private sector, avoiding the rigid (at times) administrative framework of state services and filling the void in social, educational, cultural, and environmental policies of the government. Social economy is a rapidly growing sector, which employs about 6% of the labor force and 10% of all businesses in the European Union.[13] Thus, analysis of social economy and social entrepreneurship constitutes an emerging field in the economic theory of the firm, the study of markets, and economic development.

The term social economy is based on the distinction of the private from the public sector of the economy. However, distinguishing between private and public productive activities is not always straightforward, as different criteria may designate different boundaries between the two sectors. The services offered by private and public hospitals, for example, may be similar in nature but quite different in terms of sources of finance and groups of patients admitted and/or treated by the hospital. Likewise, a municipal recreation facility may be offering private services similar to those offered by a respective private facility, nevertheless: a) it does not pursue profitability as a target over and above the welfare of the local community, and b) in the event that the operation is not financially viable, its bailout may be guaranteed by the local government. In the same line of argument, a museum that has been constructed with a private donation and requires an admission fee from visitors may offer a service that is identical to that of a public museum constructed by the Ministry of Culture (the public good offered in this particular case could be, for instance, national history). The two organizations primarily differ in the diverse ways of financing their infrastructure and operations.

> Distinguishing between private and public productive activities is not always straightforward, as different criteria may designate different boundaries between the two sectors.

SOCIAL ENTERPRISES: TAXONOMY AND DELINEATION

The types of social enterprises vary according to their stance on profit, their legal form, their relationship with their sponsors, the state, its employees, and the communities they are trying to support.[14,15,16] According to profit orientation, social enterprises can be distinguished in:

1 Purely nonprofit organizations, offering their services free of charge, supported largely by volunteer work and donations.
2 For-profit enterprises that acquire factors of production and offer goods and services in market terms, albeit maintaining focus on social and environmental issues.
3 Hybrid organizations that combine market characteristics with solidarity and philanthropy, offering services at lower-than-market prices and, correspondingly, paying lower amounts to the factors of production that they employ (e.g., their employees may not be volunteers, but receive lower remuneration than the going market rate).

Another categorization of social enterprises relates to their position across the public–private sector axis. In this analysis, social enterprises are treated as connecting different production modalities. For example, the production of public goods with the participation of the private sector, which constitutes the basis of the social enterprise, may stem from collaboration of the private sector with the government, collaboration of the private enterprise with charity organizations and, of course, collaboration of charity organizations with governments. All three types of organization may occasionally be combined. Social impact bonds for the reintegration in society of former prisoners in the state of Massachusetts constitutes a case in point (see Chapter 5).

Although a large number of organizations and individuals may be seeking to supply products of a public goods nature, social entrepreneurship has special characteristics that distinguish it from other forms of social intervention. Such characteristics include emphasis on innovation and financial viability of the enterprise and, more importantly, emphasis on production of public goods. Even though certain activities of the public and the private economy are related to social entrepreneurship, they are clearly different from it. For example, action taken by a company outside its core productive activities, for instance in the context of its marketing communication strategy, do not qualify as social entrepreneurship. Even though resources are allocated to social action, social responsibility does not constitute a big enough and important enough part of the organization's core activities. For example, a telecommunications company that sponsors a school remains a telecommunications company; it does not become an educational institution. Furthermore, in these cases, innovation and entrepreneurship center on production of private goods and services related to the core activities of the company rather than the production of public goods. For example, a telecommunications company may allocate resources to innovate by offering new subscription package services. At the same time, it may also sponsor meals to homeless people. However, the company's sponsorship of meals for the homeless cannot have the innovative characteristics of a catering enterprise that would engage in a similar action as its core business.

In the same line of reasoning, not all activist initiatives lie on the social entrepreneurship terrain. A group that cares about the environment may organize a protest against air pollution or some other event aiming to increase public awareness on the subject. This, however, is not entrepreneurial activity for it does not constitute an enterprise, whose core activity is the organization of environmental ventures based on innovation and financial viability of operations. Similarly, a private donation to help a community cope with adversity in the aftermath of a natural disaster does not make the donor a social entrepreneur. The donor would be a social entrepreneur if s/he had constructed a production mechanism that would be strategically oriented to innovatively resolving problems caused by natural disasters in a financially viable manner (Figure 1.3). Although these cases are not examples of social entrepreneurship, they do occur in the context of social economy, as the latter is a broader concept that encompasses social enterprise. Indicatively, many of the activities of charity groups and organizations with social and political interest are part of social economy, even though they do not constitute entrepreneurship.

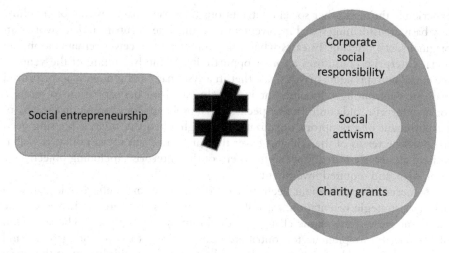

Figure 1.3 Delineating social entrepreneurship

THE SOCIAL ENTREPRENEUR AND THE EMERGENCE OF SOCIAL ENTERPRISE

Entrepreneurial risk-taking for the social enterprise

The social entrepreneur is a catalyst in the identification of opportunities for the establishment of a social enterprise; the choice of its strategic orientation, identification, organization, and exploitation of the factors of production needed to attain social impact; as well as the undertaking and management of entrepreneurial and financial risk. What distinguishes the social entrepreneur from the conventional entrepreneur is the emphasis placed by the former on combating social problems and creating social value. At the microeconomic level, creation of value involves economic outcomes that enhance welfare for society.[17] An obstacle to defining the social entrepreneur's profile is the difficulty to elucidate the social problem. For example, in certain strands of thought in economic liberalism, income inequality is not an issue; it is considered to be the outcome of individual choice and an inevitable characteristic of the market economy.[18] Likewise, homosexuality is prohibited in certain religious contexts; therefore, challenges faced by homosexual couples are not widely accepted as social problems in these communities.

> What distinguishes the social entrepreneur from the conventional entrepreneur is the emphasis placed by the former on combating social problems and creating social value.

Social enterprise starts with identification of a social problem that is important for society and is systematically overlooked by the state and other social enterprises. The creation of a social enterprise is directly related to the incentive of the social entrepreneur to contribute to society. Often social entrepreneurs have acquired experience through other social contributions they have made, usually on a voluntary basis, transforming social involvement to a full-time occupation that involves an original social offering. In cases where the entrepreneur receives remuneration, the social enterprise constitutes a career opportunity. At the beginning of the venture, the social entrepreneurs may move either in a systematic fashion, with an organized plan for confronting difficulties, or intuitively, based on her aspiration to create a social enterprise and confront the specific social problem. For example, in the case of establishment of a nonprofit organization through a bequest, there is pressing need to apply the terms of the will and cover the gap in relevant social policy, as well as to have an orderly plan about the first steps of the enterprise, including objectives, a legal form, and required investment.

A successful entrepreneur needs to have the qualities of an effective leader, who has clear strategic orientation, capability to inspire his associates and to adapt the social enterprise to dynamic changes in the business environment.[19] The aspiration of the social entrepreneur to contribute constructively to confronting social and environmental problems is a necessary condition for the establishment of the social venture, albeit not always sufficient for successful adjustment to the volatile business environment of the social enterprise. The skills of the entrepreneur as far as the organization of the productive process, the adequate management of human resources and the contacts with funding parties are concerned, along with timely adjustment to the social, economic, and political circumstances are critical for the social enterprise. Moreover, entrepreneurial skills go far beyond the initial enthusiasm and the intention to offer on the part of the social entrepreneur or the generosity of a donor, ultimately shaping effective communication with the community the social enterprise aims to support.

Similar to conventional entrepreneurs, social entrepreneurs must be capable to undertake **risk** and expose themselves to **uncertainty**. Uncertainty denotes structural causes that are unanticipated by the social entrepreneur but co-define viability of the social enterprise and capability to successfully address social and environmental problems. Uncertainty presents social enterprises with opportunities and threats and relates to both internal and external factors. Internal uncertainty is about sufficiency of organizational resources, maintaining a positive working environment for employees, as well as flexibility to adjust the organization and its operations as new challenges come up (for instance, potential conflicts arising from a change in the composition of the board of directors). External uncertainty relates to economy-wide fluctuations as well as changes in technology, regulations, and the challenges the social enterprise intends to mitigate (e.g., the outbreak of war may lead to inflows of refugees) regarding the impact of the social enterprise on society and the environment. External uncertainty also involves ambiguities in the relationship between the social enterprise and other nodes of the **social enterprise nexus**, notably the state (changes in policies and regulation), those who finance the operations of the enterprise, competitors, suppliers, other related professionals, and the community. The network structure of social

> Uncertainty denotes structural causes that are unanticipated by the social entrepreneur but co-define sustainability of the social enterprise and capability to successfully address social and environmental problems.

entrepreneurship also makes it clear that the social enterprise is not the opus of a single social entrepreneur; it stems from continuous interaction between many and diverse entities.[20]

Confronting uncertainty requires identification of as many sources of uncertainty as possible, an effort to analyze such structural causes and a plan of response to each possible outcome. Rather than adopting a fatalistic approach to the unforeseeable future, efforts should be directed to analyzing the political, economic, and social environment of the social enterprise, as well as its internal context, such that changes and challenges to be managed by the social entrepreneur can become predictable. For example, a social enterprise that provides medical care for refugees may be facing uncertainty with regard to refugee flows, which could be foreseen by analyzing the political and economic developments in the countries that refugees leave and the countries they head to. Similarly, although inflow of funds to the social enterprise for the coming year may be uncertain, the social enterprise should be able to arrive at an estimate by examining the financial condition of its main supporters. A potential economic recession might reduce funding through donations by civilians, who may nevertheless contribute with their personal work. Likewise, the prospect of funding from intergovernmental institutions, such as the European Commission, could be detected by analyzing the economic and political context of their leadership. The response of the social enterprise to different scenarios must not be fragmented; it must have a strategic orientation that will help it maintain cohesion. Uncertainty in the context of social entrepreneurship implies exposure to **change** and the management of uncertainty is equivalent to the management of change. Clearly, effective management of change is a requirement for survival and attainment of the strategic objectives of the social enterprise.[21]

As in the case of conventional enterprises, a successful response to an uncertain business environment must be innovative. For the social enterprise, innovation does not just comprise a new idea or invention, but also satisfaction of social and environmental needs in a way that secures the support of all stakeholders: those who work for the enterprise, those who finance the enterprise, other enterprises, the state, and the community. Thus, innovation denotes changes in the methods and the objectives of production of the social enterprise that result in sustainable attainment of its mission and a steadily positive contribution to social welfare. The preferences of the community that benefits from social entrepreneurship and the social framework in which the social enterprise operates define not only the content of innovation, but also its sustainability. For example, if a social enterprise supports formerly addicted individuals who sell clothing that they manufacture, its orientation and success are determined by its response to the needs of rehabilitated individuals who are striving for employment and integration in society.

Establishment of the social enterprise and business analysis

Similar to conventional enterprises, establishment of a social enterprise encompasses identification of purpose, size, legal form, location, funding, as well as organization of procedures and articulation of network. Responses to this are for the most part overlapping. Articulation of network is connected to funding, as the firm's financial supporters constitute a central node in the network, with the flow of funding signifying the edges. Funding is also connected with the size of the enterprise, as the amount of self-employed capital is one of the factors that determine the size of social enterprise. The choice of location is linked with the choice of legal form, to the extent that the enterprise must uphold the local institutional framework of the area where it resides. Moreover, the choice of location of the enterprise may be related to its objective: for example, it may choose to locate itself close to the area where the particular social problem it aims to resolve has arisen. The organization of procedures is directly linked with the objectives and the relationships of the enterprise with other nodes of its network, as well as with its legal form, which sets boundaries to the pursuit of objectives, funding, as well as operations. In the case of Greece, for example, Law 4430/2016 defines the main targets of social cooperative enterprises, their administration, as well as the way of distributing their profits (see Box 1.3 for the regulatory framework of social economy and social entrepreneurship in Greece).

> The establishment of a social enterprise encompasses identification of purpose, size, legal form, location, funding, as well as organization of procedures and articulation of network.

Box 1.3 Regulatory framework for social entrepreneurship – the case of Greece

In Greece, Law 4430/2016 defines the main types of social enterprises, the framework in which they operate, as well as the content of social and solidarity economy (Law 4430/2016 replaced Law 4018/2011 that introduced social economy in Greece).[22] The main social economy form of business organization in Greece is the Social Cooperative Enterprise,[23] which has a social mandate, while also being engaged in commercial activities.[24] Social Cooperative Enterprises are registered as Social Cooperative "Integration Enterprises" or Social Cooperative "Collective and Social Benefit Enterprises". The former are categorized as Social Cooperative Integration Enterprises for Special Groups, Social Cooperative Integration Enterprises for Vulnerable Groups, or Limited Liability Social Cooperatives. Based on Greek law, they are active in activities pertaining to sustainable development or provide social services of general interest. Social services of general interest are defined as services that are accessible by all in society, promote the quality of life and provide social protection to the elderly, infants and children, the impaired, and the chronically ill. They include education, health, social housing, social meals, childcare, long-term care, and social work. They are complementary to the general obligation of the government to exercise social policy.

Social cooperative enterprise membership is open to legal entities and individuals. Participation of the former is limited to one-third of the total number of members. The minimum number of members required for establishment of a social cooperative "integration enterprise" is seven members. In Greece, establishment of a social cooperative "collective and social benefits enterprise" requires at least five members. Each member owns at least one cooperative share. The value of each share cannot be below €100. Shares are acquired on the basis of a minimum monetary contribution, which is specified in the bylaws of each social enterprise.

All members participate in the general assembly by one vote, independently of the number of shares owned. While social enterprises may earn profits, they are not permitted to distribute dividends to their members. Instead, they are required to maintain 5% of their profit in the form of reserves. The remaining 95% is reinvested towards expansion of business operations and activities, enhancement of productivity of employees, and increase in employment opportunities.

Limited liability social cooperatives constitute a special case of social cooperative enterprises.[25] The Limited Liability Social Cooperative of the Psychiatric Health Centre of the Dodecanese established on the island of Leros, Greece in 2002 is a case in point. The purpose of the enterprise is to integrate people with psychiatric conditions in the economic and social life to the extent made possible through the enterprise's commercial character and economic activity. The enterprise is affiliated with the Public Hospital – Psychiatric Health Centre of Leros and provides help to people with socio-psychological issues. Commercial activities of the cooperative include beekeeping, production and sale of confectionaries, as well as supply chain services. Its members include professionals in the field of psychiatry (maximum 45% of the total number of members) and individuals over 15 years of age with psychiatric medical issues (at least 35% of the total number of members).

Market research prior to the establishment of an enterprise usually starts with **locating opportunities** for viable and successful entrepreneurial action.[26] The type of opportunity associated with the launching of a social enterprise demonstrates the main difference between conventional and social entrepreneurship: the prospect of low or zero profitability would not constitute reason for starting a conventional enterprise. Locating opportunity plays a catalyst role in the genesis of an entrepreneurial idea, based on comprehensive analysis of technological, demographic, political, economic, and social characteristics of its architects. In the case of the social enterprise, opportunity could be in the form of a new institutional framework that is conducive to a certain type of enterprise. Furthermore, identifying opportunity could relate to an important social or environmental problem that cannot be effectively resolved by the state or other social enterprises. Of course, recognizing opportunity does not just require identifying a social problem. It also presupposes an estimate of the extent and the dynamics of the problem and, perhaps more importantly, evaluation of the effectiveness of currently available solutions. Taking advantage of opportunity depends on the strong points of the social venture and the social entrepreneurs themselves, such as awareness of a large fraction of the population for the need to support the social purpose of the new enterprise or reinforcement of volunteerism as a political stance and way of life. For example, in the case of a social enterprise that provides legal services to socially excluded civilians, the legal background of the founders or their professional network of notaries and judges could constitute the niche of the enterprise. Furthermore, starting a venture of this type requires management of challenges, such as unavailability of funding or lack of trained personnel.

Starting a social enterprise, the entrepreneur must also confront issues pertaining to **competition**. Social enterprises do not compete against each other as conventional enterprises do by trying to increase profitability in a certain segment of the market. Nevertheless, they try to survive in a competitive environment offering their clients a price-quality combination for the products they produce that is being continuously compared and contrasted to that of rivals. For example, a social cooperative enterprise that produces and sells honey made by people with psycho-social problems is still called upon to present a final product in the market that will be superior to that of other producers.

In any event, since the purpose of the social enterprise is to confront a certain social problem, similar action taken by a number of social enterprises is positive, as it could potentially allow each enterprise to channel resources and focus on different social or environmental challenges. However, as social enterprises are productive mechanisms, just like conventional enterprises, they do face limited resources for the materialization of their productive objectives. Thus, the notion of competition appears to be multi-faceted, including access to capital funding (donors, lenders, state and supra-state funding), employment (especially specialized or volunteer work), channels of communication with the population that benefits from the social enterprise, and development of a communication and collaboration with all **stakeholders**.[27,28] For instance, government policy to confront a certain social problem (reintegrating of former convicts in Peterborough, UK) limits the expediency of the social intervention from the third sector (the government stopped some of the actions that supported that particular social innovation). Ability to differentiate a new social enterprise from private and public organizations that produce similar public goods and definition of the possibility and prospect for innovation stem from the analysis of the business environment of the private and public organizations that support the production of public goods. Furthermore, the expediency of establishment of a social enterprise is shaped by analysis of the environment in which the enterprise operates. Social entrepreneurs may choose to materialize their social purpose either through enhancement of an already existing enterprise (e.g., providing funds or volunteer work) or through establishment of a new enterprise.

Important challenges also stem on the front of human resources who often are enthusiastic **volunteers**. Organizational skills and other qualities are also required if volunteers are to constitute a factor of production the entrepreneur can count on in the longer term. In general, the cohesion and resilience of the social enterprise include facing up to a heterogeneous set of employees. Both volunteers and paid employees attending to a certain social or environmental problem start from a different basis. Volunteers tend to be educated, socially and professionally extroverted people whose main incentive is social contribution and occasionally personal enhancement. Volunteers also vary in terms of their commitment to a welfare purpose depending on gender, age: the proportion of voluntary work is higher for men than for women and for adolescents than for over-55-year-olds).[29] The difficulty faced by the social enterprise as far as management of volunteers is concerned resembles the challenges faced in terms of its leadership. The intention for social contribution and the passion for work do not always substitute for the lack of training and skills that are required for the sound operation of an enterprise and, more importantly, for the production of public goods in an innovative, effective and financially viable manner. Furthermore, potential lack of skills does not constitute a problem just for the volunteers. It is often an issue for other employees too, as very few of them are trained on issues of social economy and administration of social enterprises.[30] One more challenge in the management of employees of the social enterprise is incorporation of methods of human resources management, while maintaining the prospect of productive efficiency on the one hand and the prospect of social welfare contribution on the other.

The business plan

The **business plan** plays a decisive role in the emergence and viability of a social enterprise, just like in the case of a conventional enterprise. It is essential in **investment readiness** of the social enterprise, that is, in its acceptability by capital providers. Planning is based on the vision and the strategy of social entrepreneurs about the social problem that they intend to confront, as well as on the way that they apprehend social welfare. The business plan reflects the main scenarios for the evolution of the internal and external environment of the enterprise, as well as responses to changes in its business environment. In addition, the business plan permits the social enterprise to form a more systematic view about its future, integrate its activities, and determine the required resources it needs. Especially regarding resources, the business plan is quite helpful in raising funds (e.g., in a presentation to creditors and investors), reflecting expectations about the future, reducing uncertainty, and adjusting correspondingly the resources that the entrepreneur is willing to invest in the social venture. Moreover, the business plan may serve as a point of reference for measurement of the effectiveness of the social enterprise in terms of utilization of resources and meeting its objectives.

In general, the business plan of the social enterprise must include the elements in Figure 1.4.

♦ Social enterprise objectives, along with vision and aims of its founders. Objectives must be realistic, compatible with the vision of the social entrepreneur, and stated in both qualitative and quantitative terms, thus making the utilization of resources and the effort to materialize aims more effective.

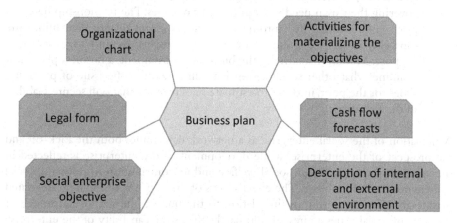

Figure 1.4 Business plan of a social enterprise

- Legal form of the enterprise, which is crucial for its viability and success.[31]
- Activities that need to be pursued to attain objectives.
- Organizational chart and basic operations.
- Description of the internal and external environment. The internal environment includes organizational resources such as organizational culture, information, management, capital, and people. The external environment includes competition (for raising funds in order to confront similar social and environmental problems), the relevant **regulatory framework**, economy-wide structures and characteristics of the capital market, the product market, and the labor market where the social enterprise operates. It also includes the political and social environment, available technology for the production of public goods, characteristics of the main stakeholders with whom the enterprise is in contact, and the natural environment that defines the environmental challenges of producing public goods.[32]
- Projection of cash flows and flows of required resources in general, such as volunteer work and donations in kind. Projections pertain to allocation of resources for the production process, revenue from the sale of public goods, and funding. They are important as they specify the capability of the social enterprise to cover the fixed and operational costs, as well as viability of the enterprise in the context of different scenarios of changes of the social economy environment. Especially in the case of social enterprises that sell public goods for a (usually low) price, cost accounting is crucial for the planning process, so that the enterprise remains viable while avoiding overcharging (as the attainment of the social target is more important than profitability). Cost accounting is also crucial for the price–quality relationship of the goods offered in comparison to similar goods produced by the private or the public sector. In this analysis, evaluation of quality denotes the way in which the specific good or service is apprehended by the consumer who pays for it. If, for example, a shoe company offers a pair of shoes to poor people for every pair it sells, its price policy must take into account the prices of rival companies, as well as the perceived benefit by consumers in both covering a social need and covering their own need to acquire a pair of shoes. The relationship between price (apprehended by customers and citizens) and quality determines the capability of the social enterprise to survive financially and attain its social purpose. Moreover, analyzing the business environment, a business plan must examine what other social action is taken to address the issue of providing shoes for the poor, in order to estimate sales revenue that will secure viability of the enterprise.

Articulation of the social enterprise as a network determines both the kick-off and the prospect of the enterprise, while development of the enterprise is reflected in the apparent impact it has on social welfare and its contribution to resolving social and environmental problems. The effectiveness of the network of funding, associated private and public institutions (in relation to the budget, the size of personnel, or the scale of social issues addressed) ultimately affects the capability of the enterprise to fulfill its mission. Failure and closure of a social enterprise comes as a result of problematic operation of this network and difficulty to adapt and be flexible so as to respond to changes in the internal and external environment (e.g., insufficient access to capital or volunteer work).

Every element of the business environment that determines the start of the social enterprise also defines its ability to survive and develop. In the first place, commencing operations based on donations and an initial capital to set up activities has a limited time horizon with respect to financial viability: at some point capital is exhausted and the lure of new donations is not always straightforward and/or feasible. Confronting this challenge often requires securing alternative sources of finance from state and supranational institutions (EU programs, local authorities resources, state investment programs, and the like), as well as access to organized money and capital markets to secure, for example, bank loans. Especially in the case of funding through banks or private investors (rather than donations), financial viability implies that the social enterprise needs to have revenues from productive and commercial activities to secure its financial viability without compromising its social character for the sake of profitability.

SOCIAL ENTREPRENEURSHIP: IMPACT MEASUREMENT

Successful coping with challenges to which the social enterprise must respond to may (also) start from measurement of effectiveness, which constitutes a useful tool for planning and controlling the production of public goods. At the same time, recording impact is a significant challenge in the field of the social economy: measurement of impact needs to be clear, functional for decision-making purposes, and adjusted to the peculiarities of the welfare purpose of each enterprise.[33]

Measurement involves several challenges (Figure 1.5).

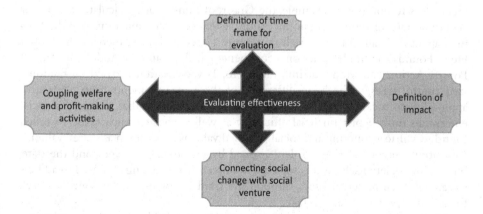

Figure 1.5 Evaluating the impact of social entrepreneurship: major challenges

1   The impact of social entrepreneurship is hard to define. For example, in the context of an effort to integrate people with mental illnesses in social and economic life, impact could be measured based on the number of persons who find a job, make a living without resorting to state support, or successfully pass psychiatric medical checks, etc. Moreover, consistent integration of people with mental illnesses affects almost every aspect of social and economic life, making it hard to focus on some of these aspects as being indicative of the impact of the social investment. Different ways of measurement highlight different aspects of social entrepreneurship and lead to different conclusions about the effectiveness of the social enterprise.

2   It is often difficult to make a connection between change in a social problem and specific action by a social enterprise.[34] For example, in the case of people with mental illnesses, a low degree of integration in the labor market would be hard to attribute to failure on the part of the social enterprise or a general deterioration of economic conditions in a certain area due to a recession.

3   The effectiveness of a social enterprise must be assessed within a given time frame (impact can neither happen at once nor be anticipated forever). Nevertheless, social change continues long after allocation of relevant resources and materialization of impact investments, rendering connection of a specific social change to a specific investment harder to make. For example, a financial literacy project for the financially excluded may yield substantial social change for many years after project implementation, extending to a time frame when impact is inevitably attributed to multiple and overlapping structural causes other than the project on financial literacy.

4   Measuring the effectiveness of a social enterprise must incorporate two occasionally conflicting aspects of the social enterprise: its business purpose versus its welfare mandate.[35]

The development of methods for measuring social impact varies according to the peculiarities of each organization, which is being evaluated on impact and management of its resources. For example, the Grassroot Fund model calculates a ten-year economic rate of return (economic value generated over capital employed), Acumen applies a Lean Data approach with project-specific impact metrics, the Robin Hood Foundation model relies on a cost–benefit analysis, and the Abdul Latif Jameel Poverty Action Lab Model of Innovations for Poverty Action is based on randomized control trials.[36] The basic difference of these measurements from alternative approaches to measurements for conventional enterprises is that metrics for social enterprises must depict financial efficiency as well as societal impact, the so-called **blended value**, economic and social (blended value is also known as shared value).[37] Evaluation outcomes are not solely assessed by investors, employees, and the state, but also by society itself. As it is society's resources that are being allocated to address social and environmental issues through the third sector of the economy, society's focus and expectations are at stake.

While analysis of organizational performance inevitably reflects the organization's profile and the special conditions that define its evolution, as well as the manifestation of the social or environmental problem it attempts to address, the wide variety of quantitative methods makes comparisons between different organizations difficult. Likewise, the mobility of labor and capital between different social purposes and different social enterprises is a challenge. Common accounting standards for recording enterprise performance may ignore variety across enterprises, but allow intertemporal, inter-sectoral and international comparisons.[38] In a similar manner, establishment of a common way of depicting the impact of social enterprises would contribute to a more effective management of their resources and would strengthen their **accountability**. It would also facilitate decision-making for social investors, social economy employees, the government that needs to confront the same social problems, as well as the civilians that are targeted (see Chapter 8 for a detailed pre-sentation on the significance, advantages, and weaknesses of organized systems of measurement of the effectiveness of social entrepreneurship).

CONCLUSION

The dynamics of social entrepreneurship has been the product of specific devel-opments in the role of the state and enterprise in the production of public goods, environmental challenges, and sustainable development; the dynamics of global capi-talism; and, ultimately, changes in perceptions and the way the community is involved in the battle against social and environmental problems.

On the one hand, the financial crisis of 2008 has showed the impasses of the mar-ket mechanism (mainly in the money and capital markets) and caused severe social problems, highlighting the need for government policy for social welfare.[39] On the other hand, the economic crisis had an adverse impact on the fiscal realm, with most governments experiencing liquidity constraints that were dealt with cuts in govern-ment spending and welfare policies.[40] Thus, private initiative comes in to fill the void and contribute to mitigating social problems, by way of expanding private activities often beyond charity and non-governmental organization of social or environmental character. Furthermore, private-sector activity may be based on creative collabora-tion with the public sector, with the latter supplying the infrastructure required to produce public goods. In this case, the public sector adopts the principles of effective management and organization to produce goods and services for social welfare just like a private enterprise.[41] Moreover, it is worth pointing out that the retreat of the public sector and the simultaneous emergence of social enterprises is not typical of crisis periods only. It has also been a basic ingredient of political proposals for reduc-tion of the public sector and replacement of the public sector by the private sector that have been put forward over the past 40 years.[42]

The coupling of the private and the public sectors and the involvement of private individuals in the production of public goods, often leaving profit considerations aside, is associated with a wide variety of organizational formations and welfare activ-ities. It ranges from the solidarity of the cooperative and collectivist organization between society members with common priorities to the entrepreneurial segment of philanthropy of very wealthy individuals. This variety emerges through different social, economic, and ethical frameworks, as well as personal trajectories, generating diverse reactions – at the collective and the individual level – and involving substantial value judgment. Participation of the private sector often improves efficiency in the production of public goods compared to production by the public sector, through application of innovative methods that economize on scarce resources and improve the production process.

Furthermore, participation of the private sector in the production of public goods increases the importance of financial viability as a yardstick for addressing a social or an environmental problem. Thus, the problem may not be addressed if the individual does not come up with the resources that are required. In other words, there must be reflection about the reliability of leaving the addressing of social problems to the private sector, where responses are often based on financial viability criteria alone. Could we risk doing without a public good because a non-governmental organization or a social enterprise is not financially viable? Reflection on financial viability is, of course, also necessary on the part of the government that produces public goods, albeit from a different angle. For example, the operation of a public hospital would continue well beyond the limits that would be dictated if private individuals managed the hospital, even if they are characterized by a strong will to make a social contribution.[43]

Moreover, production of public goods by private individuals instills these goods with the political aspirations of the producer. For example, organizing meals for poor "nationals only" substitutes for social policy that should have been conducted by the government, but projects the specific ideology of the producer of the public good (reducing poverty – providing food for the very poor nationals). Similarly, offering clothing to homeless people by a religious organization is expected to project the religious values of that organization. In the case of production of public goods by governmental institutions, the political aspiration that is instilled is that of a government that gets a vote of confidence by elected members of the parliament (continuity, however, of provision of a public service by the state may be ensured, independently of the political aspirations of a specific government in office). The question whether private sector resources are more efficient than taxes paid to the state for the exercise of social and environmental policy than being made available directly by the private sector for the production of public goods of their choice is still open, especially with reference to efficient utilization of private resources for the purposes of addressing social and environmental problems.

Social entrepreneurship may function as a pillar of social welfare and sustainable economic development. At the same time, however, it faces challenges regarding the effective management of a heterogeneous nexus that defines the social enterprise, as well as the critical limitations of the market mechanism (to which the social entrepreneur belongs) for the supply of public goods. The social enterprise stands on a very thin line that distinguishes two entirely different standpoints towards the capitalist system.[44] On the one hand, it contributes the competency of the capitalist enterprise in the battle against social problems, sparing government spending for such issues.[45] On the other hand, it may function as a social solidarity system that stands against the principles of the market economy. Thus, the form and the social impact of the social enterprise take shape through an ideological, political, and economic synthesis that determines both the nature of social problems and our choices for their resolution.

MATERIAL FOR DISCUSSION

Why social entrepreneurs are taking the lead

Rodriguez, K., 2015. Why social entrepreneurs are taking the lead. *Economist*, December 15.

Available at:

https://execed.economist.com/career-advice/industry-trends/why-social-entrepreneurs-are-taking-lead.

REVIEW QUESTIONS

1 What is a social enterprise?
2 What is the social economy?
3 What is the role of the social entrepreneur?
4 In what ways is the business plan important for the deployment of a social enterprise?
5 What is the difference between a social enterprise and a conventional business?
6 What is the importance of impact measurement in social entrepreneurship?

NOTES

1   It is worth stating at the outset that this definition does not cover all traits of entrepreneurship that affect economic activity and determine its evolutionary course. Entrepreneurship is a multi-faceted phenomenon that is critical for the reproduction and transformation of the capitalist economy, see Knight (1921), Schumpeter (1942). For an introduction to entrepreneurship, see Barringer and Ireland (2018), Zacharakis et al. (2020), and Hisrich et al. (2020).

2   On the differences between conventional and social enterprises in terms of resources, mission, and evaluation of entrepreneurial performance, see, for example, Certo and Miller (2008).

3   Innovation is a major tenet of both social and conventional entrepreneurship. See, for example, Drayton (2002).

4   Ebrahim et al. (2014), Osorio-Vega (2019). Barriers against mission drift include special limitations for acquiring or losing membership status in the social enterprise, as well as limitations that relate to resource use.

5   Indicatively, see Pindyck and Rubinfield (2018).

6   https://thistlefarms.org.

7   https://auticon.co.uk/.

8   https://livelyhoods.org.

9   For an introduction to social entrepreneurship, see, for example, Brooks (2008), Chahine (2016), and Kikcul and Lyons (2020).

10 The civil society may be defined as the set of collective, non-governmental actions of citizens that express their interests and aspirations. Non-governmental organizations,

professional associations, trade unions, charity organizations, religious organizations, and the like comprise the civil society.

11   On the motives of social entrepreneurs, see Christopoulos and Vogl (2015) and Roundy et al. (2017).

12   Vickers et al. (2017).

13   https://ec.europa.eu/growth/sectors/social-economy_en.

14   On the various types of social entrepreneurs in terms of size, objectives, and depth of the attempted social interventions, see Zahra et al. (2009).

15   On the variety of social enterprises in terms of social environment, see Defourny and Nyssens (2010) and Liu et al. (2013).

16   For a delineation of social entrepreneurship and a review of definitions see Alegre et al. (2017) and Saebi et al. (2019). The variety of definitions and categorizations of the social enterprise does have an ideological connotation. It also shapes our perception about the scope and dynamism of the social economy – Teasdale et al. (2013).

17   For example, Santos (2012).

18   Hayek (1976).

19   Leadership styles vary across the diverse cultural environments where social enterprises operate (Lee and Kelly, 2019).

20   About the network nature of social enterprises, see for example Guo and Bielefeld (2014).

21   See, for example, Eti-Tofinga et al. (2018), Akingbola et al. (2019).

22   On the solidarity economy, see indicatively Nikolopoulos and Kapogiannis (2013) and Utting (2015).

23   On the effectiveness of cooperatives as legal forms of social enterprise, see Mancino and Thomas (2005) for the case of Italy.

24   For an overview of the social economy in Greece, see Varvarousis et al. (2018).

25   According to Law 4430/2016, Limited Liability Social Cooperatives are classified as Social Cooperative Enterprise of Integration.

26   For the case of Trade Aid, whose viability was based on deployment of entrepreneurial opportunity and adequate transformation of its mission, see Doyle Corner and Ho (2010).

27   See Engelke et al. (2015) among, others for the significance of competition between social enterprises to attract specialized personnel, in the context of German social entrepreneurship.

28   On the significance of interested parties to define the profile of the social enterprise, see indicatively Neck et al. (2009).

29   See, for example, Kyriakidou and Salavou (2014).

30   Of course, under certain conditions in the case of social enterprises the devotion of employees to the social purpose is a more significant advantage than specialized training (Besley and Ghatak 2017).

31   For the importance of the choice of legal form for social enterprises, see indicatively Katz and Page (2010) and Stecker (2016).

32   On the impact of the political, cultural, and social environment on the formation of the ecosystem of the social enterprise, see indicatively Hazenberg et al. (2016).

33   Stevens et al. (2015).

34   Ebrahim and Kasturi (2014).

35   This conflict extends beyond the field of measurement, creating conflicts between stakeholders about procedures, resources, the culture of the social enterprise (Smith et al. 2013).

36   www.gbfund.org/our-approach/, https://acumen.org/lean-data/, www.robinho od.org/what-we-do/metrics/index.html, www.povertyactionlab.org/resource/introduction-randomized-evaluations.

37   On shared value in the context of social entrepreneurship, see Porter and Kramer (2011).

38   See Nicholls (2018) on the differences between financial accounting and social impact accounting.

39   Mohseni-Cheraghlou (2016).

40   Ronchi (2018).

41   On the implementation of management principles in the administration of public institutions, see indicatively Flynn and Asquer (2016).

42   Hayllar and Wettenhall (2013).

43   Dart (2004) predicts that criteria of financial viability of the individual producer will gain ground against those of social impact in the realm of social entrepreneurship, to the extent that economic authorities of the "market economy" enhance legitimization of criteria of financial viability in society.

44   Roy and Hackett (2017).

45   For example, in the case of the Aboriginals of Australia, the reduction of state income support was accompanied by an effort to support entrepreneurship amongst these people, as a mechanism for economic development – Halouva (2015). Gerrard (2017) reaches similar conclusions with regard to social entrepreneurship and social welfare for the homeless in Australia.

REFERENCES

Akingbola, K., Rogers, S.E., and Baluch, A., 2019. Social enterprise as change. *In*: K. Akingbola, S.E. Rogers, and A. Baluch, eds. *Change management in nonprofit organizations: Theory and practice*. Palgrave Macmillan, 171–186. https://doi.org/10.1007/978-3-030-14774-7.

Alegre, I., Kislenko, S., and Berbegal-Mirabent, J., 2017. Organized chaos: Mapping the definitions of social entrepreneurship. *Journal of Social Entrepreneurship*, 8(2), 248–264. https://doi.org/10.1080/19420676.2017.1371631.

Barringer, B.R., and Ireland, R.D., 2018. *Entrepreneurship: Successfully launching new ventures*. 6th Edition. Upper Saddle River, NJ: Pearson.

Besley, T., and Ghatak, M., 2017. Profit with purpose? A theory of social enterprise. *American Economic Journal: Economic Policy*, 9(3), 19–58. https://doi.org/10.1257/pol.20150495.

Brooks, A.C., 2008. *Social entrepreneurship: A modern approach to social value creation*. Upper Saddle River, NJ: Pearson Prentice Hall.

Certo, S.T., and Miller, T., 2008. Social entrepreneurship: Key issues and concepts. *Business Horizons*, 51(4), 267–271. https://doi.org/10.1016/j.bushor.2008.02.009.

Chahine, T., 2016. *Introduction to social entrepreneurship*. CRC Press. https://doi.org/10.1201/b19475.

Christopoulos, D., and Vogl, S., 2015. The motivation of social entrepreneurs: The roles, agendas and relations of altruistic economic actors. *Journal of Social Entrepreneurship*, 6(1), 1–30. https://doi.org/10.1080/19420676.2014.954254.

Dart, R., 2004. The legitimacy of social enterprise. *Nonprofit Management & Leadership*, 14(4), 411–424. https://doi.org/10.1002/nml.43.

Defourny, J., and Nyssens, M., 2010. Social enterprise in Europe: At the crossroads of market, public policies and third sector. *Policy and Society*, 29(3), 231–242. https://doi.org/10.1016/j.polsoc.2010.07.002.

Doyle Corner, P., and Ho, M., 2010. How opportunities develop in social entrepreneurship. *Entrepreneurship Theory and Practice*, 34(4), 635–659. https://doi.org/10.1111%2Fj.1540-6520.2010.00382.x.

Drayton, W., 2002. The citizen sector: Becoming as entrepreneurial and competitive as business. *California Management Review*, 44(3), 120–132.

Ebrahim, A., Battilana, J., and Mair, J., 2014. The governance of social enterprises: Mission drift and accountability challenges in hybrid organizations. *Research in Organizational Behavior*, 34, 81–100. https://doi.org/10.1016/j.riob.2014.09.001.

Ebrahim, A., and Kasturi, V., 2014. What impact? A framework for measuring the scale and scope of social performance. *California Management Review*, 56(3), 118–141. https://doi.org/10.1525%2Fcmr.2014.56.3.118.

Engelke, H., Mauksch, S., Darkow, I.-L., and Von der Gracht, H.A., 2015. Opportunities of social enterprise in Germany – Evidence from an expert survey. *Technological Forecasting and Social Change*, 90(Part B), 635–646. https://doi.org/10.1016/j.techfore.2014.01.004.

Eti-Tofinga, B., Singh, G., and Douglas, H., 2018. Facilitating cultural change in social enterprises. *Journal of Organizational Change Management*, 31(3), 619–636. https://doi.org/10.1108/JOCM-12-2016-0296.

Flynn, N., and Asquer, A., 2016. *Public sector management.* 7th Edition. London: Sage.

Gerrard, J., 2017. Welfare rights, self-help and social enterprise: Unpicking neoliberalism's mess. *Journal of Sociology*, 53(1), 47–62. https://doi.org/10.1177%2F1440783315607388.

Guo, C., and Bielefeld, W., 2014. *Social entrepreneurship: An evidence-based approach to creating social value.* San Francisco: Jossey-Bass.

Halouva, M., 2015. From self-determination to self-appreciation: Neoliberalism and social enterprise in indigenous Australia. *In*: S. Paunksnis, ed. *Dislocating globality: Deterritorialization, difference and resistance.* Leiden: Brill, 231–259.

Hayek, F.A., 1976. *Law, legislation and liberty: A new statement of the liberal principles and political economy. Volume II: The mirage of social justice.* London: Routledge.

Hayllar, M.R., and Wettenhall, R., 2013. As public goes private, social emerges: The rise of social enterprise. *Public Organization Review*, 13(2), 207–217. https://doi.org/10.1007/s11115-013-0234-y.

Hazenberg, R., Bajwa-Patel, M., Roy, M.J., Mazzei, M., and Baglioni, S., 2016. A comparative overview of social enterprise "ecosystems" in Scotland and England: An evolutionary perspective. *International Review of Sociology*, 26(2), 205–222. https://doi.org/10.1080/03906701.2016.1181395.

Hisrich, R.D., Peters, M.D., and Shepherd, D.A., 2020. *Entrepreneurship.* New York, NY: McGraw-Hill Education.

Katz, R.A., and Page, A., 2010. The role of social enterprise. *Vermont Law Review*, 35(1), 59–103.

Kikcul, J., and Lyons, T.S., 2020. *Understanding social entrepreneurship: The relentless pursuit of mission in an ever changing world.* 3rd Edition. New York, NY: Routledge. https://doi.org/10.4324/9780429270406.

Knight, F., 1921. *Risk, uncertainty and profit.* Boston and New York: Houghton Mifflin Company.

Kyriakidou, O., and Salavou, E., 2014. *Social entrepreneurship.* Athens: Rosili. In Greek.

Lee, B., and Kelly, L., 2019. Cultural leadership ideals and social entrepreneurship: An international study. *Journal of Social Entrepreneurship*, 10(1), 108–128. https://doi.org/10.1080/19420676.2018.1541005.

Liu, G., Eng, T.-Y., and Takeda, S., 2013. An investigation of marketing capabilities and social enterprise performance in the UK and Japan. *Entrepreneurship Theory and Practice*, 39(2), 267–298. https://doi.org/10.1111%2Fetap.12041.

Mancino, A., and Thomas, A., 2005. An Italian pattern of social enterprise: The social cooperative. *Nonprofit Management and Leadership*, 15(3), 357–369. https://doi.org/10.1002/nml.73.

Mohseni-Cheraghlou, A., 2016. The aftermath of financial crises: A look on human and social wellbeing. *World Development*, 87, 88–106. https://doi.org/10.1016/j.worlddev.2016.06.001.

Neck, H., Brush, C., and Allen, E., 2009. The landscape of social entrepreneurship. *Business Horizons*, 52(1), 13–19. https://doi.org/10.1016/j.bushor.2008.09.002.

Nicholls, A., 2018. A general theory of social impact accounting: Materiality, uncertainty and empowerment. *Journal of Social Entrepreneurship*, 9(2), 132–153. https://doi.org/10.1080/19420676.2018.1452785.

Nikolopoulos, T., and Kapogiannis, D., 2013. *Introduction to social and solidarity economy.* Athens: I ekdosis ton synadelfon. In Greek.

Osorio-Vega, P., 2019. The ethics of entrepreneurial shared value. *Journal of Business Ethics*, 157, 981–995. https://doi.org/10.1007/s10551-018-3957-4.

Pindyck, R., and Rubinfield, D.L., 2018. *Microeconomics.* 9th Edition. Upper Saddle River, NJ: Pearson.

Porter, M., and Kramer, M., 2011. Creating shared value. *Harvard Business Review*, January/February 1–17.

Ronchi, S., 2018. Which roads (if any) to social investment? The recalibration of EU welfare states at the crisis crossroads (2000–2014). *Journal of Social Policy*, 47(3), 459–478. https://doi.org/10.1017/S0047279417000782.

Roundy, P.T., Holzhauer, H., and Dai, Y., 2017. Finance or philanthropy? Exploring the motivations and criteria of impact investors. *Social Responsibility Journal*, 13(3), 491–512. https://doi.org/10.1108/SRJ-08-2016-0135.

Roy, M.J., and Hackett, M.T., 2017. Polanyi's "substantive approach" to the economy in action? Conceptualising as a public health "intervention". *Review of Social Economy*, 75(2), 89–111. https://doi.org/10.1080/09581596.2016.1249826.

Saebi, T., Foss, N.J., and Linder, S., 2019. Social entrepreneurship research: Past achievements and future promises. *Journal of Management*, 45(1), 70–95. https://doi.org/10.1177%2F0149206318793196.

Santos, F.M., 2012. A positive theory of social entrepreneurship. *Journal of Business Ethics*, 111(3), 335–351. https://doi.org/10.1007/s10551-012-1413-4.

Schumpeter, J., 1942. *Capitalism, socialism and democracy.* New York: Harper and Brothers.

Smith, W.K., Gonin, M., and Besharov, M.L., 2013. Measuring social business tensions: A review of research agenda. *Business Ethics Quarterly*, 23(3), 407–442. https://doi.org/10.5840/beq201323327.

Stecker, M.J., 2016. Awash in a sea of confusion: Benefit corporations, social enterprise and the fear of "greenwashing". *Journal of Economic Issues*, 50(2), 373–381. https://doi.org/10.1080/00213624.2016.1176481.

Stevens, R., Moray, N., and Bruneel, J., 2015. The social and economic mission of social enterprises: Dimensions, measurement, validation, and relation. *Entrepreneurship Theory and Practice*, 39(5), 1051–1082. https://doi.org/10.1111%2Fetap.12091.

Teasdale, S., Lyon, F., and Badlock, R., 2013. Playing with numbers: A methodological critique of the social enterprise growth myth. *Journal of Social Entrepreneurship*, 4(2), 113–131. https://doi.org/10.1080/19420676.2012.762800.

Utting, P., 2015. *Social and solidarity economy: Beyond the fringe*. London: Zed Books.

Varvarousis, A., Galanos, C., Tsitsirigos, G., Bekridaki, G., and Temple, N., 2018. *Report on the social and solidarity economy in Greece*. Athens: British Council. In Greek.

Vickers, I., Lyon, F., Sepulveda, L., and McMullin, C., 2017. Public service innovation and multiple institutional logics: The case of hybrid social enterprise providers of health and wellbeing. *Research Policy*, 46(10), 1755–1768. https://doi.org/10.1016/j.respol.2017.08.003.

Zacharakis, A., Corbett, A.C., and Bygrave, W.D., 2020. *Entrepreneurship*. 5th Edition. Hoboken, NJ: John Wiley & Sons.

Zahra, S.A., Gedajlovic, E., Neubaum, D.O., and Shulman, J.M., 2009. Motives, search processes and ethical challenges. *Journal of Business Venturing*, 24(5), 519–532. https://doi.org/10.1016/j.jbusvent.2008.04.007.

2

Social finance[1]

After reading this chapter, you will be able to:

1 Demonstrate understanding of the meaning of social finance both as an academic discipline and as a field of financial practice
2 Identify the major mechanisms of social finance
3 Identify providers of capital, recipients of capital, and flows of finance in the social finance marketplace
4 Discuss the challenges in the design and implementation of impact investments

INTRODUCTION

The term **social finance** denotes both an academic discipline and a field of financial practice. As an academic discipline, social finance is the economics of funding impact investments. As a field of financial practice, social finance is the set of processes, decisions, and institutions that are encompassed in the financing of public goods production with participation of the private sector. In this sense, social finance involves the organizations that provide financial resources for production of public goods with private-sector participation, as well as the financial operation of social enterprises. The properties of public goods are presented in Chapter 1, Box 1.1.

DOI: 10.4324/9781003230366-3

This definition of social finance leads to the following remarks:

1   Social finance studies the feasibility of impact investments, assessing whether the benefit from production of public goods with participation of the private sector exceeds the cost involved. Essentially, social finance explores the value of lifting the barriers for access to goods that have to be as non-exclusive and non-competitive as possible. Costs and benefits are calculated in monetary units, in relation to the stakeholders of social entrepreneurship: financial supporters, social entrepreneurs, citizens, and the government.

2   Social finance examines the modes of financing impact investments, including donations, loans, and own funds. Specifically, social finance studies the way financing an investment affects the benefits accrued to both the private investor and the community whose problems are addressed through the particular investment.

3   Social finance explores the way financing impact investments affect the administration of social enterprises. The identity of the organizations that are being financed is shaped, among other things, by the structure of the different priorities of those who provide financial backing. In the case of social enterprises, assessment of the structure of priorities involves investors' perceptions of social welfare.

4   Social finance studies investment decisions that aim, in addition to the monetary benefit accrued to the investor, at the creation of value for society and the environment (blended value). Investments that aim at addressing social and environmental problems include a wide variety of activities that pertain to aspects of economic development. These may include access to drinkable water, access to education, mitigation of economic and social inequalities, protection of human rights, enhancement of productivity and reduction of unemployment, access to energy, incorporation of renewable sources of energy in production and in everyday life, management of water resources, access to financing, reduction of environmental pollution, preservation of biodiversity, sustainable land use and safe access to food, pooling of funds for donations and charity purposes in general, conflict resolution, and a plethora of other actions that help address social, economic, political, and environmental challenges.[2]

5   The emergence of social finance is based on the standard ascertainment of **market failure**, where the market mechanism fails to embody the impact of transactions upon individuals who are not involved in the specific transactions. In such cases, the **price mechanism** "by itself" is not adequate to bring about efficient allocation of resources in the economy in a way that would maximize social welfare. Market failure tends to be addressed through measures such as the imposition of environmental taxes, emission fees, and subsidization of social enterprises. Especially in the case of an organized capital market (e.g., banks and the stock market), investors' expectations regarding the long-term viability of an investment, the required return and the discount rate, the optimum finance mix, and the optimum deployment of profit are often incomplete. They usually do not incorporate to a sufficient degree the social impact of production and transactions, other than the impact on the party that is

involved in production of the good (the seller) and the party that is involved in consumption of the good (the buyer). Of course, beyond market failure, the institutions of social finance aim at correcting government policy failure to resolve chronic social problems.

Failure to incorporate the relatively uncharted social impact of private investment limits **capital market efficiency**, the latter denoting that transactions and prices embody all relevant information that pertain to the traded securities. The efficient markets hypothesis constitutes the theoretical platform on which the basic propositions of finance theory are recorded, as well as one of the main scientific arguments advocating market aptitude for self-regulation without substantial or complex interventions by legislators and the government. The **global financial crisis of 2008** is considered to be a typical case of market inefficiency: the price mechanism did not incorporate sufficiently the need of society for financial stability in the case of bank loans, stocks, and financial derivatives, eradicating the expansion of credit to the real sector. As a result, the global economy was destabilized. More importantly, in many economies the content and prospect of economic freedom and regulation of economic activity underwent complete transformation.[3]

Other than epistemological objections on conventional finance,[4] this type of reflection coincides with the development of a wide network of new forms of finance that relate to social entrepreneurship, entrepreneurial philanthropy, socially responsible investment, and investment that aims at having social and environmental impact. The economic crisis marked many important changes in the fields of the social economy, social innovation, and social finance. Along with establishment of mechanisms for reinforcing systemic financial stability and enacting stricter risk management regulations, the crisis also led to the development of new methods of addressing and financing welfare objectives beyond pure profitability that is measured in monetary terms: this trajectory provides social economy and its financing mechanisms a degree of autonomy, precisely because the volume of initiatives and the increasing repercussions of their arguments contribute to the emergence of social finance as an autonomous field in the study of the economy, entrepreneurship, finance, even economics as a science.

6 The fact that certain private investments have a social character, combined with the private benefits entailed in several welfare investments, makes impact investment hard to define in a precise manner. By implication, the boundaries of social finance are hard to define. For example, the founders of a private hospital may aim at improving the standard of living in the area in addition to making profit, the founders of a private school may aim at promotion of their own ideas and aspirations about the common good through the educational process, those who provide finance for the establishment of an athletic club may aspire to support sports, etc. In addition, social finance is often about financial support of young entrepreneurs or very poor entrepreneurs who are excluded from bank loans. While the activities funded are purely for profit, such channels of finance can be part of social finance to the extent that they reduce social inequalities by giving the opportunity of wealth creation to

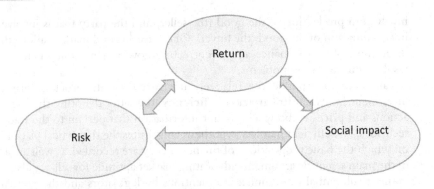

Figure 2.1 Social finance: decision-making criteria

individuals who lack capital and by increasing employment, thereby reinforcing social cohesion and economic development. The fact that a large number
of goods and services combine private and public good characteristics brings
out the need for creation of new institutions for the financing of public goods,
as well as new scientific tools for financial analysis.

7 Finance as part of microeconomic analysis needs to redefine the risk–return
relationship as the main behavioral rule, incorporating an assessment of social
impact (Figure 2.1).

As the benefit of investment and the needs for financing the daily operations
of social enterprises concern individuals who are not directly involved in financial
transactions with investors, social finance changes the meaning of key dimensions of
financial analysis, such as profit, uncertainty about investment outcomes, synthesis
and conflicts of interests between stakeholders that are involved with the enterprise,
the discount rate, the impact of taxes on the value of the enterprise, capital structure,
and payout policy. Changes in the financial landscape are depicted in new modes of
finance, as well as new risk management techniques about productive activities that
do not just aim at a monetary reward for the investor, but also target creation of value
for society and the environment. Such cases include microfinance institutions and
venture philanthropy, which transform entrepreneurship, welfare action, and financial intermediation in the direction of social benefit jointly pursued with financial
viability of private investment.

SOCIAL FINANCE MECHANISMS

Mechanisms of social finance shift with changes in the social problems addressed
by the third sector in general and social entrepreneurship in particular. In 2019, the
size of the global impact capital market amounted to 502 billion US dollars.[5] The
financing of impact investments is materialized through a dense network of financial
mechanisms. Some of these are conventional and their main goal is not to provide

support for social entrepreneurship. For example, a commercial bank could finance social enterprises in parallel to the main financial services it provides to enterprises outside the social economy terrain. Other institutions are more closely linked to the social economy and are more often involved in the financing of social enterprises and investments with developmental impact.

Microfinance institutions: Microfinance institutions are financial institutions that aim at addressing poverty by providing financial backing to those who are excluded from the conventional banking sector due to lack of property, stable income, or sound credit history (extension of loans to support female entrepreneurship in very poor areas

> Microfinance institutions are financial institutions that aim at addressing poverty by providing financial backing to those who are excluded from the conventional banking sector due to lack of property, stable income, or sound credit history.

of South Asia constitutes a typical example). For the most part, such loans involve small amounts, which are granted without collateral to small groups that undertake common responsibility for the repayment of the loan. Often the role of microfinance institutions extends beyond supporting entrepreneurship; they tend to employ mostly women (in patriarchic societies) and provide professional training and consulting services to borrowers, as well as student loans (for a discussion on microfinance, see Chapter 3). The pioneering microfinance institution is Grameen Bank in Bangladesh.

Venture philanthropy: Venture philanthropy blends social entrepreneurship with social finance. It involves application of **venture capital** techniques for the purposes of financing and helping enterprises that aim at both social impact and profit to grow. Venture philanthropy institutions extend beyond financing social enterprises and developmen-

> Venture philanthropy blends social entrepreneurship with social finance. It involves application of venture capital techniques for the purposes of financing and helping enterprises that aim at both social impact and profit to grow.

tal ventures, supporting entrepreneurs with know-how and consulting services as needed. As with conventional venture capital, the target is withdrawal of venture capital from the enterprise when the enterprise becomes financially independent. Venture philanthropy examples include Acumen, Omydiar Network, Social Venture Partners International, Social Business Trust, and others (for a discussion on venture philanthropy, see Chapter 4).

Social impact bonds: Social impact bonds are loan contracts that involve a future cash flow for the lender based on the return of the investment that is being financed. If the investment succeeds in resolving a social or environmental issue, the creditor is compensated by the institutional body that bears responsibility of addressing it and gets the loan for that purpose. As a rule, management of the borrowed funds and social intervention are conducted by an independent organization, which acquires the loan on behalf of the government and coordinates the work of enterprises and organizations that undertake the task of resolving the issue. The impact of the social investment is assessed with an independent evaluation, which determines the amount that is to be returned to the lender. These bonds are also known as **pay for performance contracts** or **pay for success contracts**. The first social impact bond was issued for the Peterborough Prison and the support services that helped those released from prison to find a job, be integrated in society, and stay out of prison for 12 months after their release (for a discussion of social impact bonds, see Chapter 5).

Crowdfunding platforms: Crowdfunding platforms are mechanisms of collecting small amounts from many financial sources and supporters to finance nonprofit-related activities, social enterprises, as well as for-profit enterprises. They are internet-based platforms for the most part. Crowdfunding constitutes a social finance mechanism to the extent that it provides financial backing to social ventures, supporting projects that are not funded by the conventional banking system, mainly because they lack collateral. Funding may take the form of a loan, equity, donation, or reward in kind (in the latter case, the supporter is paid in products produced through the production process that is being financed). Other than funding social ventures, crowdfunding through funds that come from a large number of supporters and are drawn through the internet often boosts the legitimacy of a social venture well beyond funding (for a discussion of crowdfunding, see Chapter 6). Chief crowdfunding platforms include Kickstarter, Indiegogo, GoFundMe, and Patreon.

> Crowdfunding platforms are mechanisms of collecting small amounts from many financial sources and supporters to finance nonprofit-related activities, social enterprises, as well as for-profit enterprises. They are internet-based platforms for the most part.

Socially responsible investments: Socially responsible investments comprise purchase of securities issued by enterprises which are considered by investors as having a positive impact on society and being environmentally friendly. Thus, socially responsible investments include securities issued by enterprises that are known for their socially and environmentally responsible productive activities, as well as for their active support of employee and consumer rights. Moreover, socially responsible investments may exclude securities issued by corporations in the sectors of gambling, alcoholic beverages, energy, and the arms industry (see Box 2.1). As an example, socially responsible investments comprise the portfolios of the American Hospital Association, Calvert, and Walden Asset Management. In Europe, investment in socially responsible investments exceeds 14 trillion US dollars.[6] However, socially responsible investments are often part of investment strategies that primarily pursue profit and, therefore, we could say that they lie in the periphery of social finance, rather than the core. A similar investment rationale about socially responsible investments is adopted by several commercial banks that specialize in financing social investments, social enterprises, and socially responsible enterprises, while excluding enterprises that do not fulfill social and environmental criteria. This segment of banking services is known as ethical banking or social banking.[7] Such banks are Triodos bank, GLS Bank, Charity Bank, Cultura Bank, and Alternative Bank Switzerland.

> Socially responsible investments comprise purchase of securities issued by enterprises which are considered by investors as having a positive impact on society and being environmentally friendly.

Box 2.1 Socially responsible investments: portfolio construction

In the context of socially responsible investments, portfolio construction is realized in one of the following three ways:

1 **Positive choice:** According to this approach, investors choose securities (stocks and bonds) of organizations that fulfill social and environmental criteria. Investment in renewable energy resources constitutes a typical example of positive choice.

2 **Negative choice:** According to this approach, investors preclude securities of organizations that are active in sectors that are not in congruence with social welfare (arms industry, gambling, alcoholic beverages, and the like). Moreover, they often preclude investing in companies that apply practices that are against investors' values (child labor, violations of human rights, etc.). The global portfolio value selected by negative choice exceeds 19 trillion US dollars.[8]

3 **Selecting securities issued by prominent organizations:** These are portfolios comprising securities issued by organizations that are renowned for their social and environmental performance. This approach combines elements from the other two approaches (positive and negative choice). In this case, investments are guided by published ratings of businesses based on criteria pertaining to corporate governance, sector of activity, personnel relations, environmental contribution, quality of offered goods and services, stance towards human rights, and other similar indicators. For some of these ratings, the investment strategy may only consider securities that are issued by enterprises ranked in the top 100 or top 200 in terms of the specific criteria. Morgan Stanley, KLD, and other rating agencies perform such evaluations.

Islamic Finance: Islamic finance is a system of financial institutions that abides by the rules of **Shariah**. Shariah, together with Aqidah and Akhlaq constitute the basic pillars

> Islamic finance is a system of financial institutions that abides by the rules of Shariah.

of the principles of Islam (for a discussion of Islamic finance, see Chapter 7). According to Shariah, investment in gambling, alcoholic beverages, and pornography are prohibited. Also, in congruence with **zakat** (Islamic philanthropy rule), investors are required to offer part of the realized return for public benefit purposes. Thus, Islamic finance incorporates some of the familiar practices of socially responsible investments and corporate social responsibility activities. In addition, implementation of Shariah principles excludes investment in corporations that are related to the production and sale of pork meat. Lending with interest is not allowed in Islamic finance, leading to a different structure of financial services that need to comply with religious regulations while also pursuing profit through financial intermediation and entrepreneurship. Adoption of Shariah by financial intermediaries is crucial for both their management practices, as well as their capability to respond to global economic challenges.

Credit unions: Credit unions are based on the principle of solidarity, as applied in the case of a local community. Credit unions primarily address the financial needs of a local community, the members of which are employees of the credit union, depositors, or borrowers, and elect the members of the union that conduct their management.[9] To the extent that credit unions have a mandate for the solidarity and the economic development of the local community, along with making profits from banking services, they constitute a mechanism of social finance. In 2017 there were 85,400 credit unions across 118 countries with over 274 million members. Shinkin banks in Japan bear close institutional similarity to credit unions.[10]

> The credit union institution addresses primarily the financial needs of a local community, the members of which are employees of the credit union, depositors, or borrowers, and elect the members of the union that conduct their management.

The boundaries between the institutions of social finance described here are somewhat blurred, in the sense that there are cases of financial organizations that combine elements of different institutions. For example, there are microfinance institutions that apply the rules of Islamic finance and venture philanthropy organizations that support social impact bonds. Similarly, the boundaries that separate social finance institutions from conventional banking services providers are not so clear. Conventional banks often finance impact investments, while organizations of social finance occasionally deviate from their mandate, adopting the practices of for-profit financial institutions. Box 2.2 gives an indicative list of leading impact investors in the international social finance market.

Box 2.2 Indicative list of leading impact investors

2B-Community	Enclude	Mission Driven Finance
Aavishkaar	Enterprise Community Partners	National Community Investment Fund
Accion Venture Lab	EXEO capital	New Forests
ACTIAM	Farmland	New Market Funds
Adobe Capital/New Ventures	Fledge	NonProfit Finance Fund
Alterfin	FMO	Oikocredit International
Annie E. Casey Foundation	Fondazione Sviluppo e Crescita CRT	Okavango Capital
Annona Sustainable Investments	Ford Foundation	National Community Investment Fund

Aqua-Spark	Futuregrowth Asset Management	Phitrust Partenaires
Bethnal Green Ventures	Generation Investment Management	responsAbility Investments
Beyond Capital Fund	Global Innovation Fund	Root Capital
Big Society Capital	Global Partnerships	Safer Made
Blue Haven Initiative	Goodwell Investments	Seachange Capital Partners
BlueOrchard Finance	Grace Impact	Seattle Foundation
Bridges Fund Management	Grassroots Capital Management	Shared Interest
Calvert Impact Capital	Hooge Raedt Social Venture	Sitra
Christian Super	IDB Invest	Social Ventures Australia
Clean Energy Trust	Impact Asset Management	Symbiotics
Community Capital Management	Incofin Investment Management	Temporis Capital
Community Investment Management	Inspirit Foundation	The Rockefeller Foundation
CREAS	International Finance Corporation	Triodos Investment Management
Creation Investments Capital Management	Investisseurs & Partenaires	Triple Jump
Dalio Family Office	Japan Social Impact Investment Foundation	Turner Impact Capital
Dev Equity	Living Cities	Upaya Social Ventures
DOB Equity	Lok Capital	Vital Capital Fund
DOEN Participaties	MainStreet Partners	Vox Capital
EcoEnterprises Fund	Mary Reynolds Babcock Foundation	WK Kellogg Foundation
Elevar Equity	Medical Credit Fund	WaterEquity
Enclude	Menterra Venture Advisors	Wespath Benefits and Investments
Enterprise Community Partners	Microvest Capital Management	WHEB Asset Management

Source: Global Impact Investing Network (2019)

THE NEXUS OF SOCIAL FINANCE: MAJOR TENETS

As with other financial institutions, social finance institutions constitute a social nexus of four major elements: **lenders**, **borrowers**, a **regulatory framework**, and **financial flows**. Figure 2.2 illustrates the nexus of lenders (impact investors),

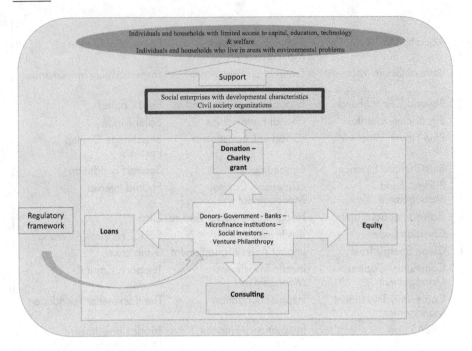

Figure 2.2 Social finance

borrowers (social enterprises), the regulatory framework and financial flows in social finance.

Providers of capital

Investors and creditors are associated with the **supply of capital**. They include governments, donors, banks, venture philanthropy organizations, and impact investors. They vary in terms of the amount of capital that they intend to supply, their view of purpose of the impact investment, as well as the mechanisms of finance that they intend to make use of. The amount of finance provided ranges from a small individual participation in a fundraising event to the underwriting of social impact bonds and large endowments for the establishment of higher education institutions.

The motivation of impact investors may vary. Although it always is a mixture of private and public benefit, its composition may differ from investor to investor. For example, a microfinance institution aims at profit that is necessary to keep it in business, but at the same time places emphasis on economic development targets by funding and training poor citizens who are excluded from the capital market and would otherwise have no prospect of becoming entrepreneurs. Similarly, financing a maritime cooperative enterprise in an island economy, the profit motive of investors is combined with the motive of contributing to the economic development of the island. The variability of motives and amounts of funds provided is closely associated with challenges stemming from different priorities and **asymmetric information** amongst capital-market participants. For example, investors in a coffee cooperative in

Kenya may be confronted on the one hand by limited information about the farmers they finance and, on the other hand, by a government policy that has completely different priorities from theirs. Such challenges make international mechanisms of finance for social investments difficult to attain, contribute to higher cost of borrowing, and render institutional change in the area of financial intermediation necessary, in order to keep borrowing costs low and facilitate the flow of cash for welfare purposes.

It is worth pointing out that the welfare and the purely financial targets of investors are not necessarily conflicting. Sometimes social investors are the nonprofit arm of corporations that are primarily for-profit. For example, the Shell Foundation is affiliated with the oil company Shell and the GS Social Impact Fund is the social investment arm of the investment bank Goldman Sachs. Involvement of a for-profit organization, such as a bank or an oil company in a welfare project to protect the environment or reduce crime, may also be conducive to enhancement of the firm's financial performance.[11,12] Beyond the narrow boundaries of social investments and social enterprises, incorporating social and environmental criteria in the provision of financial services defines the broader field of **sustainable finance**.

Recipients of capital

Demand for impact capital is associated with social enterprises and civil society organizations with a welfare mandate, such as protection of the natural environment, promotion of the fine arts, support for political programs, eradication of poverty, inequality, illiteracy, and alienation, as well as mitigating threats to public health and managing refugee flows and similar challenges. The welfare nature of these organizations does not provide immunity from management issues pertaining to operating costs and is often associated with securing revenue and financial performance (profit or loss). For example, a private not-for-profit academic institution may be established using resources from a private endowment with the mandate to promote arts and sciences in the area where it operates. The fact that the academic institution receives tuition fees in order to cover its operating costs may convince a lender (e.g., a bank) that the institution is capable of paying back the capital borrowed and that the lender's future income is secured.

Beyond social enterprises and civil society organizations, organizations that are funded through social finance may also be for-profit private enterprises, whose financial backing is deemed appropriate because of their developmental characteristics. These include enterprises established and run by the very poor. Inability of these enterprises to send a signal to their lenders about their **credibility** causes severe liquidity issues and ultimately deprives these entrepreneurs from access to capital. Entrepreneurs with little or no property assets cannot normally access bank funding. Any conventional credibility rating system used by a bank would reject financing small farmers and entrepreneurs who do not possess property that could serve as collateral, leaving them to struggle for survival in conditions of complete uncertainty. Small-scale enterprises are the main users of social finance channels in the developing economies of sub-Saharan Africa, India, and Latin America. Social finance does not merely supply funds to the very poor who are excluded from commercial bank financing. It also provides financial support for those who have a systematic difficulty accessing funds, such as women in developing patriarchic economies, recently released convicts and former drug addicts who are attempting a fresh start. To the extent that financing entrepreneurs who would otherwise have no access to capital is conducive to the economic development of the area they operate in, organizations that provide finance to them constitute part of the social finance nexus.

> To the extent that financing entrepreneurs who would otherwise have no access to capital is considered to be beneficial for the entrepreneurs and conducive to the economic development of the area they operate in, the organizations that provide finance to them constitute part of the social finance nexus.

As far as the profit-making efforts of the suppliers of capital are concerned, the challenge for the borrowers relates to the **uniqueness** of their activities, which often make discounting future profits extremely difficult to assess. For example, while financing a publisher could be based on public data on the market size of a specific book-reading audience and the financing of a hotel operation could be based on similar loans extended to the hotel's peer group, financing a public library is based on scant information regarding revenue prospects. Higher uncertainty for the investor implies higher cost of funding and, therefore, less available loanable funds. Moreover, the unique nature of the funded project prevents borrowers from convincing lenders about the pursuit of non-economic objectives. For example, while attaining a high profit margin constitutes a satisfactory indicator of return to an investment in the food industry, defining adequate return to an investment in a project that aims at reducing illiteracy is not equally straightforward to carry out (how would the reduction in the number of illiterate people be linked to the specific amount of funds that was allocated for that purpose?).

In general, the line that separates the demand from the supply of capital is rather thin in the case of social finance. For example, microfinance and venture philanthropy organizations could be both part of demand for and supply of capital. As legal entities, they are independent of their investors and lenders and are often impact investors themselves that seek funds in order to channel them to addressing the social problems that constitute their mandate. Governments may be another case where the boundaries between demand for and supply of capital are blurred. They play an important role in the capital market for social investments, as well as in organizing and materializing an impact investment. Moreover, they are the largest producers of public goods and they implement policies that shape the scope, the context, and the scale of social and environmental impact; the intergovernmental policy agenda of the United Nations Sustainable Development Goals (SDGs) is a case in point (Box 2.3). As far as securing funds is concerned, governments often seek private funds to complement public resources in the production of public goods. For example, support for the homeless and recently released former convicts involve government funds but often count on private individuals who complement the government by undertaking, financing, and materializing pertinent welfare services (e.g., the social impact bond of Peterborough Prison). As far as the supply of capital is concerned, several governments have created organizations for financing social entrepreneurship, like the Social Enterprise Investment and Development Funds established by the Australian government, and Rethink Ireland, which is co-financed by the Irish government.

Often the government does not possess all the resources that are needed in order to materialize a social welfare program but may provide funds to support it. Non-governmental organizations that address issues related to inflows of refugees serve as an example in this case. Finally, state contribution to the materialization of social welfare investments could take the form of providing experience and state care for the infrastructure needed to support private initiative. For example, the operation of a hospital that has been funded by a donation may be supported through a National Health System.

Box 2.3 The 2030 Agenda for Sustainable Development

"No one will be left behind"

The 2030 Agenda for Sustainable Development was adopted by the General Assembly of the United Nations in September 2015. The Agenda is articulated in 17 Sustainable Development Goals which span a set of 169 targets. The Sustainable Development Goals (SDGs) are:

Goal 1. End poverty in all its forms everywhere.

Goal 2. End hunger, achieve food security and improved nutrition and promote sustainable agriculture.

Goal 3. Ensure healthy lives and promote well-being for all at all ages.

Goal 4. Ensure inclusive and equitable quality education and promote lifelong learning opportunities for all.

Goal 5. Achieve gender equality and empower all women and girls.

Goal 6. Ensure availability and sustainable management of water and sanitation for all.

Goal 7. Ensure access to affordable, reliable, sustainable and modern energy for all.

Goal 8. Promote sustained, inclusive and sustainable economic growth, full and productive employment and decent work for all.

Goal 9. Build resilient infrastructure, promote inclusive and sustainable industrialization and
foster innovation.

Goal 10. Reduce inequality within and among countries.

Goal 11. Make cities and human settlements inclusive, safe, resilient and sustainable.

Goal 12. Ensure sustainable consumption and production patterns.

Goal 13. Take urgent action to combat climate change and its impacts.

Goal 14. Conserve and sustainably use the oceans, seas and marine resources for sustainable development.

Goal 15. Protect, restore and promote sustainable use of terrestrial ecosystems, sustainably manage forests, combat desertification, and halt and reverse land degradation and halt biodiversity loss.

Goal 16. Promote peaceful and inclusive societies for sustainable development, provide access to justice for all and build effective, accountable and inclusive institutions at all levels.

Goal 17. Strengthen the means of implementation and revitalize the Global Partnership for Sustainable Development.

The 2030 Agenda for Sustainable Development transforms government policies and the architecture of national economies worldwide in pursuit of sustainable development. In doing so, the Agenda rearranges the arena of the social economy. In the implementation of development goals and targets, the Agenda states that "We acknowledge the role of the diverse private sector, ranging from microenterprises to cooperatives to multinationals, and that of civil society organizations and philanthropic organizations in the implementation of the new Agenda".[13] As social economy is often based on principles such as democracy, social cohesion, and women empowerment at the level of local economies, it can foster the achievement of SDGs that rely on these principles.[14] More importantly, given the international diversity of policy priorities and performance with respect to the SDGs,[15,16] social economy can help localize sustainability objectives, support SDG "ownership" by local communities, and thus contribute to the implementation of the 2030 Agenda.[17] The 2030 Agenda highlights the importance of the institutions of social finance because the financial resources for the implementation of the SDGs cannot come from the private sector or the public sector alone: "private finance is constrained by risk and return requirements, while public finance is in scarce supply" (UNEP Finance Initiative, 2018: 8). Furthermore, the Agenda relies on principles of sustainability that many of these institutions advocate and finance, but also because SDGs 1, 2, 5, 8, and 9 are related to financial inclusion which is a fundamental aspect of social finance, especially in the context of microfinance. Indicatively, in the context of SDG 1, Target 1.4 refers to microfinance:

By 2030, ensure that all men and women, in particular the poor and the vulnerable, have equal rights to economic resources, as well as access to basic services, ownership and control over land and other forms of property, inheritance, natural resources, appropriate new technology and financial services, including microfinance.

Beyond the core of social finance, the 2030 Agenda for Sustainable Development constitutes a new context for all impact-minded financial services, including those that are primarily for-profit. For example, 100% of Nationale-Nederlanden's impact equity portfolios can be associated with SDG 8, 61% with SDG 9, and 54% with SDG 3.[18] Furthermore, the market for socially responsible investments now includes portfolios that are constructed on the basis of the sustainability merit of chosen securities in terms of SDGs; SDG-compliant Exchange-Traded-Funds have yielded profits for impact-minded investors, especially in terms of SDGs 8 and 9.[19]

Regulatory framework
Social finance regulations delineate the scale of impact investments, the sectors in which impact investors are active, and the relationship of social finance with entrepreneurship and the conventional financial sector. In addition, they safeguard stability

in the capital market for impact investments and, ultimately, shape the impact of social finance upon the developmental dynamics of the economy. As the expansion of social welfare enterprises is a somewhat recent phenomenon, the nexus of social finance institutions is constantly evolving and adapting to the broader regulatory framework for social entrepreneurship and the rules that apply in the case of conventional financial services. In the USA, for example, the Social Impact Partnership to Pay for Results Act complemented the preexisting institutional framework for social enterprises, that is, the legal forms of benefit corporations and low-profit limited liability companies. Similarly, the Jumpstart our Business Startups Act was adapted in accordance with the institutional framework of the Capital Market Committee on lending and share capital.

Financial flows

Coverage of the financial needs of impact investors encompasses a wide range of financial contracts. Depending on the priorities of the lender for repayment of capital, the right to participate in the management of the social enterprise, the timing and the amount provided, the characteristics of the finance relationship are constrained by the following triptych of choices: donations, lending, own-capital funding.[20] In each of these cases, funding mechanisms shape the mechanisms of governance of the social purpose organizations, affect the relationships between all interested parties that are associated with these organizations, and determine the effectiveness of the utilized capital.

Donations – charity

Charity is the most conventional way of private funding of welfare projects. Indicatively, charity donations in the USA stood at 424.74 billion US dollars in 2018.[21] Charity provides capital for welfare investments such as educational institutions, hospitals, orphanages, libraries, museums, etc. Less frequently, additional capital is offered to sustain operation of the social venture following completion of the investment project. The peculiar character of donations lies in that they are non-recoverable, meaning that the welfare investment does not secure any revenue for the donor to recover the capital invested, thus leading to a realized return of minus 100%. In general, charity (in finance) is defined as investment that leads to complete loss of capital. It, therefore, constitutes the typical case of an investor's priorities extending beyond the risk-return relationship. In the traditional case of charity capital, the social return expected by the investor, along with the undertaking of social risk, are exhausted in the financing phase: the need of the funding entity to contribute to social welfare is "satisfied" the moment the capital is donated to the social venture; from then on entrepreneurial risk and responsibility lie with the management of the social venture that undertakes utilization of the donation.

The fact that some investors are prepared to invest foregoing the entire capital they offer constitutes a catalyst in the formation of contracts for funding social investments and for securing accelerating social benefits in a wide spectrum of social challenges. For example, charity capital (which anticipates return equal to minus 100%) may be used as startup capital for the establishment of a productive mechanism, or for the underwriting of social impact bonds, or to provide collateral for lending a social purpose organization. This way, part of the financial risk is absorbed by charity, mitigating the risk undertaken by the other investors in the project, contributing to a more favorable risk–return relationship and an overall positive assessment of participation in the social investment. Thus, charity capital acts as a catalyst in the financing of social impact investments insofar it enhances participation by other investors.

A significant challenge in evaluating donations as financing mechanisms is the sustainability of investment following the donation of funds. Even in the few cases that money is offered for covering operating expenses of the financed institution for a long time after its establishment, donations do not cover operating expenses forever (the case of university financing via endowment funds is a case in point). Another challenge associated with donations is that they are highly cyclical: when the economy is in recession and corporate profits subside, the capability of donors to offer for welfare projects is severely limited. The decline in donations following the outbreak of the 2008 crisis is a characteristic example.[22]

In addition, donors often place restrictions, which reduce the flexibility of those who manage the funds. For example, if the donor has offered their property for the establishment of a hospital, it may be difficult to turn the hospital to a primary or secondary school if the need arises. Finally, appraisal of a donation must incorporate the costs involved – although not in the form of interest or dividends – namely, the costs associated with the resources that are being used in order to seek, raise, and manage donations. The advantages and disadvantages of donations as mechanisms of social finance are summarized in Figure 2.3.

Borrowing

Another source of finance for welfare projects is borrowing (bank loans, bonds, etc.). Debt capital is often provided by social investment finance intermediaries that specialize in financing impact investments such as Charity Bank, Triodos Bank, and ClearlySo. It can also be provided by conventional financial institutions that engage in impact financing (e.g., in 2019 HSBC launched Future Skills Innovation Challenge to finance social enterprises, jointly with Ashoka, a major impact investor). In contrast to donations, in this case the impact investor who lends funds seeks to recover the capital

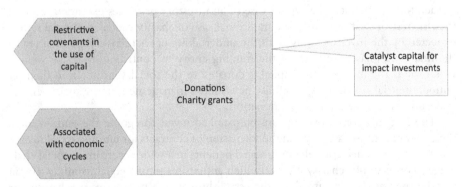

Figure 2.3 Advantages and disadvantages of donations

invested in the welfare project. In addition, the social investor seeks to collect cash for payment of interest. The financial requirements of the social investor and the operating expenses of the social enterprise actually determine the price that will be paid by the users of the welfare service. This is the case of school tuition fees or hospital fees paid to respective nonprofit institutions that are funded through loans. The benefits from borrowing stem from the limited time span of financial dependence, as well as the non-taxable nature of interest payments from the taxable income of the social investor who borrows to materialize an impact investment (although in many cases, social enterprises operate under favorable tax regimes). Moreover, after repayment of the loan the borrower can even redefine the strategy of the social investment, without the restrictive covenants that are often associated with donations.

Nevertheless, borrowing does have drawbacks. Extreme borrowing may lead a social enterprise to bankruptcy. Yet, borrowing is the most frequent form of raising funds for social enterprises compared to selling equity. According to a survey of 266 impact investors managing 239 billion US dollars, 50% of impact investments in 2018 were financed with debt, 34% private, 16% public debt.[23] Furthermore, borrowing is connected with the low rates of return that characterize social investments, as well as with the partial securing of loans with collateral (as in the case of funding social impact bonds by conventional financial institutions). The special role of borrowing in social finance is also associated with the fact that a large part of social economy action is related to finance. This is typical in the case of microfinance institutions, development banks (e.g., the European Bank for Reconstruction and Development and the World Bank), and credit unions. The unique nature of social investments impedes the dissemination of sufficient information that is required on the part of a large number of investors to establish a corporation with a broad shareholder base. For the same reason, financing social investments is for the most part carried out through private funds (generally, the loans of social enterprises do not trade in capital markets).

Borrowing is not free from the structural problems associated with social finance. Innovative social investments in areas with intense poverty and other challenges pertaining to economic development tend to be characterized by more intense informational asymmetries between lenders and borrowers. Informational asymmetries are reflected in the terms of borrowing via higher interest rates and, ultimately, prices paid by society for making use of social investments.

Own-capital financing

Own-capital funding constitutes the most important source of finance for entrepreneurship. It is capital contributed by the social entrepreneurs themselves. Especially in the field of impact investments, own-capital funding constitutes the main way of financing social enterprises in the context of venture philanthropy. Organizations such as Acumen, Omydiar Network, and LGT Lightstone often participate as owners of the organizations they finance, undertaking part of the relatively high risk associated with innovative investments that (Figure 2.4):

♦ Are difficult to liquidate in order to release the capital invested. For example, it would be impossible for an enterprise that employs solely women who live in war zones to make itself available for sale in the international capital market.

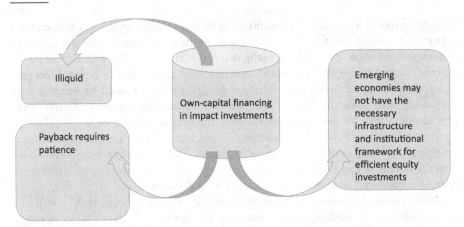

Figure 2.4 The challenges for own-capital financing in impact investments

♦ Emerge in economies characterized by intense poverty and inequality, and inadequate infrastructure and institutional framework to host innovative investments with a developmental mandate.
♦ Are expected to have a developmental impact in the distant future. As put by Acumen, such investments tend to be funded with "patient capital".

Because ownership of an enterprise is associated with access to its management, social investors are involved as partners in the enterprises they fund. Through their involvement in management, social investors may offer their expertise to prepare, materialize, and appraise social investments. The technical support associated with social finance constitutes key ammunition for sustainability of the social enterprises once the initial owners–investors pull out.

All too often the boundaries between different forms of social investment financing are not strictly defined. Many investors offer simultaneously charity donations, loans, and own-capital funding. This is the case of Ajooni in India, Mission & Co in Malaysia, Partnership for Change in Myanmar, the Rockefeller Foundation in the USA, and many others. In addition, some venture philanthropy organizations offer complex forms of finance, such as convertible loans that permit lenders to become shareholders, and convertible financial backing that permits the financial supporter to become a shareholder in the event that the social investment is successful. Moreover, social investment finance intermediaries may stand both in the demand side seeking capital from wholesale impact investors such as Big Society Capital and in the supply side providing capital for social enterprises. A further innovation in the field of social finance is **quasi equity capital**, whereby investors receive an increasing portion of profits as the profitability of the social enterprises rises (receiving part of profits may be limited to a maximum amount or time period beyond which the investor does not have the right to share the firm's revenues).

Challenges associated with planning and analysis of impact investments
Social economy and the mechanisms that fund it are expanding internationally,
attracting both attention and resources on the part of citizens, governments, owners
of capital, and the people who are in direct need of impact investments. The process
of planning and analyzing social investments is confronted by a wide spectrum of
methodological challenges, which have to do with the particular nature of impact
investments and the attempt to make use of conventional methods of financial analysis in a setting of complex decision-making criteria and limited access to organized
capital markets.

Measurement and valuation
The social and financial performance of an impact investment must be assessed
through an integrated evaluation process and, to the extent possible, through integrated measurement. In addition to the well-known challenges of **causality** between
investment – impact and non-exclusivity and non-rivalry of public goods, evaluating
impact investments necessitates the examination of social and financial performance
in terms of both their distinct impact, as well as their combined impact, as elements
that comprise one, integrated target.

Measurement and forecasting of the impact
of social investments is necessary to portray
social impact in monetary terms and thereby
make evaluation of investment choices possible. Specific valuation requirements and
the potential of incorporating algorithms for

> Measurement and forecasting of the
> impact of social investments is neces-
> sary to portray social impact in mon-
> etary terms and thereby make evalu-
> ation of investment choices possible.

investment appraisal in social finance decision-making depend on the availability of
data and the priorities of those who generate and those who make use of mechanisms
of financial analysis. Consequently, the use of financial valuation methods cannot pos-
sibly be objective. Nevertheless, it ought to offer an instructive analysis of the financial implications of a social investment to stakeholders. The subjectivities of all those
involved in social investments are particularly important, precisely because most of
these investments have a time horizon that goes well beyond the control and accountability of those who manage the invested capital (e.g., achieving social cohesion or
protection of the environment extends to the distant future). In that context, different
interests and preferences of the parties involved tend to influence estimations about
the plausibility of different scenarios regarding the outcome of impact investments,
measurement of impact and its expression in monetary units, approximation of the
discount rate, and analysis of causality between the social investment and social or
environmental change.

The requirements for the valuation of social investments mentioned earlier
drive the processes of formation of information models about social investments.
Standardization is necessary to reduce uncertainty about the aggregate (social and
monetary) value produced by the social investment. Requirements for organized
information express the needs of diverse impact investors: those who supply capital
funds, those who manage the funds, and those who ultimately make use of the capital invested to attain social impact. Those include donors, institutions, governments,
small- and large-scale capital market investors, organized investment capital, and, of

course, social enterprises. These institutions are also associated with demand for and supply of information in the impact investment market. Demand for information on behalf of investors leads, to a certain extent, to the supply of systematic information and vice versa, the supply of systematic information reduces the uncertainty associated with investment opportunities, encouraging more investors to come forth. The relationship between development of the social investment sector and development of an organized and widely accepted system of measuring social impact and establishment of a financial information taxonomy is almost bidirectional.

Risk-return: extending the analysis to account for social impact

One of the key difficulties associated with this new financial landscape is the functional incorporation of the expected social benefit with the risk associated with the investment. Social finance is about investments that are imprinted in the triptych **risk, return, social impact**. While return and risk are well-defined notions in financial theory and their size may be expressed with recognized statistical measures, social impact is a lot more difficult to measure and equally difficult to match to a specific investment.

Impact investments often display the characteristics of a positive relationship between risk and return. Let us assume that an impact investor wishes to finance research on Alzheimer's disease. One way would be to fund the building of infrastructure, where patients will receive medical care or even brief hospitalization. This is a low risk–low return approach, in the sense that it is highly likely to improve the lives of patients, supporting them in coping with their condition (of course, practical threats associated with challenges pertaining to operation of the infrastructure or the responsiveness of patients are always there). Nevertheless, it is a low social risk–low social return investment, because it addresses the symptoms of the disease (and, secondarily, social problems that stem from the patient's condition), rather than the deeper causes of the disease. A different approach to dealing with challenges associated with Alzheimer's disease is financing research for the production of medicine that would cure the disease. This would be a much riskier investment, because of the particularly high level of uncertainty about research outcomes, testing, and distribution of the medicine to the wider public. In case of success, the return to the investment would be quite significant, invariably larger than that of the mere addressing of the disease symptoms. Thus, the special character of medical innovation renders comparisons for the purposes of mapping effectively expected return and risk an extremely difficult exercise.

As a rule, impact investments are unique in the sense that they adapt to the historical context of the social problem they attempt to address. Indicatively, investment in the building of infrastructure for vocational training of women in a developing country is quite specific to the development context of that country and would, therefore, be inappropriate to compare its rate of return to that of a similar project in a different country. The unique character of such investments affects the assessment of the risk involved, the latter being defined as uncertainty that is associated with estimating the plausibility of different scenarios of investment outcomes.[24] Similarly, the uniqueness of incidents that underlie the undertaking of impact investments renders the evaluation of potential estimates subjective, especially when it comes to the probability of occurrence of phenomena that do not tend to repeat themselves, thus making it difficult to treat probability as frequency.[25] Nevertheless, such impediments do not alleviate the need for quantitative analysis and probabilistic estimate: full-scale valuation of social investments must incorporate quantitative imprints for both private and social benefits associated with a specific social investment. Recently established systems of impact measurement, such as IRIS and EngagedX, constitute the basis for the systematic valuation of social investments and, by implication, expression of social investment value in monetary terms.

In mainstream financial analysis, the required return for investors is used as the **discount rate** for bringing the value of cash flows to the present in order to compare them to the cost of undertaking the investment. The required return varies with the motivations and preferences of different social investors. Some investors are content with achieving social impact and receiving a monetary return that is limited to a riskless bank deposit. Others consider investments in poor countries with weak institutional frameworks to be extremely risky and expect rates of return that exceed 20%.[26] The first scenario of extremely low discount rates is mainly applicable to investments that are undertaken by state and development banks.[27] Low discount rates in the process of valuation keep the weight attributed to the future benefits high (the expected cash flows from an investment over many time periods after initiation of the investment that are discounted by a high discount factor end up having limited impact on of the present value). In general, however, the risk-free rate is not adequate for social investment appraisal. The reason is simple and has to do with the fact that impact investors face a wide range of investment alternatives, which vary not only in terms of expected social impact, but also in terms of probable outcomes and, therefore, in terms of risk. Thus, a measure based on the assumption that the expected return is common to all investors (the risk-free rate), indicating that the risk involved is common to all investment alternatives, actually being equal to zero, is not appropriate.

Impact investment scale and conventional capital markets

As a rule, social economy institutions are small-scale organizations, in the sense that the capital funds they utilize are less than those utilized by conventional enterprises that operate in the same field. For example, a social grocery store is always smaller in size than a super-market chain and a microfinance institution tends to be smaller than a conventional commercial bank. This practically precludes social finance mechanisms from financing large infrastructural projects that determine the dynamism of economic development in the very societies they try to bring change to. Change of scale in the case of social organizations presupposes changes in terms of the business model, communication channels with society, perceptions about social contribution, as well as changes in the relationship of the organization with money and capital markets. While large scale may be necessary in the case of social investment in order to impact more citizens and address more significant issues pertaining to economic development, the access

> As a rule, social economy institutions are small-scale organizations, in the sense that the capital funds they utilize are less than those utilized by conventional enterprises that operate in the same field.

of social investors to mechanisms of conventional finance is subject to severe issues and challenges.[28]

One reason behind limited availability of capital for social finance – beyond issues pertaining to the calculation of return, risk, and social impact of the investment – is that social entrepreneurs (who represent the demand-for-loanable-funds side in the financial market) often lack the skills or the mindset that is needed to implement radical organizational changes that would allow their organization to transform in terms of size and to become a larger-scale entity, such as more systematic management and a more flexible strategy. Indeed, they may have reservations with regard to changes that are being brought about by a critical increase in the scale of the social organization, fearing that pecuniary motives will prevail and political motives will be downgraded to being more conventional, as the new owners of capital may not share the nonprofit priorities of the founders.

A case in point is Banco Compartamos, the largest microfinance institution in Mexico, which offered 30% of its share capital to new investors through an IPO in 2007, giving astonishing profits to the original non-governmental organizations that founded it (such as Accion and the World Bank). As microfinance institutions tend to offer credit at higher interest rates (because of lack of collateral), the combination of high interest rates for lending low-income Mexican women and extraordinary profits realized by stock market investors constitutes a characteristic example of the risks and contradictions that may emerge in the event that social finance mingles with conventional capital.[29]

One solution to the problem of scale of impact investments would be the establishment of organized capital markets especially for impact investments, independently of conventional capital markets. Establishment of stock markets for attracting and trading capital for impact investment purposes would facilitate the flow of information in the market and increase liquidity, reducing uncertainty for investors and, therefore, reducing the cost of financing social ventures.

However, there is a major issue with this type of finance that needs to be addressed: the fact that social enterprises produce public goods and, therefore, do not pursue maximization of private profits makes it difficult to attract funding from the broad pool of investors who often seek to exercise power on the organizations they back in proportion to the capital invested. In addition, social enterprises tend to be small scale businesses that operate in an economic environment of high regulatory and financial risk. The uniqueness of each development project tends to keep investors' expediency of intentions away from the dynamism of a capital market that is primarily secondary in nature. Nowadays, there are several networks that operate as platforms of providing information for social ventures and act as channels for carrying out impact investments (SASIX in South Africa, Social Venture Conexxion in Canada, and Ethex in the UK).

Time horizon
An additional special feature of social investments is the very long time horizon. To the extent that the purpose of impact investments is to address social and environmental problems, their time horizon must be quite extended. Acumen, for example,

refers to "patient capital", determining a time horizon for social investments of seven to ten years, while other approaches assume an even longer time horizon.[30] Acumen finances Broadreach, an organization that offers medical services to low-income AIDS patients in South Africa. In such a case of a chronic disease, investors must be patient and must take into consideration all factors affecting the effectiveness of the investment, such as government health policy. Of course, extension of the time horizon reinforces the challenges associated with social and environmental investments with respect to matching investment initiatives to observed impact: as the time horizon gets longer, the factors that affect the dynamics of a social phenomenon are increasingly diverse.

Duration of the time horizon is more than just a prerequisite for the attainment of social impact; it is also an integral part of the preferences of the investor and, therefore, needs to be evaluated by the investor in the context of the triptych of criteria for engaging in impact investment (risk, return, and social impact). Thus, the time horizon of the investor expresses, in a way, the balance between the social and financial objectives. Investors with a shorter time horizon by and large place greater emphasis upon financial return rather than supporting sustainability, which has a longer gestation period.

Addressing these challenges expands the field of social and environmental issues addressed by social finance. More importantly, it increases investment projects that are ready to receive finance (ready in the sense that they operate in the context of a sufficiently developed institutional framework and have a comprehensive business plan). This is the key issue in many cases, where the inadequacy of the business plan and the institutional framework restricts investment readiness and deprives social welfare actions from much needed funds. For example, although there is a huge need for impact investments in Sub-Saharan Africa, social finance pioneers are mostly found in the UK, the USA, South East Asia, and Latin America.[31]

CONCLUSION

Social finance is the field of economics that studies the financing of impact investments. Social finance also denotes the financing of public goods production, combining private benefit and economic development priorities on the one hand with investment financing mechanisms such as state funding, donations, loans, and own capital on the other. The adoption of social finance is associated with the development of social economy institutions and social entrepreneurship. It is also associated with limitations pertaining to government policy and the failure of traditional market mechanisms to evaluate with precision and to manage effectively social inequalities, eradication of poverty, environmental protection, wide access to education and the arts, and to address refugee crises. Facing up to such social issues through social finance is carried out through a nexus of social enterprises and innovative financing mechanisms. Social impact bonds, crowdfunding platforms and venture philanthropy have changed the landscape of traditional charity in the form of donations and have helped redefine the role of finance for the purposes of addressing social problems and challenges associated with the process of economic development.

In these circumstances, financial analysis extends beyond the traditional risk-return framework of analysis to incorporate the impact of investments upon society and the environment. In the financial analysis of social welfare investments, financial benefits and positive social change coexist in a new landscape of finance that entails challenges for both lenders and borrowers, as well as for the institutions that undertake the task of generating a new regulatory framework. These challenges embody the methodological issues associated with conventional finance, expanded to include challenges stemming from the distinct nature of social investments: lack of widely accepted accounting standards and methods of measuring social impact, as well as lack of organized secondary markets to provide finance for social enterprises.

MATERIAL FOR DISCUSSION

EUR 65 million of EU financing for 430 social enterprises in the Netherlands, Belgium, Spain, and France

European Investment Fund, 2018. EUR 65 million of EU financing for 430 social enterprises in the Netherlands, Belgium, Spain and France. April 12.

Available at:

www.eif.org/what_we_do/microfinance/news/2018/easi-triodos-bank-euclid-network.htm.

REVIEW QUESTIONS

1 What is the object of study of social finance?
2 What are the principles of financial analysis in impact investments?
3 What are the most important mechanisms of social finance?
4 What are the main sources of finance in the context of the social economy?
5 What are the advantages and the disadvantages of donations, loans, and own-capital funding as mechanisms of financing social investments?
6 What are the challenges facing financial valuation in impact investments?

NOTES

1 A version of this chapter has been published in the *International Review of Financial Analysis:* Andrikopoulos, A., 2020. Delineating social finance. *International Review of Financial Analysis*, 70, July.

2 https://the giin.org.

3   The popular term "real sector" denotes all economic activities outside the financial sector. In fact, banking services are no more and no less "real" than the services of travel agencies, hospitals, or schools.

4   See, for example, Andrikopoulos (2013), Hodgson (2009).

5   Mudaliar and Dithrich (2019).

6   Global Sustainable Investment Alliance (2018).

7   Ethical banking is not always identical to social banking, but often these terms are used interchangeably to describe similar banking activities.

8   Global Sustainable Investment Alliance (2018).

9   See McKillop et al. (2020) for a review of cooperative financial institutions.

10   World Council of Credit Unions (2018).

11   See, for example, Lu et al. (2017), Ghoul et al. (2018), Caroll and Shabana (2010), Dhaliwal et al. (2011).

12   Especially with regard to corporate social responsibility (CSR), it is worth stressing that CSR activities are often criticized for morally legitimizing profit in conditions of social inequality, helping for-profit companies improve their public image and increase customer loyalty, ultimately enhancing profitability (see, for example, Patten, 1992; Cho et al., 2010). Disclosing CSR activities improves the flow of information from the company to investors, reducing uncertainty on the part of investors and, by implication, leading to lower return on the capital invested and, ultimately, higher levels of finance for corporations. Thus, systematic involvement of corporations in CSR activities may be conducive to gaining favorable access to capital markets.

13   www.un.org/ga/search/view_doc.asp?symbol=A/RES/70/1&Lang=E

14   UNRISD (2017).

15   Forestier and Kim (2020).

16   Moyer and Hedden (2020).

17   Jones and Comfort (2019).

18   Schramade (2017).

19   Miralles-Quirós et al. (2018).

20   Nichols and Emerson (2015).

21   https://givingusa.org/giving-usa-2019-americans-gave-427-71-billion-to-charity-in-2018-amid-complex-year-for-charitable-giving/.

22   See Meer et al. (2017).

23   Mudaliar and Dithrich (2019).

24   For example, uncertainty denotes a situation where the value of an investment after six months is unknown, while risk denotes a situation where the future value of an investment is unknown, yet it may be inferred that the probability of the investment value going up is 40% and the probability of the investment value going down is 60%.

25   De Finetti (1989). The subjectivity of estimating the probability of a social phenomenon to occur highlights the potential of Bayesian statistics in social investment valuation.

26   O'Donohoe et al. (2010).

27   Freeman et al. (2018).

28   Schmidt (2010); Varga and Hayday (2018).

29   Ashta and Hudon (2012).

30   https://acumen.org/about/patient-capital.

31   Oleksiak et al. (2015).

REFERENCES

Andrikopoulos, A., 2013. Finance: An essay on objects and methods of science. *Cambridge Journal of Economics*, 37(1), 35–55. https://doi.org/10.1093/cje/bes027.

Ashta, A., and Hudon, M., 2012. The Compartamos microfinance IPO: Mission conflicts in hybrid institutions with diverse shareholding. *Strategic Change*, 21(7–8), 331–341. https://doi.org/10.1002/jsc.1912.

Caroll, A.B., and Shabana, K.M., 2010. The business case for corporate social responsibility: A review of concepts, research and practice. *International Journal of Management Reviews*, 12(1), 85–105. https://doi.org/10.1111/j.1468-2370.2009.00275.x.

Cho, C.H., Roberts, R.W., and Patten, D.M., 2010. The language of US corporate environmental disclosure. *Accounting, Organizations and Society*, 35(4), 431–443. https://doi.org/10.1016/j.aos.2009.10.002.

De Finetti, B., 1989. Probabilism: A critical essay of probability and the value of science. *Erkenntnis*, 31(2/3), 169–223. https://doi.org/10.1007/BF01236563.

Dhaliwal, D.S., Li, O.Z., Tsang, A., and Yang, Y.G., 2011. Voluntary nonfinancial disclosure and the cost of equity capital: The initiation of corporate social responsibility reporting. *Accounting Review*, 86(1), 59–100. https://doi.org/10.2308/accr.00000005.

Forestier, O., and Kim, R.E., 2020. Cherry-picking the sustainable development goals: Goal prioritization by national governments and implications for global governance. *Sustainable Development*, 28(5), 1269–1278. https://doi.org/10.1002/sd.2082.

Freeman, M., Groom, B., and Spackman, M., 2018. *Social discount rates for cost-benefit analysis: A report for HM treasury.* https://assets.publishing.service.gov.uk/government/uploads/system/uploads/attachment_data/file/935551/Social_Discount_Rates_for_Cost-Benefit_Analysis_A_Report_for_HM_Treasury.pdf.

Ghoul, S.E., Guedhami, O., Kim, H., and Park, K., 2018. Corporate environmental responsibility and the cost of capital: International evidence. *Journal of Business Ethics*, 149(2), 335–361. https://doi.org/10.1007/s10551-015-3005-6.

Global Sustainable Investment Alliance, 2018. *Global sustainable investment review 2018.* http://www.gsi-alliance.org/wp-content/uploads/2019/03/GSIR_Review2018.3.28.pdf.

Hodgson, G.M., 2009. The great crash of 2008 and the reform of economics. *Cambridge Journal of Economics*, 33(6), 1205–1221. https://doi.org/10.1093/cje/bep050.

Jones, P., and Comfort, D., 2019. A commentary on the localisation of the sustainable development goals. *Journal of Public Affairs*, 20(1), e1943. https://doi.org/10.1002/pa.1943.

Lu, L.Y., Shailer, G., and Yu, Y., 2017. Corporate social responsibility disclosure and the value of cash holdings. *European Accounting Review*, 26(4), 729–753. https://doi.org/10.1080/09638180.2016.1187074.

McKillop, D., French, D., Sobiech, A.L., and Wilson, J.O.S., 2020. Cooperative financial institutions: A review of the literature. *International Review of Financial Analysis*, 71. https://doi.org/10.1016/j.irfa.2020.101520.

Meer, J., Miller, D.H., and Wulfsberg, E., 2017. The great recession and charitable giving. *Applied Economics Letters*, 24(21), 1542–1549. https://doi.org/10.1080/13504851.2017.1319556.

Miralles-Quirós, J.L., Miralles-Quirós, M.M., and Nogueira, J.M., 2018. Diversification benefits of using exchange-traded funds in compliance to the sustainable development goals. *Business Strategy and the Environment*, 28(1), 244–255. https://doi.org/10.1002/bse.2253.

Moyer, J.D., and Hedden, S., 2020. Are we on the right path to achieve the sustainable development goals? *World Development*, 127, 104749. https://doi.org/10.1016/j.worlddev.2019.104749.

Mudaliar, A., and Dithrich, H., 2019. *Sizing the impact investing market*. New York: Global Impact Investing Network.

Nichols, A., and Emerson, J., 2015. Social finance: Capitalizing social impact. *In*: A. Nicholls, R. Patton, and J. Emerson, eds. *Social finance*. Oxford: Oxford University Press, 1–41.

O'Donohoe, N., Leijonfvud, C., Saltuk, Y., Bugg-Levine, A., and Bradenburg, M., 2010. *Impact investments: An emerging asset class*. New York: JP Morgan Global Research, The Rockefeller Foundation, Global Impact Investing Network.

Oleksiak, A., Nicholls, A., and Patton, R., 2015. Impact investing: A market in evolution. *In*: A. Nicholls, R. Patton, and J. Emerson, eds. *Social finance*. Oxford: Oxford University Press, 207–249.

Patten, D.M., 1992. Intra-industry environmental disclosures in response to the Alaskan oil spill: A note. *Accounting, Organizations and Society*, 17(5), 471–475. https://doi.org/10.1016/0361-3682(92)90042-Q.

Schmidt, R.H., 2010. Microfinance, commercialization and ethics. *Poverty and Public Policy*, 2(1), 99–137. https://doi.org/10.2202/1944-2858.1020.

Schramade, W., 2017. Investing in the UN sustainable development goals: Opportunities for companies and investors. *Journal of Applied Corporate Finance*, 29(2), 87–99. https://doi.org/10.1111/jacf.12236.

UNEP Finance Initiative, 2018. *Rethinking impact to finance the SDGs*. Geneva: UNEP Finance Initiative.

UNRISD, 2017. *Localizing the SDGs through social and solidarity economy*. Geneva: UNRISD.

Varga, E., and Hayday, M., 2018. *A recipe book for social finance*. Luxembourg: Publications Office of the EU.

World Council of Credit Unions, 2018. Statistical report. www.woccu.org/documents/2018_Statistical_Report.

Part II

Institutions of social finance

3

Microfinance

After reading this chapter, you will be able to:

1 Outline the characteristics of microfinance institutions
2 Identify the challenges facing microfinance
3 Assess the advantages of microfinance
4 Explain the impact of microfinance on economic development

INTRODUCTION

Microfinance consists in funding individuals and organizations that do not have access to the conventional banking system, because they either do not possess property or have very low income. Microfinance is the showcase institution of social finance. The year 2005 was proclaimed by the United Nations as the international year

> Microfinance consists in funding individuals and organizations that do not have access to the conventional banking system, because they either do not possess property or have very low income. Microfinance is the showcase institution of social finance.

of microcredit. Financial inclusion via microfinance is incorporated in Target 1.4 of the United Nations' 2030 Agenda for Sustainable Development, in the context of

DOI: 10.4324/9781003230366-5

SDG 1 that is about ending poverty in all its forms. In 2006 Muhammad Yunus was awarded the Nobel Prize for establishing Grameen Bank, the emblematic mechanism in the war against extreme poverty through microcredit. Grameen bank currently has more than 9 million members, of whom 97% are women.[1] It constitutes a characteristic example of combining financial viability with welfare, in the sense that through microfinance individuals who would otherwise be excluded based on pure profit-seeking solvency and risk-return analysis are given the opportunity to create wealth and improve their standard of living.

The spread of microfinance across a large number of countries, capital markets, users and providers of capital contributes to the advancement of structured discourse, as well as to the development of an institutional framework in this novel field of finance. In general, the field of microfinance experiences ongoing expansion in different aspects of the financial network. For example, organizations evaluating credit risk in microfinance, such as Microrate, M-CRIL, and a relevant S&P division have sprung up, specializing in microcredit rating. The landscape of borrowers who target the microfinance market, financial institutions that are involved in the extension of microcredit, the pertinent regulatory framework, and, more importantly, the boundaries that separate microfinance from the conventional financial system framework are also in continuous flux. A financing mechanism that targets those who are excluded from the banking system and capital markets faces an extensive plexus of challenges (Figure 3.1).

1 Defining financial stability in microfinance and its influence on systemic stability of the financial system as a whole (many **microfinance institutions** are not part of the banking sector regulatory framework, generating novel challenges for financial stability).
2 Managing credit risk, market risk, and operational risk.

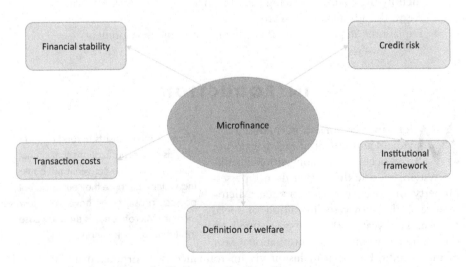

Figure 3.1 The main challenges of microfinance

3 Managing increasing transaction costs, as well as the weak and asymmetric information that characterizes microfinance, because those who receive funding are – almost by definition – outside the radar of bank information systems.

4 Utilizing the institutional toolbox of organized capital markets and commercial banking, while preserving the social character of microfinance (e.g., credit rating programs to assess the creditworthiness of borrowers).

5 Evaluating the notion of welfare that defines the boundaries between microfinance mechanisms and conventional banking.

This chapter offers an introduction to microfinance. Its target is to define the basic pertinent concepts, present the differences between microcredit and conventional ways of lending, and identify the key challenges associated with the design of microfinance regulations and entrepreneurship.

BASIC CONCEPTS

Economic entities that do not possess property for hypothecation and lack a steady flow of income that would ensure paying their creditors back find it hard to secure funding. Funding in such cases is cumbered by the particularly high degree of uncertainty and level of cost associated with the measurement of credit risk in the absence of a credit record for the borrower and unknown prospects for the borrower's enterprise. Thinking conservatively, commercial banks tend to exclude such customers, as they do not wish to be burdened by the costs of potential credit events or to be forced to generate a special category of high interest rate loans of undefined prospects. However, with no access to credit for their small enterprises, low-income citizens in developing economies are highly likely to remain poor.

Microfinance is about the supply of financial services to individuals and enterprises with minimal ownership of property and very low income.[2] Actually, finance mechanisms for the poor have been in place in different parts of the world for several centuries. The term microfinance denotes the plexus of institutions that developed over the past few decades, mainly since the 1970s. Muhammad Yunus' Grameen Bank constitutes a remarkable example of the contemporary meaning of the term "microfinance". This area of finance is oriented towards three principal objectives (Figure 3.2).

1 Addressing poverty of the local population, rather than enhancing the creditors' wealth.

2 Supplying financial services that are economically viable for the creditor.

3 Supplying financial services that are oriented to those excluded from the banking system.

These points imply that microfinance, as a developmental mechanism, differs from state subsidization of credit, where – usually via development or agricultural banks – the government subsidizes interest rates drawing on state resources. In addition,

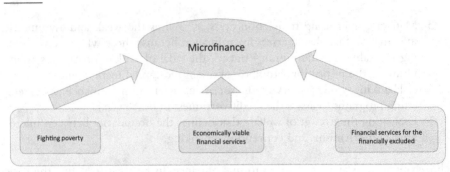

Figure 3.2 Microfinance: principal objectives

emphasis on those excluded from the banking system justifies the systematic focus of microfinance to female loan applicants, the target being boosting economic development through empowerment of women.[3] Finally, microfinance activities tend to extend beyond lending. Microfinance institutions offer additional services, including deposits, money transfer, life insurance, small business consulting, young professionals' training, and the financing of development investment projects in sanitation facilities and access to drinkable water.[4] BRAC, the Bangladeshi NGO that preceded Grameen Bank, constitutes a typical example of a microfinance organization offering a wide variety of financial services outside loans.

THE DEVELOPMENT OF MICROFINANCE OVER THE PAST 40 YEARS

Microfinance transformed the landscape of banking services, highlighting the poor and financially excluded as credible borrowers. As **financial exclusion** implies, among other things, exclusion from entrepreneurial activities, microfinance serves mainly as an apparatus that aims to convert low-income farmers to small-scale entrepreneurs, rendering entrepreneurship a mechanism for combating poverty.[5] Remarkably, microfinance was initiating significant change in the financial system at the same time that another radical change in the field was taking place – in fact in the opposite direction – namely the **financial engineering** revolution. During the same period that special financial institutions for women, the poor, and those subject to financial exclusion emerged, providing these groups with small amounts of money in order to sustain their businesses, a whole new world of financial derivative products was growing in conditions of ongoing deregulation, which targeted organizations of high financial caliber and access to mechanisms of complex scientific analysis. Thirty years later, towards the end of the first decade of the 21st century, microfinance was already established as a pillar of economic development in the areas of the world that were striving to escape poverty. At the same time, financial engineering was heavily criticized for the role it played in the global financial crisis, through financial derivative products that exposed the global financial system to risky bets. In actual fact, of course, financial innovation mechanisms (such as microfinance or financial engineering) have the potential to make significant contributions to economic development. The substance of the financial innovation is defined by the historical trajectory of the economies and societies that instigate it.

Microfinance started in the early 1970s as a parallel system of credit with a loose institutional structure, which is typical for the onset of social innovations in low-income countries, such as Indonesia, Bolivia, and Bangladesh. From the very beginning, microfinance combined the need for financial viability of the creditor with the motive of economic development for the local economy. Muhammad Yunus, the pioneer of microfinance with Grameen Bank in Bangladesh, has repeatedly stated that addressing poverty constituted the primary motive for the establishment of Grameen Bank. The fact that Grameen Bank started operations in January 1977 but officially acquired the charter to operate as a bank six years later is indicative of its innovative nature.[6] Moreover, a special characteristic of the developmental nature of Grameen Bank was its focus on women who were excluded from the banking system of Bangladesh to that point. Yunus extended small loans to groups of women. Group lending helped with loan monitoring, reinforcing organized collective intervention on the part of women to transform their prospects in the local society. Another characteristic of the credit policy of Grameen Bank was the extension of small loans to be repaid in quite frequent installments. For example, a 150 USD loan could be paid back in one year, with payments being made every week or every fortnight. Payments were made in public meetings of borrowers with Grameen bank clerks.

> Microfinance serves mainly as an apparatus that aims to convert low-income farmers to small-scale entrepreneurs, rendering entrepreneurship a mechanism for combating poverty.

Nowadays, Grameen is a profitable bank. Twenty-four percent of the bank is owned by the Bangladeshi government and the rest is owned by its members (depositors and borrowers).[7] Its members are more than 5% of the Bangladeshi population and include over 109,000 beggars (loans to beggars are interest free; their goal is to eliminate the begging profession and create employment for beggars). Total assets were 2.6 billion US dollars, loans outstanding were 1.5 billion US dollars, and only 0.33% of loans were overdue in 2018. Lending interest rates peak at 20% and deposit interest rates peak at 12%. Most loans are business ("loans for income generating activities") and housing loans, the average loan amount being 478 US dollars in 2018.[8] Loans are given without collateral and the bank is not taking legal action against customers who are unable to pay loans back. The bank's policy for extending a loan is such that the prospective borrower's poverty increases the probability of the borrower getting a loan.[9] The entrepreneurial model of Grameen Bank for combating poverty is applied by many microfinance institutions throughout the world. In 2018 it had a loan portfolio of a loan portfolio of 124 billion USD and 140 million borrowers (80% women).[10] In terms of the number of borrowers, South Asia has the largest share in the global market, 61%. However, in terms of the value of the loan portfolio and the number of microfinance institutions, Latin America and Caribbean lead the market with 39% and 27%, respectively. The market is concentrated with 11% of microfinance institutions having 76% of the global loan portfolio.[11]

The role of the World Bank is substantial in the microfinance market: through the International Finance Corporation, the Bank offers consulting services and funds to microfinance institutions in 95 countries.[12]

Rapid development of the international network of microfinance over the past 40 years is accompanied by a wide variety of microfinance institutions in terms of size, geographical dispersion, credit policy, and legal form. Microfinance institutions evolve, trying to attain financial viability (through appropriate selection of borrowers and interest rate determination), while distancing themselves from government subsidization of interest rates as well as incorporation of commercial banking processes and, at the same time, maintaining the target of combating poverty by way of financing entrepreneurship. The legal form of microfinance institutions is critical in determining the direction of the pertinent regulatory framework.[13] For example, issues relating to capital adequacy, credit risk and market risk management, corporate governance and taxation are different for banks, NGOs, or non-bank financial institutions. An appropriate regulatory framework is extremely important given the wide geographical dispersion of microfinance mechanisms, which gives poverty, inequality, economic development, and structural change a completely different texture. The law enacted by the state of Andhra Pradesh in India in 2010 is a characteristic example of legislation that specifically aimed at protection of borrowers from the payment collection practices of SKS Microfinance.

CHARACTERISTICS OF LOAN CONTRACTS

The landscape of microfinance mechanisms varies widely and is in continuous flux. As result, business and cash flow planning on the part of microfinance institutions, as well as formation of a pertinent regulatory framework need to take into account a number of essential matters. In the first place, lending groups of borrowers (as opposed to individual borrowers) pose challenges for the determination of credit rating and the impact of lending upon social and economic development. Furthermore, repayment of loans in public (in the presence of members of the local society) needs to be evaluated in terms of the message and the incentives it conveys regarding entrepreneurship, credit, poverty, and social monitoring in these communities. Also, the frequency of payments – usually inversely related to the level of payments – needs to be analyzed in terms of its impact on both the ability of borrowers to fulfil their obligations and the viability of the microfinance organization. In addition, it is necessary to examine the degree to which microfinance institutions should expand in the field of services beyond lending (e.g., saving, insurance, risk management). Last but not least, perhaps the most fundamental challenge pertains to measurement of the social impact of microfinance institutions: measuring the percentage reduction in the level of poverty and, more importantly, the extent to which mitigation of poverty comes as a result of microcredit, as opposed to being the result of other actions that have similar objectives in a given community (e.g., training programs for the unemployed, housing and heating support for the poor, etc.).

Group lending

Most microfinance institutions mainly supply loans to small groups of borrowers implementing the entrepreneurial model of Grameen Bank. This practically means that if a member of the group fails to pay back the corresponding proportion of the installment, the other group members are responsible for covering the payment.[14] The size of funded groups varies. Indicatively, the National Bank for Agricultural and Rural Development in India gives loans to groups of four to ten individuals.[15]

The primary objective of group lending is addressing basic challenges to which the borrower needs to respond in the context of microfinance: lack of sufficient information about the creditworthiness of borrowers and lack of property to be placed as collateral for the loan. When responsibility for loan repayment is shared by the group, monitoring for the creditworthiness and timely repayment of the loan is partly transferred from the lender to the group. Group members are vigilant of one another for consistency with regard to payments and preclusion of bad borrowers. The fact that the group members reside in the same area makes **social monitoring** of payments more effective. Group structure is important in enforcing loan repayment. For example, evidence from Sierra Leone has shown that a group's structural cohesion affects repayment up to a point, beyond which cohesion may deter punishment of inconsistent group members and thereby result in worse repayment rates.[16]

Naturally, adoption of such methods has certain weaknesses. First, social monitoring (aiming at prompt loan repayment) might disrupt relations amongst team members, constituting an obstacle to social cohesion (which happens to be one of the main objectives of microfinance).[17] In addition, because group lending frees the lender from the task of loan monitoring, it essentially transfers part of the cost of lending to the borrowers it aims to help.[18] In certain occasions, the lender proves to be more effective in loan monitoring than a group of borrowers. In Kenya, for example, group microcredit appears to demonstrate a higher proportion of bad loans in comparison to individual credit.[19,20] Even in terms of the motivation for prompt loan repayment, it is not always certain that individual borrowers will be willing to undertake credit risk on the part of the rest of the borrowers in the team, along with the burden of monitoring and disciplining of the team. Moreover, in the case of for-profit microfinance institutions, the phenomena of extended violence to maintain borrowers' compliance are not uncommon. This was the case of SKS Microfinance in India, where the government had to step in to protect the citizens of Andhra Pradesh from SKS Microfinance employees who made use of violence to enforce repayment of loans.

The focus of microfinance institutions on group lending – as opposed to individual loan contracts – is useful to the extent that the benefits are higher than the costs associated with the process. In the Philippines, microfinance group lending is not associated with lower default rates compared to individual lending.[21] Similarly, in Mongolia group lending does not generate improved repayment rates compared to individual lending, even though it is found to positively impact the establishment of businesses and household food consumption.[22]

Payment in public

In the same line of argument, the rationale behind payment of installments against a loan in public needs to be evaluated, weighing not only the positive impact of group dynamics, but also the practical aspects involved. On the one hand, a public repayment schedule may increase social pressure for consistency of loan recipients. However, as debt collectors are deployed to neighborhoods, labor and transaction costs increase for the provider of financial services, thereby pushing interest rates up. Moreover, debt collection in person may at time entail violence, thus standing counter to the principal objective of microfinance, that is, to improve the lives of the socially and financially excluded.[23] Addressing the issue of labor-intensity in microfinance, there are now mobile-banking services that help the implementation of microcredit contracts (M-PESA, owned by Vodafone, is a case in point; starting in Kenya in 2007, it now offers payment services to many African countries, Eastern Europe, and India). In Rwanda, Urwego Opportunity Bank (a microfinance institution) introduced mobile banking in microcredit and achieved lower default rates and cost savings.[24] Still, the efficiency of payment methods (e.g., in public versus electronic) has to be assessed in terms of its effect on microfinance institutions' social mandate and financial performance.

Frequency of payments

A key feature of repayment contracts is the frequency of payments and the corresponding payment amount. On the one hand, frequent payments reveal the ability or willingness of the borrower to pay back, thus mitigating the uncertainty for the lender. More frequent payments are appropriate for borrowers who do not possess a bank account (microfinance is often relevant in these very cases) and find it difficult to save large amounts of money. On the other hand, extremely frequent payments require the use of resources for materialization and monitoring of payments (e.g., payments in public), to the extent that they counterweigh at least in part the benefits stemming from frequent payments. For example, Grameen bank started with daily payments and then moved on to weekly and fortnightly payments to deal more effectively with the administrative costs of the payments system.

Dynamic incentives

Dynamic incentives is a type of lending that involves increasingly higher amounts lent out as a reward for prompt repayment. Thus, if the first three-month loan to the borrower is 50 euros, the second could be

> Dynamic incentives is a type of lending that involves increasingly higher amounts lent out as a reward for prompt repayment.

75 and the third 100, provided that the borrower keeps up with the repayment schedule. If the loan is not paid back, the borrower is excluded from future credit by the particular lender. In the case of group loans within the dynamic incentives

system of lending, if one group member does not pay back, all group members are excluded from future borrowing. This way, the incentive of rewarding consistency reduces the cost of loan monitoring for the lender, as well as losses associated with potential credit events.

Managing credit risk through dynamic incentives is related to two main challenges. The first challenge has to do with that borrower who intends to borrow only once and does not intend to rely on microfinance ever again in the future; in this case the dynamic incentives system fails to motivate the borrower to pay the loan back. The second challenge is related to the first. It is about borrowers who have access to many microfinance institutions. In such cases, the borrower has an incentive not to pay back one organization and then seek a loan from another. This challenge could be overcome through the establishment of a database with the credit history of each borrower, similar to the databases typically used by commercial banks. However, this would be outside the traditional scope of microfinance, which addresses borrowers who are excluded from the commercial banking system precisely because they do not possess sufficient property, income, or sound credit history.

The breadth of financial services offered by microfinance institutions

Microfinance is not just about microcredit. Although the operations of microfinance and social targeting have, for the most part, to do with extension of loans to socially and financially excluded individuals, additional services have sprung up over the past few years. Other than lending for business purposes or confronting extreme circumstances (e.g., natural disasters or public health issues), microfinance institutions also offer money transfer services and provide financial services that often serve a specific cause, such as children's education or marriage (for example, Grameen offers scholarships for secondary education and interest-free loans for higher education). In addition, they offer insurance services, such as retirement pensions, life insurance, and property insurance.

While these are essential and commonly offered services by commercial banking institutions, they constitute a relatively recent development in the case of microfinance. There are two reasons for that. First, the cost of supplying such services is relatively high in relation to the limited amounts that are involved in such services and, therefore, the profit margin may be too low. Second, demand for these kinds of services on the part of individuals and organizations who choose microfinance mechanisms for funding tends to be low. Other than extreme poverty – low demand is attributable to lack of **financial literacy**, a field microfinance institutions are often active in (financial education and the development of money and capital markets are attributes of developed economies).[25]

MICROFINANCE AND ORGANIZED MONEY AND CAPITAL MARKETS

Given that several commercial banking practices are also adopted by microfinance institutions, any discussion on the commercialization of microfinance denotes solely the extent to which microfinance and conventional banking are coupled on the axis that distinguishes them from each other, namely the active pursuit of profit as a priority behind the extension of credit (Figure 3.3).[26] On the one hand, the criticism against commercialization of the credit system of microfinance underlines that emphasis on profit on the part of the lender shifts the priorities of microfinance away from economic development and emphasis on the local society, ending up with lower rather than greater availability of resources for the very poor, superseding the main objective of microfinance.[27,28] On the other hand, enhanced profit associated with microcredit attracts more capital, thus aiding microfinance institutions to respond to increased demand for microcredit in many developing areas around the globe. In addition, the risk management mechanisms used by for-profit financial institutions appear to be appropriate for some of the capital market requirements of microfinance. In 2006, for example, Morgan Stanley materialized the investment project BOLD "Blue Orchard Loans for Development 2006–1", through which securitization of the loan portfolios of 21 microcredit institutions took place, providing over 100 million US dollars to microfinance institutions, thus helping them cover their capital needs.[29]

Although microcredit and organized money and capital markets are separate fields, their interaction is inevitable. For example, funding microfinance institutions may come from commercial banks and, likewise, the cash of microcredit may be made available for deposits and other conventional banking services. Other than inflows of capital, capital markets may assist these organizations to accumulate own capital. Large microfinance institutions have drawn capital from IPOs in organized capital markets (e.g., Bank Rayat Indonesia, Equity Bank, Banco Compartamos, SKS Microfinance, Equitas Holdings, Ujivan Financial Services, etc.). Beyond organized exchanges, microfinance institutions also collect funds from private placements.

While microfinance institutions' access to organized capital markets helps raise much needed capital, it does not leave their developmental orientation intact. The intense pursuit of profitability may lead to reckless expansion of lending and soaring interest rates charged on loans in order to cope with the frequent credit events. For example, just before the IPO of Banco Compartamos, the interest rate on microcredit

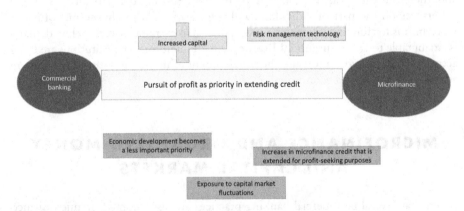

Figure 3.3 Microfinance and commercial banking

stood at 100%.[30] The market evaluated Banco Compartamos in a positive manner and the IPO issue was oversubscribed 13 times, resulting in huge profits for big investors, at a time when borrowers were paying extraordinarily high interest rates.[31] Moreover, exposure to organized capital markets renders microfinance institutions vulnerable to market volatility, even to financial crises. The degree of contagion of a liquidity crisis or a stock market crash in the area of microcredit is also dependent on the degree to which microcredit organizations are dependent on organized capital markets for funding. For example, in the federal state of Andhra Pradesh in India, crisis in microfinance followed the global financial crisis at the end of the first decade of the 21st century. By then, India was the area with the highest development in microfinance and Andhra Pradesh was the center of the largest microfinance institutions in the country (Box 3.1).

Box 3.1 SKS Microfinance and the microfinance crisis in India

SKS Microfinance was established in 1997 by Vikram Akula, a US citizen of Indian origin who had studied political science at the Universities of Chicago and Yale. SKS was established as a nonprofit in 1997 and was converted to a for-profit organization in 2005. The global reach of this endeavor was corroborated not only by the rapid growth of SKS Microfinance, but also by the awards Vikram Akula received from the World Economic Forum and *Time* magazine during the 2000s. In its first steps, SKS Microfinance seemed to follow the footsteps of Grameen Bank, addressing poverty through the financing of micro-entrepreneurship, as explained in Akula's book, *A Fistful of Rice: My Unexpected Quest to End Poverty through Profitability* (Harvard Business Review Press, 2010).

However, towards the end of the first decade of the 21st century, Akula sought growth for SKS Microfinance by implementing conventional commercial banking methods in organized capital markets. The growth in the scale of banking services of SKS Microfinance meant that the financial services offered would be standardized and the bank's capital would be increased by big investors and structures of organized capital markets. Participation of investment houses such as Sequoia Capital and Quantum Fund, as well as successful entry of SKS Microfinance in the stock market in July 2010, constitute characteristic examples. SKS Microfinance raised 155 million USD from the IPO. The price of the stock increased by 11% on the first day of trading in the stock market, benefiting the initial investors. However, just a few weeks later the price of the stock collapsed. With its recently acquired capital, SKS Microfinance enjoyed a leading position in the Indian State of Andhra Pradesh, where it held its headquarters and where another 400–600 microfinance institutions were also active.[32] Stock market entry rendered the bank increasingly accountable to shareholders and investors whose only purpose was the acquisition of profit in sharp contrast to the basic principle of microfinance as a developmental mechanism against poverty. Profit is not the primary objective of Grameen Bank, for instance. The pursuit of higher profits resulted in tremendous loan expansion to low-income individuals and, as a result, higher credit risk for the bank. Towards the end of 2010, 84% of households had acquired two or more loans, while 58% of the households had acquired four or more loans. Real annual rates of interest in Andhra Pradesh exceeded 50%.[33]

Furthermore, shared responsibility for loan repayment in accordance with the Grameen model created more challenges than it resolved in an environment of rapidly growing speculative credit expansion. The relations between group members were often uncontrollable and suicides related to microfinance borrowing became commonplace. The situation got completely out of hand in October 2010. On October 15, 2010, the government of Andhra Pradesh responded with a legislative decree, referring to 30 suicides in 45 days and overcharging borrowers through extremely high interest rates. According to the decree, microfinance institutions were not allowed to exercise any kind of violence or use their agents to force loan repayment. One week later, microfinance institutions faced severe liquidity issues, thus being forced to announce interest rate cuts on loans. Some borrowers turned to small-group solidarity microfinance, which was subsidized by the local government. Of course, neither aspect of the financial system was immune to this financial crisis that led to limiting capital and credit, bringing into light both the need for regulation of microfinance as well as the limitations of microfinance with respect to conventional banking practices.

In 2011 Vikram Akula stepped down from the leadership of SKS Microfinance.

The distance between priorities and regulations of commercial banking and microfinance may be bridged if commercial banking maintains the local character of microfinance credit, placing the emphasis on trust and solidarity, instead of pursuing solely geographical expansion and profit.[34] Furthermore, the commercial microcredit sector may incorporate both traditional practices of microfinance as well as commercial banking practices, if the two systems become more complementary than antagonistic by focusing on different market segments. Conventional microfinance is more appropriate for small group loans to very poor borrowers, while its commercial version of individual loans of higher amounts are more appropriate for individuals who are in a better financial condition.

Indeed, this is the objective of **microfinance in developed countries**. For example, Procredit bank, the German microfinance group, is a bank that finances small and medium-size enterprises. Its practices differ substantially from the business model of Grameen bank and other organizations whose objective is to address extreme poverty.[35] Even in the context of commercial banking for small-scale entrepreneurs and individuals, microfinance makes bank credit accessible to low-income households.[36] State development banks that are active in microfinance, such as Instituto de Credito Oficial in Spain, are also different from the classic model of Grameen Bank. Similarly, in the case of the European Union, microfinance is not defined as credit to combat extreme poverty, but in the context of the Employment and Social Innovation Programme it denotes loans of less than 25,000 euros that are granted to microenterprises that employ less than ten employees and have total annual turnover or balance sheet size less than 2 million euros.[37]

EVALUATING THE IMPACT OF MICROFINANCE

Microfinance was originally based on the expectation that access to funding for the poor and the financially excluded parts of the population would be effective in combating poverty and social inequality. However, as the field of microfinance develops, attracting the interest of policy-makers, regulators, investors, and a broad spectrum of stakeholders, measurement of the effectiveness of microfinance becomes increasingly important. Identifying and evaluating the impact of microfinance is essential to determine and direct the flow of resources and the design of a regulatory framework for microfinance in the immediate future. The answer to the question of measurement determines whether resources devoted to combating poverty are to be directed to microfinance or to other priorities, such as addressing illiteracy, reducing crime, and improving hygiene conditions.

The social impact of microcredit is difficult to assess. This is true for social finance activities in their entirety, as well as for social and economic policy in general. In the first place, evaluating a policy for economic development such as support for microcredit has an ideological connotation in terms of consistency: evaluation of the policy includes consistency of the policy to its principles. In a field where capital market practices are mingled with the political quest for inequality and poverty reduction, it is hard to identify the boundaries that separate consistency to the developmental mission of microfinance from speculative credit expansion that may worsen people's lives instead of helping them out. Moreover, it is unclear whether economic and social change can be attributable to microfinance. For example, construction of a road transport network in a certain area with widespread poverty, along with the building of new schools and the establishment of microfinance institutions, make it hard to calculate with accuracy the percentage of poverty reduction that is due to microfinance as opposed to other activities. Change in poverty circumstances may be owed to a broader set of factors rather than targeted interventions, as in the case of natural disasters or recessions that hit economies in their entirety.

In such cases one significant question is what would have happened to the population in the absence of access to microfinance. One answer to the methodological challenge is isolation of similar groups of the population and comparison of the evolution of those who accessed microfinance for funding and those who did not, given that all other attributes of the population groups are similar. This is the rationale behind the methodology of **randomized control trials,** in the context of which the differences between two groups – the control group and the treatment group – are being compared. The treatment group is the group that has access to microfinance. Of course, it is not easy to identify two groups of the population with sufficient size that are identical in all respects except for access to microfinance. Even if there are similarities in many instances, the group that received microcredit may comprise individuals and organizations that had already developed entrepreneurial activity and managed to expand their activities further following access to microcredit, whereas the group that did not receive microfinance may comprise individuals who never had any entrepreneurial activity nor have any prospects of having entrepreneurial activities in the future, thus being unable to utilize the opportunities offered by microfinance in the combat against poverty.

Research on the measurement of the impact of microfinance covers a wide spectrum in geographical, cultural, and economic context. The financial and social performance of microfinance institutions varies substantially and research has shown that – as in the case of conventional financial institutions – their performance varies with factors such as governance, type of financing, size,

> Research on the measurement of the impact of microfinance covers a wide spectrum in geographical, cultural, and economic context.

maturity, macroeconomic and political conditions.[38] One study on microfinance in Hyderabad, the capital of Andhra Pradesh, shows that demand for microloans was neither homogeneous nor popular amongst low-income citizens (two out of three were not interested). Moreover, while extension of microcredit contributed to the expansion of entrepreneurial activities, it failed to lead to higher profits or consumption for borrowers and, more importantly, failed to impact welfare sectors, such as healthcare, education, and the role of women in society.[39,40] Similar findings are reached for the impact of microfinance on income, consumption, and welfare for poor segments of the agricultural population of rural areas in Morocco.[41] In the Philippines, with real annual interest rates around 60%, expansion of microloans did not bring about increase in consumption, employment, or individual welfare of borrowers. More importantly, it failed to reduce informal lending. In contrast to the findings for the case of Morocco, microfinance in the Philippines contributed to improving social cohesion of local societies, helping them to manage risks more effectively.[42] In Bangladesh, home of Grameen Bank, the impact of microfinance on combating extreme poverty was a catalyst, contributing not only to increasing the wealth of many of the poorest Bangladeshi citizens (through increasing ownership of arable land), but also reducing the incidence of usury at the expense of low-income farmers, mitigating illiteracy, and improving hygiene conditions.[43]

In terms of **economic growth**, the impact of microfinance institutions is positive. In a study of 119 countries and 2,382 microfinance institutions for the 1995–2012 period, microfinance expansion (in terms of customer numbers, profitability, serviced loans) had a positive impact on GDP, savings, employment, and the money supply.[44] Investigating the impact of microfinance on economic development at the international level, it appears that microfinance has contributed to alleviating income inequality, reducing the value of the Gini Index and the number of individuals living on less than $1.25 per day.[45] A further study on microfinance institutions operating in 64 different countries has shown that microcredit helps reduce child mortality: a) microfinance institutions usually focus on women who devote part of their income to the healthcare of their children and of themselves; b) microfinance institutions often provide special loans for access to healthcare services.[46]

At first glance, conflicting research findings on the effectiveness of microfinance for economic development point to the fact that microfinance does not necessarily contribute to the economic development of the communities it addresses. Such a conclusion would imply that microfinance should not be allocated resources or be subject to favorable regulation. Instead, resources should be directed to other activities that confront poverty, such as public services in the areas of education and healthcare or – in the area of finance – government subsidization of interest rates on loans to the financially weakest segments of the population. However, such a view is far from being complete. As social finance in general and microfinance in particular are fairly young and developing institutions, research findings are currently not sufficient to permit a thorough evaluation of microcredit. For the same reason, research on the long-term impact of microfinance that could give a more accurate picture of its developmental dynamics is not currently available.

CONCLUSION

The experience of microfinance to this point is helpful in deriving useful conclusions for social finance in general. The fact that microfinance and related financial services may contribute to the reduction of poverty brings into light the areas that need to be emphasized in goods and money markets, combining the pursuit of welfare in conjunction with economic profit.

First of all, the rapid development and wide impact of microfinance indicate that in social finance, as in other financial services, the design of financial contracts plays a vital role in the welfare of all parties involved. One significant conclusion that stems from the seminal finance literature on capital structure is that the quality of financial contracts – measured on the basis of the impact that funding has upon each of the parties involved – depends on: a) the way in which the contracts address the problem of asymmetric information between lenders and borrowers, and b) the incentives to fulfill the terms of the contracts in order to extend credit to those who need it and, at the same time, avoid adverse selection of borrowers who are likely to impose a moral hazard on the institution by failing to pay the loan back. Innovation in microfinance aims at dealing with these issues, pointing to the fact that success in social finance must be based on financial contract innovation. This was achieved through the introduction of simple innovative attributes, such as frequent payments, payments in public, group lending, and dynamic incentives that involve higher amounts lent out as a result of prompt repayment of installments. Nevertheless, taking into account the failures of microfinance mechanisms, we may conclude that the design of social finance networks must focus on the particular needs of the places and the individuals it aims to support, adapting financial contract terms accordingly.

Furthermore, the experience of microfinance shows that expansion of social finance must take place cautiously. Microfinance has been associated with credit crises in India and Bolivia. This means that lack of an organized regulatory framework and the occasional uncontrollable infusion of conventional commercial banking activities in microfinance may result in developments that lead to financial crisis: there is a thin line that separates social finance from conventional mechanisms of capital and money markets. Finally, regarding evaluation of the impact of social finance upon economic development and mitigation of poverty, the evidence stemming from recent research on microfinance is rather positive, although it appears to be difficult to match the funding network of social finance with transformation of the standard of living of groups of microcredit recipients.

In addition, research in the field of microfinance indicates that depicting the failures of social finance in a way that would benefit the design of financial contracts, the economic activities and needs of those who receive funds is of vital importance. It is only the analysis of the diversity of experiences of social finance – in social and historical context – that could lead to the redesign of finance mechanisms and enhance the impact of microfinance upon the economy and society.

MATERIAL FOR DISCUSSION

London Stock Exchange welcomes ASA International Group Plc to the main market
Available at:
www.lseg.com/markets-products-and-services/our-markets/london-stock-exchange/equities-markets/raising-equity-finance/market-open-ceremony/london-stock-exchange-welcomes-asa-international-group-plc-main-market.

REVIEW QUESTIONS

1 What are the main characteristics of a microfinance institution?
2 What are the principal challenges facing microfinance?
3 What are the main characteristics of a loan contract in microfinance?
4 What is the importance of microfinance as a mechanism for economic development?
5 What is the impact of microfinance on the combat against poverty?
6 What are the advantages and disadvantages of the inclusion of microfinance institutions in the stock market?

NOTES

1   Grameen Bank (2019).
2   See, for example, Sabin (2015).
3   Except for providing credit to women, microfinance institutions figure more prominently as employers of women compared to conventional banks – Øystein Strøm et al. (2014). In addition, women participation in the leadership of microfinance institutions has a positive impact on the financial performance of these institutions – Mersland and Øystein Strøm (2009).
4   The supply of services beyond finance – like professional training and consulting for new enterprises establishment – ends up being conducive to enhancement of the quality of loans: It reinforces customer loyalty to the creditor and reduces the number of bad loans with delayed payments. For a relevant study on 77 countries, see Lensink et al. (2018).
5   Wahlen (2017).

6   See M.Yunus's speech from the Nobel Prize award ceremony in 2006 (www.nobel prize.org/nobel_prizes/peace/laureates/2006/yunus-lecture-en.html).

7   https://grameen.com.

8   Grameen Bank (2019).

9   For Grameen Bank a member is considered to have moved out of poverty if her family fulfills the following criteria:

1   The family lives in a house worth at least Tk. 25,000 (twenty-five thousand) or a house with a tin roof, and each member of the family is able to sleep on a bed instead of on the floor.

2   Family members drink pure water of tube-wells, boiled water, or water purified by using alum, arsenic-free purifying tablets, or pitcher filters.

3   All children in the family over six years of age are all going to school or finished primary school.

4   The minimum weekly loan installment of the borrower is Tk. 200 or more.

5   The family uses a sanitary latrine.

6   Family members have adequate clothing for everyday use, warm clothing for winter, such as shawls, sweaters, blankets, etc., and mosquito-nets to protect themselves from mosquitoes.

7   The family has sources of additional income, such as a vegetable garden, fruit-bearing trees, etc., so that they are able to fall back on these sources of income when they need additional money.

8   The borrower maintains an average annual balance of Tk. 5,000 in her savings accounts.

9   The family experiences no difficulty in having three square meals a day through-out the year, i.e. no member of the family goes hungry any time of the year.

10   The family can take care of their health. If any member of the family falls ill, the family can afford to take all necessary steps to seek adequate healthcare.

10   www.convergences.org/wp-content/uploads/2019/09/Microfinance-Barome ter-2019_web-1.pdf.

11   The study of Kar and Swain (2018) on microfinance in Peru, the Philippines, India, Ecuador, and Indonesia for the 1996–2010 period finds that the microfinance market has many monopolistic competition characteristics, which explains the high interest rates associ-ated with microcredit.

12   www.ifc.org/wps/wcm/connect/industry_ext_content/ifc_external_ corporate_site/financial+institutions/priorities/mesm/microfinance.

13   On the significance of the legal form of microfinance institutions for the financial risk they undertake, see Gietzen (2017).

14   For an overview of group lending and its impact on microfinance institutions, see Rathore (2017).

15   www.nabard.org/content.aspx?id=2.

16   Sabin and Reed-Tsochas (2020). In general, the credit risk that microfinance institu-tions have to manage is affected by the general institutional structure of the local economies where they operate – Lassoued (2017).

17   See Lindvert et al. (2019) on the possibility of female borrowers' conflicting priori-ties with respect to their family and their lending group.

18   On the transfer of credit monitoring from the lender to the group of borrowers who receive credit, see Stiglitz (1990). While the effectiveness of social monitoring as a mechanism of enforcing consistency in loan repayment is significant, it is also true that the task of loan

monitoring falls on individuals who do not possess resources or skills to carry it out effectively (the team members).

19   Kodongo and Kendi (2013).

20   Even in the case that the lender undertakes full monitoring of credit risk, the special attributes of microfinance render it less appropriate for standardized monitoring of credit scores (see, for example, Van Gool et al. [2012]).

21   Giné and Karlan (2014).

22   Attanasio et al. (2015).

23   Maîtrot (2018).

24   Uwamariya et al. (2019).

25   On the role of capital markets in economic development, see for example, Rapp and Udoieva (2018), Bruhn and Love (2014). In contrast, Henderson et al. (2013) advocate that the benefits from financial expansion tend to be accumulated more in developed economies than in underdeveloped ones, underlining the need for careful planning of financial institutions in developing economies.

26   On the typologies of microfinance institutions and the features of commercial banking that are present in microfinance mechanisms, see Koveos and Randhawa (2004).

27   Haldar and Stiglitz (2016) underline the importance of solidarity and trust as the main success factors of Grameen Bank and, correspondingly, the speculative extension of microcredit as the main factor underlying the failure of SKS Microfinance.

28   Hoque et al. (2011) studied the impact of commercial banking on microfinance for an international sample of 24 microfinance institutions. According to their findings, implementation of commercial bank practices ended up reducing funding, the primary mission of microfinance, to the very poor segments of the population, because the microfinance institutions studied seemed to choose safer destinations for their credit.

29   Callaghan et al. (2007). In the context of that project, Morgan Stanley developed mechanisms for evaluation of credit risk associated with microfinance institutions themselves – Arvello et al. (2008).

30   Sabin (2015).

31   Drift from impact to profit as organizational objective need not be the outcome of a top-down institutional shift materialized with an exposure to organized capital markets. It may also be the outcome of field-level practices of implementing standard microfinance services (Maîtrot, 2018).

32   Haldar and Stiglitz (2016).

33   Mader (2013).

34   The issue with this approach does not appear to be geographical expansion per se, but the broadening of banking activities offered by microfinance institutions on the basis of profitability criteria. Growth may have a positive impact on the viability of nonprofit microfinance institutions, allowing them the attainment of economies of scale – Hartarska et al. (2013).

35   http://procreditbank.gr.

36   Brown et al. (2016).

37   https://ec.europa.eu/social/main.jsp?catId=1482&langId=en.

38   Hermes and Hudon (2018).

39   Banerjee et al. (2015).

40   Nevertheless, microfinance in Andhra Pradesh is not characteristic of the general picture of microfinance. It constituted a case of rapid credit expansion and speculative microcredit. These characteristics led to the credit crisis of 2010, resulting in shrinking of

microfinance mechanisms and reform against loan collection practices in the area of Andhra Pradesh.

41   Crépon et al. (2015).

42   Karlan and Zinman (2011).

43   Ahmed (2009), Islam et al. (2015).

44   Lopatta and Tchikov (2016).

45   Lacalle-Calderon et al. (2019), Lacalle-Calderon et al. (2018).

46   Posso and Athukorala (2018).

REFERENCES

Ahmed, S., 2009. Microfinance institutions in Bangladesh: Achievements and challenges. *Managerial Finance*, 35(12), 999–1010. https://doi.org/10.1108/03074350911 000052.

Akula, V., 2010. *A fistful of rice: My unexpected quest to end poverty through profitability*. Boston: Harvard Business Review Press.

Arvello, M., Bell, J.-L., Novak, C., Rose, J., and Venugopal, S., 2008. Morgan Stanley's approach to assessing credit risks in the microfinance industry. *Journal of Applied Corporate Finance*, 20(1), 124–134. https://doi.org/10.1111/j.1745-6622.2008.00175.x.

Attanasio, O., Augsburg, B., De Haas, R., Fitzsimons, E., and Harmgart, H., 2015. The impacts of microfinance: Evidence from joint liability-lending in Mongolia. *American Economic Journal: Applied Economics*, 7(1), 90–122. https://doi.org/10.1257/app.20130489.

Banerjee, A., Duflo, E., Glennerster, R., and Kinman, C., 2015. The miracle of microfinance? Evidence from a randomized evaluation. *American Economic Journal: Applied Economics*, 7(1), 22–53. http://dx.doi.org/10.1257/app.20130533.

Brown, M., Guin, B., and Kirschenmann, K., 2016. Microfinance banks and financial inclusion. *Review of Finance*, 20(3), 907–946. https://doi.org/10.1093/rof/rfv026.

Bruhn, M., and Love, I., 2014. The real impact of improved access to finance: Evidence from Mexico. *Journal of Finance*, 69(3), 1347–1376. https://doi.org/10.1111/jofi.12091.

Callaghan, I., Gonzalez, H., Maurice, D., and Novak, C., 2007. Microfinance – On the road to capital markets. *Journal of Applied Corporate Finance*, 19(1), 115–124. https://doi.org/10.1111/j.1745-6622.2007.00130.x.

Crépon, B., Devoto, F., Duflo, E., and Parienté, W., 2015. Estimating the impact of microcredit on those who take it up: Evidence from a randomized experiment in Morocco. *American Economic Journal: Applied Economics*, 7(1), 123–150. http://dx.doi.org/10.1257/app.20130535.

Gietzen, T., 2017. The exposure of microfinance institutions to financial risk. *Review of Development Finance*, 7(2), 120–133. https://doi.org/10.1016/j.rdf.2017.04.001.

Giné, X., and Karlan, D., 2014. Short and long term evidence from Philippine microcredit lending groups. *Journal of Development Economics*, 107, 65–83. https://doi.org/10.1016/j.jdeveco.2013.11.003.

Grameen Bank, 2019. *Grameen bank annual report 2018*. https://grameenbank.org/wp-content/uploads/bsk-pdf-manager/gb_annual_report_2018.pdf.

Haldar, A., and Stiglitz, J.E., 2016. Group lending, joint liability and social capital: Insights from the Indian microfinance crisis. *Politics and Society*, 44(4), 459–497. https://doi.org/10.11 77%2F0032329216674001.

Hartarska, V., Shen, X., and Mersland, R., 2013. Scale economies and input price elasticities in microfinance institutions. *Journal of Banking and Finance*, 37(1), 118–131. https://doi.org/10.1016/j.jbankfin.2012.08.004.

Henderson, D.J., Papageorgiou, C., and Parmeter, C.F., 2013. Who benefits from financial development? New methods, new evidence. *European Economic Review*, 63, 47–67. https://doi.org/10.1016/j.euroecorev.2013.05.007.

Hermes, N., and Hudon, M., 2018. Determinants of the performance of microfinance institutions: A systematic review. *Journal of Economic Surveys*, 32(5), 1483–1513. https://doi.org/10.1111/joes.12290.

Hoque, M., Chrishty, M., and Halloway, R., 2011. Commercialization and changes in capital structure in microfinance institutions: An innovation or wrong turn? *Managerial Finance*, 37(5), 414–425. https://doi.org/10.1108/03074351111126906.

Islam, A., Nguyen, C., and Smyth, R., 2015. Does microfinance change lending in informal economies? Evidence from Bangladesh. *Journal of Banking and Finance*, 50, 141–156. https://doi.org/10.1016/j.jbankfin.2014.10.001.

Kar, A.K., and Swain, R.B., 2018. Are microfinance markets monopolistic? *Applied Economics*, 50(1), 1–14. https://doi.org/10.1080/00036846.2017.1310999.

Karlan, D., and Zinman, J., 2011. Microcredit in theory and in practice: Using randomized credit scoring for impact. *Science*, 332(6035), 1278–1284. https://doi.org/10.1126/science.1200138.

Kodongo, O., and Kendi, L.G., 2013. Individual lending versus group lending: An evaluation with Kenya's microfinance data. *Review of Development Finance*, 3(2), 99–108. https://doi.org/10.1016/j.rdf.2013.05.001.

Koveos, P., and Randhawa, D., 2004. Financial services for the poor: Assessing microfinance institutions. *Managerial Finance*, 30(9), 70–95. https://doi.org/10.1108/03074350410769281.

Lacalle-Calderon, M., Larrú, J.M., Garrido, S.R., and Perez-Trujillo, M., 2019. Microfinance and income inequality: New macrolevel evidence. *Review of Development Economics*, 23(2), 860–876. https://doi.org/10.1111/rode.12573.

Lacalle-Calderon, M., Perez-Trujillo, M., and Neira, I., 2018. Does microfinance reduce poverty among the poorest? A macro-quintile regression approach. *Developing Economies*, 56(1), 51–65. https://doi.org/10.1111/deve.12159.

Lassoued, N., 2017. What drives credit risk of microfinance institutions? International evidence. *International Journal of Managerial Finance*, 13(5), 541–559. https://doi.org/10.1108/IJMF-03-2017-0042.

Lensink, R., Mersland, R., Vu, N.T.H., and Zamore, S., 2018. Do microfinance institutions benefit from integrating financial and nonfinancial services? *Applied Economics*, 50(21), 2386–2401. https://doi.org/10.1080/00036846.2017.1397852.

Lindvert, M., Patel, P.C., Smith, C., and Wincent, W., 2019. Microfinance traps and relational exchange norms: A field study of women entrepreneurs in Tanzania. *Journal of Small Business Management*, 57(1), 230–254. https://doi.org/10.1111/jsbm.12407.

Lopatta, K., and Tchikov, M., 2016. Do microfinance institutions fulfill their promises? Evidence from cross-country data. *Applied Economics*, 48(18), 1655–1677. https://doi.org/10.1080/00036846.2015.1105924.

Mader, P., 2013. Rise and fall of microfinance in India: The Andhra Pradesh crisis in perspective. *Strategic Change*, 22(1–2), 47–66. https://doi.org/10.1002/jsc.1921.

Maîtrot, M., 2018. Understanding social performance: A "practice drift" at the frontline of microfinance institutions in Bangladesh. *Development and Change*, 50(3), 623–654. https://doi.org/10.1111/dech.12398.

Mersland, R., and Øystein Strøm, R., 2009. Performance and governance in microfinance institutions. *Journal of Banking and Finance*, 33(4), 662–669. https://doi.org/10.1016/j.jbankfin.2008.11.009.

Øystein Strøm, R., D'Espallier, B., and Mersland, R., 2014. Female leadership, performance and governance in microfinance institutions. *Journal of Banking and Finance*, 42, 60–75. https://doi.org/10.1016/j.jbankfin.2014.01.014.

Posso, A., and Athukorala, P.-C., 2018. Microfinance and child mortality. *Applied Economics*, 50(21), 2313–2324. https://doi.org/10.1080/00036846.2017.1394976.

Rathore, B.S., 2017. Joint liability in a classic microfinance contract: Review of theory and empirics. *Studies in Economics and Finance*, 34(2), 213–227. https://doi.org/10.1108/SEF-02-2016-0040.

Rapp, M.S., and Udoieva, I.A., 2018. What matters in the finance growth nexus of advanced economies? Evidence from OECD countries. *Applied Economics*, 50(6), 676–690. https://doi.org/10.1080/00036846.2017.1337867.

Sabin, N., 2015. Microfinance: A state in flux. *In*: A. Nicholls, R. Patton, and J. Emerson, eds. *Social finance*. Oxford: Oxford University Press, 156–184.

Sabin, N., and Reed-Tsochas, R., 2020. Able but unwilling to enforce: Cooperative dilemmas in group lending. *American Journal of Sociology*, 125(6), 1602–1667.

Stiglitz, J.E., 1990. Peer monitoring and credit markets. *World Bank Economic Review*, 4(3), 351–366. https://doi.org/10.1093/wber/4.3.351.

Uwamariya, M., Loebbecke, C., and Cremer, S., 2019. Mobile banking impacting the performance of microfinance institutions: A case study from Rwanda. *International Journal of Innovation and Technology Management*, 17(1), 1–18. https://doi.org/10.1142/S0219877020500017.

Van Gool, J., Verbeke, W., Sercu, P., and Baesens, B., 2012. Credit scoring for microfinance: Is it worth it? *International Journal of Finance and Economics*, 17(2), 103–123. https://doi.org/10.1002/ijfe.444.

Wahlen, S., 2017. *Microfinance: An economic analysis of banking to the poor*. Bloomington: Archway Publishing.

4

Venture philanthropy

After reading this chapter, you will be able to:

1 Demonstrate understanding of the mandate, the structure, and the business practices of venture philanthropy organizations
2 Distinguish between venture capital and venture philanthropy
3 Assess the contribution of venture philanthropy in mitigating social problems
4 Assess the regional diversity of venture philanthropy organizations
5 Explain the challenges facing venture philanthropy organizations

INTRODUCTION

Venture philanthropy is a social finance mechanism that made its debut in the 1980s.[1] The difference from other forms of social finance lies in the adoption of practices pertinent to **venture capital**, which provides financing to innovative entrepreneurship and startups. Application of venture capital processes in philanthropy constitutes, in a way, a case where the entrepreneurial spirit

Venture philanthropy involves financing mechanisms beyond donations, incorporating investors who pursue social and environmental impact alongside financial viability of social projects.

DOI: 10.4324/9781003230366-6

"colonizes" an area traditionally "dominated" by government social and development policies.[2] At the same time, venture philanthropy constitutes a major technological change, aspiring to equip impact investments with more than just the capital required, notably with the expertise needed for efficient implementation of innovation in impact investments. Thus, an important difference between donating and venture philanthropy is that in the case of the latter, the donor monitors closely the development of the activities that are financed, seeing that the allocated resources are utilized in an optimal manner and the desired social impact is attained.[3] Outside the narrow framework of philanthropy (in the form of donations), the term "venture philanthropy" incorporates aspects of the social economy where venture capital principles are applicable. Thus, venture philanthropy involves financing mechanisms beyond donations, incorporating investors who pursue social and environmental impact alongside financial viability of social projects.

In the case of venture philanthropy, the relationship between suppliers and recipients of finance is long term. Moreover, interaction between them is frequent (monthly or even weekly), covering aspects relating to financing, operation, and strategy of the social purpose organization. According to the **European Venture Philanthropy Association**, "Venture Philanthropy (VP) is a high-engagement and long-term approach whereby an investor *for* impact supports a social purpose organisation (SPO) to help it maximise its social impact".[4] The main features of venture philanthropy are the following (Figure 4.1):

♦ Venture philanthropy provides non-financial support to social purpose organizations.
♦ Financing of social purpose organizations is adapted to the particular context of each different investment.
♦ Impact measurement is required in the recipient social purpose organization's planning and assessment.

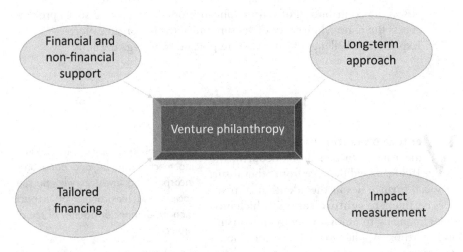

Figure 4.1 Venture philanthropy

Similar to venture capital, the search for capital by the social entrepreneur takes place along with planning for social impact activities, such that the potential and the priorities of suppliers and recipients of capital are matched. At the stage of portfolio formation and choice of social enterprises and impact activities to be financed, venture philanthropy administrators analyze investment alternatives, hold meetings with representatives of the recipient organizations, visit the sites where premises are located and social activities are deployed, assess investment readiness, and select the organizations that will be incorporated in the particular venture philanthropy portfolio.

In line with venture capital (and in contrast to conventional donating), venture philanthropy financing is not limited to the supply of capital. The supplier of capital is actively involved in constructing the business plan of the social purpose organization, determining the corporate governance structure, establishing a network of collaborations, even putting together the management team that will run the social purpose organization (Figure 4.2).[5] Once the social purpose organization starts operations, a venture philanthropy administrator takes part in the management of financial resources of the recipient organization, in the management of operations, as well as in business planning. The diversity in forms of collaboration between recipient organizations and venture philanthropy also implies

> Venture philanthropy financing is not limited to the supply of capital. The supplier of capital is actively involved in constructing the business plan of the social purpose organization, determining the corporate governance structure, establishing a network of collaborations, even putting together the management team that will run the social purpose organization.

variation with respect to forms of funding, duration of collaboration with the recipient social purpose organization, conditions of impact investor withdrawal, intended financial outcomes, measurement of return of the social investment and the way this is communicated with stakeholders, geographical focus of the social venture, as well as the social impact of the allocated venture philanthropy capital. Thus, venture philanthropy financing may take the form of donation, loan, or share capital participation, depending on the degree to which the social activity pursues profit. The expected rate of return varies from −100% (in the case of a donation where the donor foregoes the entire capital invested) to relatively high rates of return (exceeding 10%), proportionate to the risk undertaken by the impact investor who finances the social venture.

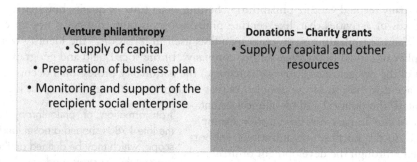

Venture philanthropy	Donations – Charity grants
• Supply of capital • Preparation of business plan • Monitoring and support of the recipient social enterprise	• Supply of capital and other resources

Figure 4.2 Venture philanthropy versus donating

One distinguishing feature of venture philanthropy in comparison to donating and venture capital is reflected in the way the relationship between the supplier and the recipient of capital is concluded. In the case of donating, the relationship simply ends with the donation of a certain amount of money or resource(s). In contrast, in the case of venture capital the relationship ends (or is radically transformed) when the recipient social purpose enterprise is ready to expand by way of seeking capital in an organized capital market through an IPO. Moreover, withdrawal of the supplier of capital in the context of venture philanthropy is part of the business plan and generally implies that the recipient organization is ready to carry out its social purpose in an autonomous manner. For this reason, the term "graduation" is often used to describe conclusion of the relationship between the supplier and the recipient of capital. For the most part, venture philanthropy maintains ties and collaborates with the recipient organization for long periods, offering ongoing expertise in the area of impact investments.

Financial and other support for organized public goods production through venture philanthropy enhances the social legitimacy of large-scale businesses and wealthy individuals beyond action pertaining to corporate social responsibility, donating, or paying taxes. Moreover, capital out of profit and wealth acquired through capital markets and the internet that is channeled to venture philanthropy substitutes for government spending and state priorities for financing sectors such as education, healthcare, and culture. With venture philanthropy, the responsibility for the conduct of social policy by a government that is both directly and indirectly accountable to voters is essentially transferred to private individuals. Thus, it is private individuals, who – while being part of the relevant institutional framework and a broad social economy network – decide on an "individual" basis how to address challenges, such as poverty, social cohesion, and access to basic needs public goods, that affect society as a whole.[6,7]

VENTURE PHILANTHROPY IN THE USA

Venture philanthropy developed in the USA mainly in the 1980s. By the end of that decade, several prominent organizations had been established, transforming the social economy terrain and laying the foundations for the field of social finance that was eventually termed venture philanthropy. Setting exact time or quality boundaries for a plexus of activities that, like venture philanthropy, is quite diverse is not an easy task. Venture philanthropy diversity manifests itself in terms of a) the identity of the supplier of capital (individual, family, company); b) the social field and geographical area of the project that receives financing; c) the nationality, professional occupation, and age distribution of the population that is supported through the impact investment; d) the political and ideological orientation of the impact investment. For example, some social purpose organizations support welfare through the development of small and medium-scale enterprises, while others support

Transformation of philanthropy in the late 1980s shaped a novel landscape, which may be defined on the basis of the practices it adopts.

development through the promotion of Christian principles and values. Similarly, some social purpose institutions are subsidiaries of multinational corporations (such as the Shell Foundation), while others constitute independent social economy networks that place emphasis on local society needs. Nevertheless, transformation of philanthropy in the late 1980s shaped a novel landscape, which may be defined on the basis of the practices it adopts. This novel landscape is venture philanthropy, where the pursuit of social impact is maintained, but the way it is materialized is transformed through implementation of new methods of entrepreneurship, where the social venture is treated as a network of cooperating institutions, and adoption of the principles of venture capital in the organization of investments with social impact.[8]

Until the late 1980s, philanthropic work in the USA mainly concerned the supply of capital required for the social purpose organization that was to receive financing. Philanthropic institutions were assessing the expediency of financial support for various welfare purposes, comparing alternatives based on planned action, infrastructure, and social impact, providing funds based on their own priorities, and monitoring the evolution of the financed project in its first steps.[9] In contrast, venture philanthropy was based on entrepreneurial practices of the "new economy" of the 1990s, with the development of the internet, the evolution of the financial sector frenzy, the accompanying swelling of the financial system and the emergence of a nouveau riche class of philanthropists in the USA. While some individuals from this new class of wealthy people adopted the rationale commonly prevailing amongst past generations and donated sums for the development of the arts and the sciences or directly financed the construction of public buildings and infrastructure, another group started applying some of the principles familiar to them from their professional experience to support projects with social impact. They reckoned that if American capitalist entrepreneurship helped them flourish through successful business, it could also help those who aspired to address social problems that were endemic in the very economy that helped them enhance their wealth: support for the homeless, access to education and employment for ethnic minorities, reduction of crime in inner city areas etc.[10]

In the context of this new form of social impact, investment alternatives are appraised based on clear criteria of expected rates of return. Moreover, support for financing proposals in terms of business plan, legal support, market entry, and securing necessary infrastructure are provided just like in the case of financial venture capital. In that spirit, in 1987 the **private equity** firm General Atlantic established Echoing Green, an organization providing financing and support to social entrepreneurs. General Atlantic was co-founded by Charles F. Feeney, the billionaire co-owner of Duty Free Shoppers Group Ltd. and Edwin Cohen, previously a partner of McKinsey. Feeney and Cohen were seeking philanthropy initiatives with the originality and enthusiasm that characterized the companies they financed in the profit-seeking arms of their businesses. They did not just accept applications for financing impact investments, but were actively seeking innovative philanthropic plans to which they offered the technical expertise of their profitable business ventures. Similarly, George R. Roberts, co-Chairman of the Board and co-Chief Executive Officer of the investment group KKR Management LLC, established the Homeless Economic

Development Fund in 1989.[11] The Homeless Economic Development Fund was subsequently renamed Roberts Enterprise Development Fund (REDF), which has been operating in social entrepreneurship and venture philanthropy since 1997. REDF accumulates and manages capital aimed for organization and support of social enterprises that hire employees otherwise excluded from the labor market, such as the homeless. To this day, 27,000 people have found employment in social enterprises developed under the auspices of REDF.[12]

The prospect of contributing to social ventures has spread well beyond large-scale private equity organizations, attracting investors from capital markets at large, especially from a different category of novel and powerful nodes in the deranged global financial system of the past three decades, namely the **hedge fund**. Hedge fund managers apply principles of financial engineering to support their social impact activities. For example, Paul Tudor Jones, successful hedge fund manager and one of the wealthiest people in the world,[13] established in 1988 the Robin Hood Foundation, whose objective is to address poverty, education, and employment challenges for socially excluded individuals who live in New York City. The Robin Hood Foundation differs from traditional philanthropic institutions in several ways. First, it comprises a large network of donors, social entrepreneurs, and welfare actions. Second, its financing covers a wide range of projects, which extend beyond the supply of welfare services to include lending and investing in the enterprises of individuals who are socially excluded from money and capital markets (e.g., immigrants). Third, support for the financed projects is not limited to donating a certain amount of money. It includes business consulting and technical support for the deployment of the social enterprises that receive capital. Finally, significant emphasis is placed upon impact measurement and the financial viability of the projects that are financed: "for every dollar spent, we effectively raise the living standards for low-income New Yorkers by $12".[14,15]

In the years that followed, venture philanthropy and social entrepreneurship embraced the leaders, the capital, and the practices of the emergent **internet economy**. In that context, in 1997 a group of entrepreneurs, including Paul Brainerd (co-founder of the Aldus Corporation, which released PageMaker, the first page formatting software for Apple and Windows) and Paul Shoemaker (who subsequently led the transformation of Social Venture Partners to a global impact investments network) established Social Venture Partners in Seattle. Similarly, social entrepreneur Kim Smith and successful venture capitalists John Doerr (biotechnology and healthcare) and Brook Byers (information systems) established the NewSchools Venture Fund in 1998. Perhaps the most characteristic example of implementation of "new economy" principles to impact investments is that of Omidyar Network, established in 2004 by Pierre Omidyar, the founder of the e-commerce platform eBay. Omidyar Network is a hybrid organization, operating simultaneously as a nonprofit organization under regulation 501(c)(3) and as a limited liability company. As venture philanthropy, Omidyar Network invests in both for-profit and not-for-profit enterprises, combining the attributes of the donor to those of the shareholder and seeking innovative investment opportunities that are financially viable and have the potential for growth. Intended social impact covers a wide range of impact investments, from education to access to technology and financing. Finally, the case of the venture philanthropy organization Acumen, which was also established around that time, is worth exploring in greater detail, especially with regard to its blended goal of pursuing both social impact and financial return (Box 4.1).

Box 4.1 Acumen

Acumen, founded and led by Jaqueline Novogratz, a social entrepreneur previously working in investment banking, is a venture philanthropy organization that was established in 2001. Acumen was financed by the Rockefeller Foundation, the Cisco Systems Foundation, and the donations of three philanthropists. Acumen's objective is to address poverty throughout the world, especially in Central Asia, Africa, and South America. For this purpose, Acumen provides financial and technical support to innovative entrepreneurship, which is thought to drive even the lowest income brackets of the population in those regions into the dynamic of economic development. The organizations financed by Acumen are usually for-profit businesses that find it hard to secure financing through conventional money and capital markets, as they undertake investments that are subject to high financial risk. Acumen finances such investments, to the extent that it considers their success as being helpful for addressing poverty and economic stagnation.[16] For instance, Acumen provides financial support and consulting services to Cacao de Colombia, high quality chocolate production in Colombia, where the deterioration of the international price of cocoa has financially exhausted local producers. In the field of financial services, Acumen finances First Access, an enterprise that has created a data analysis mechanism for the evaluation of the creditworthiness of borrowers in Tanzania. Reliable evaluation of creditworthiness contributes to the extension of loans to individuals who would not otherwise be financed due to lack of data on their wealth and income. Increased availability of information implies lower interest rates on loans and financing for entrepreneurial projects in the context of a developing country. Acumen also supports nonprofit organizations, such as the Aga Khan Rural Support Program, which is involved in the construction of hydroelectric units in North Pakistan to provide safe and affordable energy to the local population.

Acumen considers its impact investments to be "patient capital". This practically means that Acumen is involved in high-risk investments, characterized by long repayment periods of the capital that was invested. Capital is usually supplied in the form of a loan or in the form of share capital (but not as a donation). Thereafter, Acumen pursues its social impact objective in parallel with the financial success of the financed investment. Beyond covering financing needs of enterprises in developing areas, the rationale behind the supply of "patient capital" is to also provide the necessary technical and business consulting support for the impact investment to be materialized. Acumen's aptitude to support financially and technically investments that aim to mitigate poverty is based on the deployment of a wide network of affiliates that includes charity organizations and businesses in almost every sector: the Bill and Melinda Gates Foundation, the IKEA Foundation, the MetLife Foundation, the Skoll Foundation, Goldman Sachs, General Electric, Ernst & Young, Barclays, American Express, Mitsubishi, Unilever, and many others. Since the beginning of its operations in 2001, Acumen has invested 128 million US dollars in 128 enterprises in 14 countries.

These organizations laid the foundations for venture philanthropy, paving the way for implementation of innovative and profitable entrepreneurial practices on nonprofit, social purpose organizations, thus increasing the effectiveness of conventional organizations in social economy and civil society. In addition, such initiatives financed by leaders of capitalist innovation in the USA redefine the discourse on social acceptability of profits realized by big businesses and the production of public goods outside the framework of the government and the pertinent parliamentary control on government action.

THE EUROPEAN EXPERIENCE

Similar to other areas of business, the US pioneered social entrepreneurship and social economy action, constituting a model for Europe, starting from the United Kingdom. In the UK, the ascent of social economy was reinforced by changes brought about by the labor government of Tony Blair, as well as by a strong tradition of innovation in the third sector of the economy, dating back to the socialist utopia of Robert Owen in the 19th century, on to the Open University of Michael Young and the Action Aid of Cecil Jackson-Cole in the 20th century, to the design of capital markets for impact investments by Sir Ronald Cohen in the 21st century.[17] The United Kingdom led impact investing with investors whose goals included the simultaneous pursuit of profit and social impact (for instance, Bridges Ventures), as well as promotion of social and financial innovation through initiatives such as the social impact bond of Peterborough prison. The Social Business Trust, presented in Box 4.2, constitutes a characteristic example of venture philanthropy in the United Kingdom.

Box 4.2 Social Business Trust

The Social Business Trust is a venture philanthropy organization established in the UK in 2010 by Sir Damon Buffini, co-founder of Permira, an international investment firm that manages assets worth 32 billion GBP, and Adele Blakebrough, a social entrepreneur with long experience in the administration of social purpose organizations such as Community Action, which provides networking opportunities and support to social entrepreneurs, and the Kaleidoscope Project, which provides support to individuals addicted to toxic substances. Outside Permira, the affiliation network of the Social Business Trust includes companies like IBM (technology), Bain & Company (management consultancy), British Gas (energy), Clifford Chance (legal services), Ernst & Young (accounting), Credit Suisse (financial services), Thomson Reuters (media).

The Social Business Trust focuses on social enterprises that seek to expand the scale of their operations, exceeding a certain sales revenue threshold (e.g., 1,000,000 GBP). The Social Business Trust donates to such organizations for the purposes of covering their capital needs and, more importantly, provides advice on how to manage the transformations they undergo as they grow and broaden their social impact. The purpose of management consulting is to help those social enterprises become financially independent and efficient, beyond the time horizon covered by the donations received at the start. Overall, the Social Business Trust has offered 20 million GBP worth of assistance (cash and in kind), including 40,000 hours of business support to social enterprises.[18]

On the continent, Dr. Rob John pioneered in 2004 the founding of European Venture Philanthropy Association (EVPA), a member of the European Venture Capital Association – now known as Invest Europe. EVPA contributed decisively to the spread of venture philanthropy throughout Europe. The goal of EVPA is to effectively match private capital that seeks to be invested in social impact activities with social purpose organizations that have a systematic view of social problems that need to be tackled, but do not possess the organizational and governance mechanisms or the resources required for effective deployment of their potential in addressing specific social problems. This matching led to the establishment of social enterprises and philanthropy action that are completely different from traditional charity, which is exhausted in mere donations. Social enterprises are now part of a capital market network, utilize modern management techniques, as well as financial technology for the management of risk. Each year the Association holds an annual conference in a European city (from Amsterdam in 2004 to The Hague in 2019). The annual conference is the main event of the Association and a meeting point for social economy networking, including donors, social enterprises, impact investors, universities, microfinance institutions, banks and companies that are active in Corporate Social Responsibility, impact investment professionals, charity institutions, and, of course, venture philanthropy organizations.

Several venture philanthropy organizations that are located in Europe have expanded their activities internationally, thus contributing to remedying social and environmental problems in some of the poorest areas of the planet (NESsT, for example, initially active in supporting social entrepreneurship in Central and Eastern Europe after the fall of the Berlin wall, is now supporting impact projects in Latin America). Although deployment of social entrepreneurship and venture capital networks is necessary for the development of synergies in addressing a wider plexus of social issues in many countries, effective operation of the network is not to be taken for granted. The challenges confronted by such endeavors have to do with the heterogeneity of the institutional framework in different countries, the diverse nature of social problems, as well as wide variety in capital adequacy, level of expertise, and ideological orientation of impact investors. For example, LGT Lightstone is a venture philanthropy organization, part of the LGT private banking and asset management group, owned by Liechtenstein's Princely House and headed by the Prince of Liechtenstein.[19] Social entrepreneurship supported by LGT Lightstone is located in Kenya, Brazil, and India. LGT Lightstone support (with cash and know-how) development finance organizations in India, such as AYE Finance and Varthana. Along these lines, LGT Lightstone supports Brazilian organizations involved in supplying drinking water and healthcare services, such as dr.consulta and General Water. In terms of regulation of financial services, there are significant differences between

Switzerland, where LGT Lightstone is incorporated, and, for example, India, where the regulatory framework for social finance mainly supports microfinance institutions. In general, the content, impact, and importance of social investment of an organization like LGT Lightstone are defined by the variety of social problems, economic conditions, and regulatory frameworks in the diverse environment of Eastern Africa, South Asia, and Latin America.

It is worth noting that beyond the enhanced influence of the entrepreneur and their organization upon society and the legitimization of profit realized from capitalist entrepreneurial activities in the eyes of that part of society that are reluctant to accept the notion of profit, engagement of entrepreneurs with venture philanthropy has to do with their personal experiences, religious beliefs, and the political orientation of the impact investors involved. For example, the British organization Christian Aid, member of the European Venture Philanthropy Association, constitutes a universal network of welfare action that originated in the English and the Irish Churches. Similarly, Cordaid Investment Management, which provides finance and financial risk management services, is an arm of the Dutch Catholic Organization for Relief and Development Aid.

VENTURE PHILANTHROPY IN ASIA

Venture philanthropy in Asia has developed rapidly since the 1980s. Expansion of venture philanthropy has essentially taken place in a parallel fashion with microfinance mechanisms, addressing similar social problems, albeit in a different manner and with different effects in these countries. The development of venture philanthropy in Asia is associated with the rapid growth and development experienced over the past decades, based on the local form of capitalism, entrepreneurship, and correspondingly on an emergent class of very wealthy capitalists. The number of **high net worth individuals** (individuals whose net worth exceeds 1 million US dollars) has soared in Asia, approaching rapidly the wealth level of high net worth individuals in Europe and North America. In 2010 high net worth individuals in Asia and Pacific amounted to 3.3 million, with total wealth of 10.8 trillion US dollars. By 2019 high net worth individuals reached 6.5 million, with their wealth standing at 22.2 trillion US dollars.[20] This increase in high net worth capitalists in some of the Asian economies led to the expansion of philanthropic organizations and social entrepreneurship in a manner similar to that of the emergence of the third sector of the economy in the developed capitalist economies of the West.

Economic growth in Southeast Asia and the Pacific has certain special characteristics, thus lending special characteristics to venture philanthropy organizations in those areas. Specifically, the wealth that has been accumulated has a strong family character, special relationships with the state, and is relatively recent as most of the entrepreneurs are self-made. These peculiarities explain the reluctance of Asian entrepreneurs to get involved in organized initiatives of "Western-type" philanthropy like Giving Pledge: while the very wealthy capitalists from Asia and the Pacific outnumber their American counterparts, Giving Pledge membership is largely populated by individuals from

North and South America.[21] In contrast, big Asian businesses have their own network of entrepreneurial philanthropy, namely the **Asian Venture Philanthropy Network** (AVPN), which has approximately double the number of members and accumulates much more capital compared to the European Venture Philanthropy Association. In line with its European counterpart, EVPA, AVPN brings together a variety of parties that are interested in impact investments: philanthropic organizations, social entrepreneurship technocrats, organizations that specialize in corporate social responsibility and social entrepreneurship, universities, non-governmental organizations, supragovernmental organizations like the Organization for Economic Cooperation and Development (OECD), banks, legal firms that offer specialized services for impact investing, microfinance institutions, etc. Following the establishment of EVPA in 2004, Dr. Rob John co-founded AVPN in 2010. AVPN is characterized by extraordinary diversity in terms of the support it provides to social enterprises (financing, consulting), as well as in terms of fields of action for the social enterprises that receive support (unemployment, healthcare services, social exclusion, addressing poverty, environmental protection).

In spite of the local characteristics of Asian capitalism and the respective philanthropy, capitalism has a universal character. Thus, the philanthropic practices deployed in capitalist countries are also universal. Reference to European and Asian philanthropy networks of venture philanthropy does not imply purely European or Asian impact investments in terms of country of origin and utilization of capital and expertise. Venture philanthropy in Asia is materialized by organizations that operate all over the world. Several European and American organizations in the field of social economy operate in Asia and Africa (e.g., The Ground_Up Project from Switzerland, Give2Asia from the US, and the King Baudouin Foundation from Belgium). In addition, several philanthropy and social entrepreneurship organizations are structured as international networks, comprising organizations that have a national focus, like United Way and ChildFund. In human capital terms, the pioneers of social entrepreneurship at the national level are institutions possessing supranational skills that are typical of big capitalist businesses. Raj Gilda, for instance, having acquired long working experience with Deloitte and Citibank in New York, co-founded Lend-A-Hand India, an organization focused on financing vocational education and training for young Indians who live in extreme poverty.

Despite their global reach, impact investments are inevitably shaped by regional characteristics: entrepreneurial philanthropy in Asia is confined to the entrepreneurial, social, and political context of that area. In this respect, China constitutes a special case in the field of venture philanthropy. Government control of a large part of the economy precluded the development of such organizations up until the late 1980s. Until then, the "government organized non-governmental organizations" aimed at addressing poverty issues in the country. Indicatively, the China Foundation for Poverty Alleviation was established in 1989 and the Soong Ching-ling Foundation was established in 1982 (Soong Ching-ling served as the Vice President of the People's Republic of China from 1959 to 1975; in 1981 she became Honorary President of the People's Republic of China). For several years, these institutions operated under the leadership Chinese Communist Party officials and were primarily supported by state funds. It is worth pointing out here that the dividing line between non-governmental organizations that are controlled by the government and those that are independent is generally quite thin. The tradition of non-governmental organizations that are associated with the government, the state, or a specific political party is not limited to China. Instead, it is present and continuously evolving in several countries.[22] One of the first institutions that enjoyed a high degree of autonomy from the Chinese government was Amity Foundation of the Chinese Christian Church, which was established in 1985. In China there are currently over 7,000 foundations[23] that are active over the entire spectrum of the social economy.

VENTURE PHILANTHROPY: CRITIQUE

Venture philanthropy constitutes social economy innovation in the way social impact is supported and deployed. Moreover, it supplies part of the capital that is needed to achieve the SDGs and implement the 2030 Agenda for Sustainable Development, sustainable economic growth (SDG 8) and clean energy (SDG 7) being at the focus of private-equity impact investors.[24] However, despite its significant social impact, venture philanthropy is subject to several criticisms. First, the wealth of venture philanthropy pioneers may be seen as the flip side of the global economic inequality that is being addressed through their own impact investments. Furthermore, in the case of impact investments, implementation of the principles of successful entrepreneurship, such as support for startups offered by venture capital, may be hard to combine with key public goods characteristics (non-rivalry, non-excludability).[25] In addition, venture philanthropy stumbles on issues pertaining to the measurement of social impact and the quantification of public goods production. For instance, measuring the benefits to a local community from the construction of a cultural center and attributing a certain portion of the economic development of that community to the cultural center is not a straightforward exercise.

In the same line of argument, financial viability of venture philanthropy is subject to a similar critique: emphasis on financial returns is for the most part against the tradition of public goods production through philanthropy.[26] Manufacturing of Kalydeco, the prescription drug for cystic fibrosis, is a case in point. Aurora Biosciences and, subsequently, Vertex, which bought out Aurora Biosciences in 2001, produced the drug, receiving financial support from the American Cystic Fibrosis Foundation.[27] In this particular case, the Cystic Fibrosis Foundation acted as a venture philanthropist, while the companies involved act in a fully for-profit manner. As the number of patients suffering from cystic fibrosis is relatively small (about 30,000 in the US and 70,000 internationally), production of the drug by the private sector is not viable, hence financial support from the impact investor, the Cystic Fibrosis Foundation, is indispensable. Yet, due to the small market size and the profit-making criteria of Vertex, Kalydeco was made available at a market price of 311,000 US dollars per year of treatment for each patient (subsequent Vertex drugs for cystic fibrosis were sold at a similar price). Thus, the market price of the drug made access to treatment extremely difficult for many of the patients. The case of Kalydeco highlights both the potential and the limitations of the market mechanism to produce public goods and address social problems.

It is worth pointing out that while these are reasonable concerns, the practice of venture philanthropy – with measurable objectives, a business plan, and outcomes assessment – is confronted by a challenge that is all too common in both private and public goods production, namely the scarcity of resources. The need for business organization and budgeting on the part of private producers of public goods stems from the need to attain the best possible outcome out of a given amount of resources (for example, there is no public health service that is offered abundantly, regardless of considerations of cost). However, implementation of venture philanthropy practices in the production of public goods is legitimized to the extent that the outcomes are substantially superior to those of conventional forms of social action. There is, for example, no conclusive evidence that the construction of a school complex in the context of venture philanthropy is socially more effective compared to the construction of a school complex through conventional philanthropy donation and, even less so, through the government budget, where revenue comes from taxation.

A further criticism on venture philanthropy and other social impact initiatives has to do with the fact that public goods production is motivated by specific priorities and, therefore, is fragmented and isolated from the broader plexus of social policy. For example, the establishment of an organization that offers free-of-charge legal services to socially excluded citizens, for example refugees, because the latter are financially unable to get such services paying the relevant fees, may not necessarily be part of a holistically organized initiative that would include action on housing, schooling, and healthcare services for refugees. Several venture philanthropy organizations support a diversified portfolio of social impact actions, aiming at holistic interventions in addressing social problems. Nevertheless, the broadest possible way to confront social policy challenges rests with the government, as the government has the budgetary and political responsibility to address social problems in their entirety, throughout the geographical area and for the whole of the population in the country. The synergies that are involved in a holistic, large-scale planning approach necessitate central planning and, to a great extent, implementation by the central government. In addition, precisely because such policies affect society in its entirety, implementation requires consensus by all citizens. In turn, consensus passes through parliamentary control of the central government and, in the case of local societies, local government control.

At this point, the political question on venture philanthropy that needs to be addressed is the following. How does venture philanthropy ensure that social policies exercised by private venture philanthropy satisfy the priorities of the philanthropist entrepreneurs, the needs of those who are directly benefiting from their action, and, most importantly, a broader social consensus about the allocation of resources and the substance of economic development and welfare?

CONCLUSION

Venture philanthropy is a novel institution of social finance. Its share in the global capital market is relatively small, especially compared to conventional venture capital.[28] However, venture philanthropy is pioneering social finance as it expands the entrepreneurial, financial, and social choices of the social economy, enriching the latter with the logic of venture capital. This approach functions in a complementary fashion with state and other social economy activities and mechanisms of funding whose goal is to address social problems. It also functions in a competitive fashion, in the sense that it competes with other organizations for access to the limited capital and human resources that are available to the social economy. Success of venture philanthropy as a social finance institution depends on responding successfully to the challenges it faces.

First, venture philanthropy needs to acquire its own space in the social economy discourse, with terminology that distinguishes it from other forms of social finance. The terms "exit" (describing the withdrawal of philanthropy investors), "due diligence", "business plan", "social investment", "social impact", "philanthropy", and "venture capital" need to be clearly defined in order to encourage discourse to facilitate the flow of capital, labor, and ideas in the area of social finance.[29] Otherwise, the already blurred boundaries between different mechanisms of finance become even more confusing. As with other mechanisms of social finance, the most important term to clarify in venture philanthropy is social impact. Determining social or environmental changes as the result of an impact investment and particularly measuring impact on all parties affected by venture philanthropy in a clear manner constitute a requirement for the expansion of social finance networks in general and novel institutions like venture philanthropy in particular.

Furthermore, because it shares methods with venture capital, venture philanthropy needs to embrace its main attribute, namely its adaptability to the financial needs of novel forms of entrepreneurship. The social economy offers new ways of addressing social and environmental challenges. Therefore, the management of scarce resources and capital requirements must adapt to the needs of each different social project, blending social impact with sustainable financial innovation. The flexible nature of venture philanthropy means that it can embody efficiently different financing options, in sharp contrast with charity (donation), which implies a -100% rate of return for the donor. A blend of social impact bonds, crowdfunding platforms, microfinance – along with conventional for-profit lending and private investment mechanisms – may enhance financial synergies, thereby boosting the social impact of venture philanthropy.

Like conventional venture capital, venture philanthropy could become a sustainable mechanism of financing social innovation to the extent that it would support effectively social enterprises for a long period after granting the initial capital.[30] Support includes providing guidance to social entrepreneurs to help them materialize their business plan, strategic re-orientation in a dynamic environment of social challenges and financial limitations, and deployment of strategic alliances for the innovative social enterprise. More importantly, like conventional venture capital, successful venture philanthropy requires a specific exit mechanism from the financed social enterprise in a way that secures ongoing social impact and the financial resources necessary to achieve that.

MATERIAL FOR DISCUSSION

Bill Gates announces further investment in Alzheimer's research, taking on disease detection

Tindera, M. 2018. Bill Gates announces further investment in Alzheimer's research, taking on disease detection. *Forbes*, July 17.

Available at:

www.forbes.com/sites/michelatindera/2018/07/17/bill-gates-announces-further-investment-in-alzheimers-research-taking-on-disease-detection/#2074b86b147b.

REVIEW QUESTIONS

1   What are the differences and similarities between venture capital and venture philanthropy?
2   How can venture philanthropy contribute to remedying social problems?
3   What are the differences between venture philanthropy and charity?
4   What are the characteristics of venture philanthropy in Asia?
5   What are the differences and similarities between venture philanthropy in Europe and venture philanthropy in the USA?
6   What are the main criticisms against venture philanthropy in terms of its contribution to social problems?

NOTES

1   John and Emerson (2015).
2   Rodger (2013).
3   On the principles of venture philanthropy, see Letts et al. (1997).
4   https://evpa.eu.com/about-us/what-is-venture-philanthropy.
5   For an analysis of stages of materializing social investments by venture philanthropy organizations, see Gordon (2014).
6   Boyce (2013).
7   For example, Williamson (2018) refers to the P_TECH schools network that is being financed by IBM and constitutes part of the Smart Cities program of IBM, which is about the redesign, governance, and economic development of cities. Similarly, XQ: The Super School Project is a school network established by Laurene Powell, the widow of late Apple founder and CEO Steve Jobs. The project has several venture philanthropy traits, promoting the principles of startups and the "new economy" of Silicon Valley, thus distancing itself from the educational system of public schools.
8   For network attributes of the investment community of venture philanthropy, see Mair and Hehenberger (2014).
9   John and Emerson (2015).

10   The term philanthropocapitalism, among other terms, is used to describe the introduction of capitalist and business practices in the domain of addressing social and environmental challenges. For an introduction to philanthropocapitalism, see Bishop and Green (2015).

11   The investment group KKR & Co. L.P. (Kohlberg, Kravis & Roberts) is involved in real estate management, financial risk management, healthcare services, energy, and construction. The value of assets managed by the group exceeds 158 billion US dollars (www.kkr.com/).

12   http://redf.org.

13   www.forbes.com/forbes-400/list/4/#version:static.

14   www.robinhood.org.

15   The analysis of pioneer investors in venture philanthropy in the USA presented here is inevitably indicative. For an extensive presentation of venture philanthropy, see Pepin (2005) and John and Emerson (2005).

16   https://acumen.org.

17   On the development of social entrepreneurship in the United Kingdom.

18   www.socialbusinesstrust.org.

19   www.lgtlightstone.com/en/.

20   Capgemini (2017, 2020).

21   https://givingpledge.org.

22   For example, the organization CARE (Cooperative for Assistance and Relief Everywhere) was established in the USA in the context of the humanistic support of the US government towards certain European governments in the context of the Marshall Plan after World War II. Nowadays, in addition to its charity work, CARE is involved in social finance, being active in several aspects including microfinance in developing countries. On the boundaries of non-governmental organizations and their historical relationships with governments, states, and political parties, see, for example, Hasmath et al. (2019).

23   http://en.foundationcenter.org.cn/mission.html.

24   IFC (2019).

25   For example, Di Lorenzo and Scarlata (2019) report that venture philanthropy is more effective in reducing income inequality when social enterprises that receive impact capital exhibit collectivistic – rather than utilitarian, market-minded – orientation in their organizational identity.

26   Nielsen (2017).

27   Feldman and Graddy-Reed (2014).

28   Mair and Hehenberger (2014) note that venture capital in Europe is about 60 times higher than venture philanthropy.

29   On the importance of "language" limitations in the deployment of venture philanthropy, see Katz (2005) and John (2006).

30   See John (2006).

REFERENCES

Bishop, M., and Green, M., 2015. Philanthrocapitalism comes of age. In: A. Nicholls, R. Patton, and J. Emerson, eds. Social finance. Oxford: Oxford University Press, 113–129.

Boyce, B.A., 2013. Philanthropic funding in higher education: Carrot and/or stick. Quest, 65(3), 255–265. https://doi.org/10.1080/00336297.2013.791873.

Capgemini, 2017. *World wealth report 2017.* https://www.capgemini.com/wp-content/uploads/2017/09/worldwealthreport_2017_final.pdf.

Capgemini, 2020. *World wealth report 2020.* https://www.capgemini.com/nl-nl/wp-content/uploads/sites/7/2020/07/World-Wealth-Report-WWR-2020.pdf.

Di Lorenzo, F., and Scarlata, M., 2019. Social enterprises, venture philanthropy and the alleviation of income inequality. *Journal of Business Ethics*, 159, 307–323. https://doi.org/10.1007/s10551-018-4049-1.

Feldman, M.P., and Graddy-Reed, A., 2014. Accelerating commercialization: A new model of strategic foundation funding. *Journal of Technology Transfer*, 39(4), 503–523. https://doi.org/10.1007/s10961-013-9311-1.

Gordon, J., 2014. A stage model for venture philanthropy. *Venture Capital*, 16(2), 85–107. https://doi.org/10.1080/13691066.2014.897014.

Hasmath, T., Hildebrandt, T., and Hsu, J.Y.J., 2019. Conceptualizing government-organized nongovernmental organizations. *Journal of Civil Society*, 15(3), 267–284. https://doi.org/10.1080/17448689.2019.1632549.

IFC., 2019. *Creating impact: The promise of impact investing.* Washington: International Finance Corporation.

John, R., 2006. *Venture philanthropy: The evolution of high engagement philanthropy in Europe.* Working paper. Oxford: Oxford University Press.

John, R., and Emerson, J., 2015. Venture philanthropy: Development, evolution and scaling around the world. *In:* A. Nicholls, R. Patton, and J. Emerson, eds. *Social finance.* Oxford: Oxford University Press, 185–206.

Katz, S.N., 2005. What does it mean to say that philanthropy is "effective"? The philanthropists' new clothes. *Proceedings of the American Philosophical Society*, 149(2), 123–131.

Letts, C.W., Ryan, W., and Grossman, A., 1997. Virtuous capital: What foundations can learn from venture capitalists. *Harvard Business Review*, 75(2), 36–44.

Mair, J., and Hehenberger, L., 2014. Front-stage and backstage convening: The transition from opposition to mutualistic coexistence in organizational philanthropy. *Academy of Management Journal*, 57(4), 1174–1200. https://doi.org/10.5465/amj.2012.0305.

Nielsen, A.E., 2017. Perceived inconsistency in new philanthropy. *Management Communication Quarterly*, 31(3), 492–498. https://doi.org/10.1177%2F0893318917699524.

Pepin, J., 2005. Venture capitalists and entrepreneurs become venture philanthropists. *International Journal of Nonprofit and Voluntary Sector Marketing*, 10(3), 165–173. https://doi.org/10.1002/nvsm.10.

Rodger, J.J., 2013. "New capitalism", colonization and the neo-philanthropic turn in social policy: Applying Luhmann's systems theory to the big society project. *International Journal of Sociology and Social Policy*, 33(11/12), 725–741. https://doi.org/10.1108/IJSSP-02-2013-0022.

Williamson, B., 2018. Silicon startup schools: Technocracy, algorithmic imaginaries and venture philanthropy in corporate education reform. *Critical Studies in Education*, 59(2), 218–236. https://doi.org/10.1080/17508487.2016.1186710.

5

Social impact bonds

After reading this chapter, you will be able to:

1 Identify the characteristics of pay-for-performance/pay-for-success contracts
2 Identify the counterparties, stakeholders, and processes in a social impact bond
3 Assess the diversity of social impact bonds across different social, financial, and institutional frameworks
4 Explain the challenges facing social impact bonds

INTRODUCTION

A distinct mechanism of financing social ventures is the pay-for-success or pay-for-performance contract that involves financial return based on social impact. In this case, a chronic social problem is identified by the public sector and impact investors supply the capital required for addressing it. The capital required is not supplied directly from suppliers of capital to the public sector or the supplier of social services. Most of the times, a non-governmental intermediary undertakes coordination of action and monitors delivery of the impact investment. Subsequently, suppliers of social services (usually non-governmental organizations that carry out social work in that particular area) offer the service to the affected parts of the

DOI: 10.4324/9781003230366-7

population. During the phase of implementation, an independent evaluator measures the impact achieved, in terms of both mitigation of the social problem and saving of public resources, and determines the amount to be repaid by the public sector to the supplier of finance: the better the outcome, the higher the amount to be repaid.[1]

Social impact bonds constitute a showcase of pay-for-success contracts. They are loan contracts signed by central or local governments or by public organizations, through which the supplier of finance receives payments according to the financial benefits incurred from accomplishment of a specific social purpose. Essentially, this type of financing takes the form of up-front capital outlay. Social impact bonds are a relatively recent tool of financial innovation that may also be considered as social innovation, because in their context the effort of governments to address social problems is associated with implementation of new forms of financing and delivery of social policy.[2] Social impact bonds are based on partnership between social purpose organizations, the government, and the private sector. The investment community in particular uses social impact bonds as a vehicle for participating in efforts to address social issues. Like risk management in government pension funds, impact bonds constitute a most representative way of blending private profit with state policy for the sake of mitigating social problems. In addition, social impact bonds have a longer time horizon in addressing a specific social problem than most government policies do. For example, policy to address unemployment may change even during the term in office of the same government, while the term to maturity of a social impact bond that would raise funds to address this problem would tend to be longer than five years.

The terms of social impact bond contracts are negotiated between all stakeholders involved (rather than just between the government and the lender), based on different priorities, resource availability, and financial capability of each party. Loan contracts specify the success criteria of the impact investment. Satisfaction of success criteria determines repayment to bondholders. For example, a bond that supports protection of the environment in a certain area will make payments through the amount that will be saved by the local government from mitigating environmental deterioration and contributing to prosperity and development in the region as a result of improved environmental conditions. Similarly, financing the reduction of crime in a certain area indirectly promotes economic development, as it frees resources devoted to the prison system for investments in other areas. The amount saved from mitigation of the social problem addressed is used to repay the bond, with accomplishment of more significant social impact being positively related to investors' return.

Moreover, the contract terms in the case of social impact bonds tend to be very specific. For example, they may specify reduction of inmates' bed days in prison as the measure of crime reduction. The first ever social impact bond was issued for Peterborough Prison in the UK. Its goal was to reduce the proportion of former inmates who were reconvicted after their release and returned to prison. Another social impact bond, through which Goldman Sachs lent 9.6 million USD to the City of New York, aimed at supporting inmates of 16 to 18 years of age in Rikers Island Prison. In that case, the loan was guaranteed by Bloomberg Philanthropies and was to be paid off by the City of New York, based on the cost savings of the prison system from the reduction in crimes committed by recently released convicts.[3] Thus, in contrast to other public-sector areas, where measurement of performance matters but is not fully embodied in the decision-making process, in the case of social impact bonds measurement of social impact is fully incorporated and features prominently in the respective bond contract, determining repayment of the bond to its holders.

A basic difference with conventional measures of social policy effectiveness is that in the case of social impact bonds, the sole determinant of the rate of return is social change, rather than mere evidence that a certain public good or service is being supplied. As an example, in the case of a social impact bond to help reduce drug addiction, what matters is the reduction in the number of drug addicts, reflected in closing down the relevant public service offered to address drug addiction for instance, rather than just the number of therapy sessions or the work hours put into such sessions. Moreover, because the emphasis is placed on social impact rather than on recorded efforts, social ventures financed through social impact bonds are highly flexible.

SOCIAL IMPACT BONDS: NODES OF THE NETWORK

The connections between the basic nodes that define the social impact bonds are shaped by negotiations, in the context of the pertinent legal framework and the stakeholders' needs and relative power (Figure 5.1).

The most important node in the network is the government. The government (or the local government) identifies the social problem to be addressed, borrows through the social impact bond, and is obligated to repay creditors through the savings it will

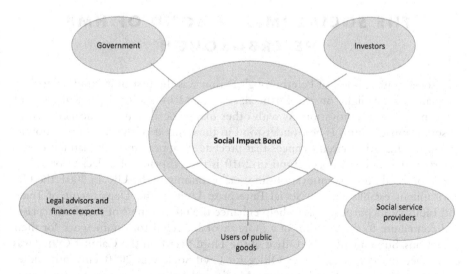

Figure 5.1 Social impact bond network

make from impact investment success. A further key node in the network is investors, who actually supply the funds for delivering the social venture (e.g., charity organizations, institutional investors, high net worth individuals, financial companies, etc.). Their objectives usually include both achieving social impact and securing financial profit. Politics aside, the relationship between social benefit and investor profit is clear: higher social benefit implies higher profits for the investors. However, as the rate of private return is associated with attainment of social impact, uncertainty about the social impact achieved implies uncertainty about financial return. Uncertainty is accentuated by the lack of complete information on the impact investment itself (note that beyond organized capital markets, legal frameworks, and structured contracts, each investment is historically unique). More importantly, uncertainty is further reinforced by the lack of an organized secondary market for social impact bonds.

The organizations that deliver the social service associated with the impact investment (e.g., the specific organization that offers vocational training to the unemployed or to recently released convicts) constitute another important node. The effectiveness of these organizations in delivering the social service is critical to boost the profit for the social impact bond's creditors. Other nodes in the social impact bond network include legal advisors and financial markets experts who undertake contract design, as well as organizations that bring together all stakeholders and mediate in the negotiation process on specific aspects of financing the impact investment. Finally, yet importantly, the users of the public goods that are produced in the context of the impact investment (e.g., the unemployed, patients, single parents, recently released convicts, etc.) constitute a separate node in the social impact bonds network. Both social welfare and the financial return to the impact investment are determined by the quality of the services and the magnitude of the benefit from the particular services accrued to citizens.

THE SOCIAL IMPACT BOND OF HMP PETERBOROUGH

The social impact bond of Peterborough Prison was the first of its kind. Therefore, its analysis sheds light on the financial, social, and institutional particularities of this type of social innovation. As with other major social changes, the significance of social impact bonds is best understood in the context of the specific economic, social, and historical circumstances that precede its appearance. The launch of the Peterborough Social Impact Bond in 2010 is the offspring of a decade of policy, regulatory, and business innovations in social economy in the UK. In 2001, the UK government established the Social Enterprise Unit in the Department of Trade and Industry. Its purpose was to help enhance the effectiveness of social enterprises and contribute to the creation of a more favorable regulatory framework for their operations. Subsequently, the Office of the Third Sector in the Cabinet Office was established in 2006 (renamed as Office for Civil Society in 2010, currently under the Department for Digital, Culture, Media and Sport); its role is to offer advisory services on strategic planning for social economy and social entrepreneurship development. Moreover, the government established funding organizations for social economy such as the Financial Inclusion Fund established in 2005 (HM Treasury, 120 million GBP), the Social Enterprise Investment Fund established in 2007 (Department of Health and Social Care, 100 million GBP) and the Communitybuilders Fund established in 2009 (Ministry of Housing, Communities and Local Government, 70 million GBP). In terms of legal reform, the first decade of the 21st century in the UK witnessed the introduction of the Community Investment Tax Relief in 2002, which encouraged impact investments, and the introduction of the Community Interest Company in 2005, which operated under specific rules with respect to impact-oriented use of its assets and limitations to payouts to investors. Furthermore, the launch of the Peterborough Social Impact Bond was also preceded by the emergence of important impact investors in the UK such as Bridges Ventures (later Bridges Fund Management) and Adventure Capital Fund (later Social Investment Business).

Placement of the Peterborough bond was based on the interest of the central government to confront crime on the one hand and the financial interest of impact investors, the social orientation of philanthropic organizations, and the legal expertise of finance professionals on financial engineering contract design on the other. The beginning of the process dates back to the spring of 2007 when the UK government established the Council for Social Action, inviting all those interested to participate in action addressing social problems. The nonprofit organization Social Finance, a key social finance institution in the UK, also participated in this effort. The UK government established the Social Outcomes Fund, whose goal was to support investments that had the characteristics of social impact bonds. In addition, deployment of the Peterborough bond was based on the understanding that, irrespectively of the specific political party in power, the private and the public sectors needed to work together in order to address social problems more effectively. Thus, while the bond had been issued during the term of the Labour party, the coalition government of the Conservatives and the Liberals that followed suit reinforced the role of impact investors and offered support for the Peterborough social impact bond (it is indicative that the relevant political argument was named "Big Society", as opposed to "Big Government").[4]

In that context, the first social impact bond was launched in March 2010, its goal being reduction of crime amongst convicts who had spent one year or less in prison. Thus, the objective of the social impact bond was prevention of recidivism on the part of recently released prisoners. The bond was issued under the auspices of the UK Ministry of Justice for prisoners released from HMP Peterborough.[5] The set of actions taken to achieve social impact through the bond on Peterborough was called One Service. The main stakeholders were as follows:

♦ The UK Ministry of Justice.
♦ Social Finance: The nonprofit organization that coordinated the entire project. The joint venture of the Ministry of Justice with Social Finance was named "Social Impact Partnership".
♦ Big Lottery Fund: A public-sector organization that manages part of the revenues from the UK National Lottery for charity purposes. Big Lottery Fund

would repay the loan, in conjunction with the UK Ministry of Justice, in the event that the target of crime reduction would be successfully accomplished.

♦ Impact investors: 17 organizations, including Tudor Trust, Friends Provident Foundation, Johansson Family Foundation, Rockefeller Foundation, and many others.

♦ Independent assessors who, upon completion of the project, would measure outcomes and determine payments to investors. The independent assessment was delivered by the University of Leicester and QinetiQ, the latter being a private firm active in the defense industry. Overall evaluation of the social impact bond was conducted by RAND Europe.

♦ Providers of social services, namely the organizations that undertook to offer support services for the prisoners: St Gilles Trust, Peterborough and Fenland Mind, YMCA, Sova, Ormiston Trust, and others.

    ♦ St Gilles Trust is a charity organization that supports the homeless, the unemployed, those addicted to substances, as well as individuals with deviant behavior, and the very poor.

    ♦ Sova is a UK charity organization that focuses on supporting socially excluded and deviant individuals.[6]

    ♦ Peterborough and Fenland Mind, now operating as Cambridgeshire Peterborough and South Lincolnshire Mind, is a nonprofit organization delivering psychiatric care services.[7]

    ♦ Ormiston Families is a charity organization that supports children and youngsters, mainly by way of delivering education and healthcare services to them.[8]

    ♦ Young Men's Christian Association (YMCA) is a nonprofit institution established in 1844 in London. Based on Christian values and principles, YMCA offers youngsters education, as well as hospitality, healthcare, advisory, and sports services.[9] YMCA entered the initial Peterborough prison social impact bond, offering its facilities for meeting sessions between professionals and project volunteers, but was subsequently replaced by Sova for most of its services.

The nominal value of the bond was approximately 5 million GBP Its term to maturity was seven years. The goal was to help inmates with relatively short-term imprisonment, both during their time in prison as well as after their release, in order to ensure their reintegration in society in the smoothest possible manner. Evaluation of social impact was to take place in stages, examining the behavior of three different groups of 1,000 inmates each. The main requirement for repayment of the loan was a minimum average reduction in the crime rate by 7.5% or by 10% in at least one of the three groups that participated in the project. Attainment of that target would give investors an annual rate of return of 7.5%. The maximum annual return could be up to 13%, depending on the scale of reduction in reconvictions (Disley et al., 2011). The government was not to repay more than 8 million GBP over the seven-year maturity period of the bond. The first group of inmates would participate in the program from September 2010 to June 2012, the second from July 2012 to

June 2014, and the third from July 2014 to June 2016. The services offered to former inmates would have a one-year duration following their release, that is, to the summer of 2013, 2015, and 2017 respectively. Because loan repayment depended on the outcome, that is, on the actual change in crime rate (committed by former inmates) following implementation of the program irrespectively of the means that this was achieved by, it was relatively easier to introduce novel methods of crime prevention as part of the program. Thus, the Peterborough bond was characterized by substantial flexibility. Each institution that partnered with One Service specialized in a particular type of social action according to its past experience and mandate, while the form of collaboration with the program was flexible (each social services provider offered different services based on the needs of each inmate, contributing to the accomplishment of the overall goal of the program).

The effort to meet program objectives started with taking a record of the immediate needs of former inmates upon their release from prison: securing housing, opening a bank account, registering with public services. Inmates' enrollment in the program started while they were still in prison. Enrollment was on a voluntary basis. Inmates could leave the program even after they had enrolled. The financial return for investors was calculated on the basis of the new crimes committed by released prisoners as a proportion of the entire group that qualified for the program, rather than as a proportion of those registered in the program only. This particular clause of the bond contract discouraged providers of public services from "cheating" by selecting "easy cases" of former inmates who were unlikely to go back to jail, in order to forge a falsely positive outcome. On the contrary, this way social services providers had an incentive to take action to encourage inmates' participation in the program. Nevertheless, the long maturity period of the bond implied that the institutions involved in the delivery of the program had an incentive to continue working with the same individuals, even if they were reconvicted.

The reduction in crime had to stem directly from the social intervention in the context of which the social impact bond was financed. Commitment of illegal action by prisoners released from Peterborough was not vaguely compared to UK historical crime rates. Instead, it was compared against the recidivism of former inmates with equivalent crime record, age, and nationality. The significance of this feature for the design of relevant financial contracts relates to the fact that the use of different benchmark groups may lead to different conclusions about the overall effectiveness of the program. Obviously, the need for creating a benchmark group for the purposes of comparison renders international implementation of such a program almost impossible, as prisoners' progress is comparable within the same country (e.g., the UK), but it is not comparable across different countries (e.g., Italy or Greece).

Inmates' participation was of critical importance, from the imprisonment period until several months after their release. For the first group of 1,000 inmates, participation rates stood at 74% during imprisonment, 64% on release day, 10% three months after release, and 5% six months after release. For the second group, respective figures stood at 87%, 86%, 20%, and 13%. The initial outcomes were encouraging. In 2014, in the first group of inmates the crime rate fell by 8.4%, which exceeded the 7.5% threshold but was lower than the 10% required for loan repayment. In the second group, the reduction in the crime rate was 9.74%, bringing the average for both groups to about 9%.[10,11]

In spite of its apparent success, the UK government ended the program in 2014. The summer of 2015 was the last period inmates received the services of One Service. The reason the operations of One Service were intercepted was implementation of a different structural reform system that had started in 2013, known as "Transforming Rehabilitation", which required participation of released prisoners in rehabilitation programs that had been assigned to private companies known as Community Rehabilitation Companies. As the reduction in crime rate exceeded 7.5% on average for the first two groups of inmates, the investors got fully repaid. For the third group, One Service operated on a fee-for-service basis.

In general, in spite of interception of the program, the experiment of the social impact bond for rehabilitation of Peterborough prisoners was useful not least because it demonstrated the benefits stemming from private- and public-sector partnerships on social policy issues, as well as benefits from the use of financial innovation to mitigate challenges that pertain to economic development. This rationale allowed implementation of social impact bond financing in other countries. Ultimately, it is the structure of the bond that determines financial comparability between different bond cases in different social contexts. The Peterborough bond was only the beginning. One hundred and seventy-six have been contracted (as of January 1, 2020) and 47 have been completed, with more than half of them yielding positive returns for investors.[12]

THE SOCIAL IMPACT BOND OF RIKERS ISLAND PRISON IN NEW YORK

The social impact bond of Rikers Island was the first US social impact bond. Launched in 2012 when Michael Bloomberg was mayor of New York, the program sought to mitigate recidivism of young men (16–18 years of age) who were released from Rikers Island, the largest prison in New York. Nearly half of the young prisoners released from prison tended to commit crimes again and returned to jail within 12 months from their release.

The main counterparties in the Rikers Island bond issue were:

♦ Manpower Demonstration Research Corporation (MDRC): a nonprofit organization that functioned as the general coordinator of the project. MDRC received the capital required for delivery of the program from Goldman Sachs.
♦ The City of New York: The city has the political and administrative responsibility of Rikers Island and therefore had to make the payments to MDRC. In turn, MDRC would repay the lender if recidivism of prisoners released

from Rikers Island were significantly reduced. The city, however, would repay MDRC even if the program failed to achieve its 10% target reduction in former inmates' recidivism. Specifically, the city would pay MDRC 4.8 million USD for any improvement between 8.5% and 10% but would make no payment for improvement below the 8.5% threshold. In general, repayment was tied to the reduction of recidivism attained. For extraordinary improvement in excess of 20%, the maximum repayable amount was 11.712 million USD.[13]

♦ Osborne Association: A nonprofit organization whose goal is to support individuals who are jailed for law violations, as well as their families. In the context of the Rikers Island social impact bond, Osborne Association undertook delivery of the social intervention that addressed recidivism after former prisoners were released from prison. The model of intervention was named Adolescent Behavioral Learning Experience (ABLE) and was based on the principles of Moral Reconation Therapy.[14]

♦ Goldman Sachs Urban Investment Group: It supplied MDRC with the capital required for the project (9.6 million US dollars). According to the loan contract, Goldman Sachs would be repaid only in the event of a reduction in the crime rate of 10% or more.

♦ Bloomberg Philanthropies: A philanthropic organization led by the then mayor of New York, Michael Bloomberg. It undertook the task to compensate Goldman Sachs up to 7.2 million USD in the event that the program did not bring about the expected outcomes, in which case the city would not make any payments for the services supplied.

♦ Vera Institute of Justice: The independent evaluator of the social intervention program.

The measure of effectiveness of the program were the bed days of youngsters who participated in ABLE program sessions. By use of randomized control trials on the youngsters who enrolled in the program, ABLE program outcomes were compared against cases of recidivism of the youngsters who did not participate. Results were publicized and the program was terminated on August 31, 2015. The findings of Vera were that reduction in recidivism as a result of the program was not statistically significant in relation to the changes observed for the control group (the control group was constructed in such a way to allow comparisons with the group of youngsters enrolled in the ABLE program, in terms of both demographic and crime profiles). Indeed, Vera documented an increase in recidivism, which was attributable to factors irrelevant to the program.[15]

Goldman Sachs was compensated by Bloomberg Philanthropies for a large fraction of the amount it invested, but still had losses. Nevertheless, in spite of interception of the program, the outcome was considered to be quite satisfactory by both the main supplier of finance, Goldman Sachs, and Bloomberg Philanthropies.[16] This shows that effectiveness of such programs is open to different interpretations, thus bringing about new challenges in measuring the effectiveness of impact investments and the interventions attempted through social impact bonds. On the part of the suppliers of finance, the reasoning behind program success was based on the following three factors:

1 The citizens of New York City were spared the financial burden associated with action to address a specific social problem. Normally, taxpayers carry the financial burden of such action, irrespective of the outcome.
2 The data that were collected in the context of the program constitute a unique resource that can be used for (re)designing social policy action.
3 The program paved the way for financial innovation when fiscal discipline restricts the availability of funds for the conduct of social policy.

THE SOCIAL IMPACT BOND FOR THE RECIDIVISM OF YOUNGSTERS RELEASED FROM MASSACHUSETTS PRISONS

The contract of the social impact bond for the recidivism of youngsters released from Massachusetts prisons, launched as the Massachusetts Juvenile Justice Pay for Success Initiative, was signed in January 2014 and amended in November 2016.[17] The objective of this program was to reduce the crime rate amongst former inmates and enhance their employment opportunities in Massachusetts: Boston, Springfield, and Chelsea. The main nodes in the network defined by this contract are the Commonwealth of Massachusetts, the non-governmental organization Roca, and the non-governmental organization Youth Services Inc. (YSI).

An organization that helps gang members, school dropouts, young unmarried mothers, and other groups who are prone to living lives in extreme poverty and crime, Roca was established in 1988 by Molly Baldwin, a former street worker and community organizer. Roca applies its own intervention model, whose goal is to transform the behavior of young people. Youth Services Inc. is part of Third Sector Capital Partners, a non-governmental organization that specializes in the management of pay-for-success programs (see Box 5.1).

Box 5.1 Third Sector Capital Partners

Third Sector Capital Partners is a US nonprofit organization established in 2011. Its goal is to address social problems that are related to unemployment, justice, children's welfare, and extreme poverty, by making use of pay-for-success contracts. For that purpose, it collaborates with the public sector, private investors, and other nonprofit organizations. It has organized several bond issues in the US and has taken part in social impact investments worth over 800 million USD, approximately 95% of it being government funding.[18] As a non-governmental organization, Third Sector Capital Partners' target is to enhance the effectiveness of social policy. Other than social impact bonds, Third Sector Capital Partners offers consulting services to the federal government as well as to state authorities, aiming to deliver social innovation with measurable impact to help mitigate social problems.

Third Sector Capital Partners programs are delivered in four stages. In the first stage, the social problem is identified and the network of organizations that will be involved in addressing the problem is formed. In the second stage, the social impact bond contract is drafted, incorporating the priorities of the parties involved and the characteristics of the pertinent social problem. In the third stage, the social intervention is optimized through measurement of social impact and program redesign as needed to attain the best possible outcome. In the fourth stage, successful social impact bonds constitute the basis for the design of new ones, aiming to attract new impact investors.

As with all social impact bonds, funds are not directly payable to the government but to the intermediary that organizes the social intervention/investment and coordinates the project. In the case of Massachusetts Juvenile Justice Pay for Success Initiative, that intermediary is YSI. As service provider, Third Sector Capital Partners is expected to manage the project, collaborating with a network of institutions of the Commonwealth of Massachusetts, including the Executive Office for Administration and Finance, the Department of Youth Services with the Executive Office of Health and Human Services, the Office of the Commissioner of Probation, the Department of Criminal Justice Information Systems within the Executive Office of Public Safety and Security, and the Executive Office of Labor and Workforce Development.[19] The recipients of services ("customers") are 1,036 males aged 17–24 who exhibit high probability of imprisonment and are on probation by the Department of Youth Services.[20] The model implemented by Roca comprises two years of supply of services to "customers" and two years of follow-up services offered by specialists in skills development and behavioral change. The duration of the project is seven years and can be extended by another two years.

The maximum amount to be paid by the state of Massachusetts is 28 million USD based on the outcome. Funding comes from loans and philanthropic capital. The loan originates mainly from Goldman Sachs (8 million USD – Goldman Sachs Social Impact Fund), as well as from Kresge Foundation and Living Cities (1.33 million USD each).[21] The interest rate on Goldman's priority loan is 5%, while the interest rate on the other two non-priority loans is 2%. Except for lending, contributions to the financing of the loan come from donations by philanthropy organizations: the Laura and John Arnold Foundation (3.34 million USD), New Profit Inc. (1.81 million USD), Boston Foundation (300,000 USD). The US Department of Labor offered a 11.7 million USD grant for payments and administration costs (grant was contingent on the project exhibiting early-stage success). The independent evaluator of the project, initially Sibalytics and subsequently Urban Institute,[22] conducts performance evaluation, which is audited by an **independent validator**, Public Consulting Group, a public-sector management consulting and operations improvement firm that collaborates with the

Commonwealth of Massachusetts. The Social Impact Bond Technical Assistance Lab of the Kennedy School of Business of Harvard University offered free technical support.

The amounts to be paid back by the Commonwealth of Massachusetts depend on the reduction of former prisoners' recidivism. In any case, the loan is not to be repaid if the reduction in recidivism is less than 5% (5.2% is the minimum reduction that must be attained so that the Commonwealth can proceed to payments). Twenty-one million USD is to be repaid if the reduction is at least 40%. The cap fee for Roca is 18.53 million USD.[23] Except for the reduction in crime and the direct benefits accrued to the recipients of services from the program, the Commonwealth of Massachusetts is expected to make savings of 22 million USD if bed days are reduced by 40% or 33 million USD if bed days are reduced by 55%. Savings are realized from lower expenditure for inmates' social reintegration. The goal of the program is reduction of bed days by 223,577, which corresponds to 40% and increase in employment for former inmates enrolled in the program by 1,266 employment quarters.

Similar to other bond contracts, the social impact bond of Massachusetts faces challenges pertaining to contract design, so that appropriate incentives are provided to counterparties to comply with contract terms. Lenders have an incentive to push Roca to report a positive outcome, implying an improvement over the current situation. The Commonwealth of Massachusetts would benefit from an understatement of projected outcomes in terms of reduced payoffs to creditors and might also benefit from an overstatement of project outcomes in terms of attracting support from investors and stakeholders for similar projects in the future. Moreover, the state of Massachusetts has an incentive to change the laws that apply to the social impact bond, altering contractual terms in its favor. Furthermore, all involved parties have the incentive to exert pressure on the independent evaluator.[24]

To address these challenges the following action is taken:

1 The data of program participants are accessible to all counterparties. Special care is taken for personal data protection and privacy.
2 Once the groups of inmates are identified, individuals to receive program services are randomly selected by an independent evaluator.
3 Roca prepares quarterly reports on the progress of the program.
4 Roca was selected for this task because of its good record in support programs for youngsters. It bears part of the credit risk associated with the project by sharing part of the cost of operations (3.26 million USD in backlog, on top of the up to 18.53 million US dollars fee, to be repaid according to project outcome). Fifteen percent of quarterly fees owed to Third Sector Capital Partners will also be deferred.
5 The evaluator, the validator, and Roca cannot be replaced without the consent of the lenders.

The program financed by the social impact bond of Massachusetts is currently active. An important challenge faced by the program is its commitment to the behavioral model of Roca, which may be giving the program structured social intervention tools on the one hand, but severely restricts its flexibility in addressing the diverse needs of individuals who make use of its services on the other.

SOCIAL IMPACT BONDS: PROS AND CONS

The main advantage of social impact bonds is that participation of private investors and institutions in the conduct of social policy transfers part of the financial risk associated with impact investments to private investors. In addition, the scale of services supplied to society can be expanded, especially at times of economic recession, when state funds are severely restricted (Figure 5.2).

The pros of social impact bonds may be summarized as follows:

1 Social impact bonds constitute a profitable investment opportunity for impact investors who seek profit along with making an impact on society.
2 Through social impact bonds, the market for impact capital is expanded and nonprofit organizations secure access to capital required for their projects, thus given the opportunity to produce outcomes in accordance with their mission.
3 Society enjoys social services that are not paid for through central or local government budgets.
4 Because investors are repaid based on the social impact attained by the investment, social impact bonds are focused on evaluating social policy outcomes, providing incentives and enhancing the accountability of the institutions that deliver social policy, and motivating investors who benefit only through delivery of successful outcomes.[25]
5 Participation of private investors may reinforce innovation both in the financial planning process for impact investments, as well as in the operation of the social services delivered.

Equally, however, social impact bonds are subject to several challenging complications. Addressing such complications is essential for expansion of social impact bonds as a mechanism of financing social impact investments. The main challenges faced by social impact bonds are presented as follows:

1 Measuring social impact and attributing social transformation to a specific mechanism of funding and a specific social intervention can be complicated,

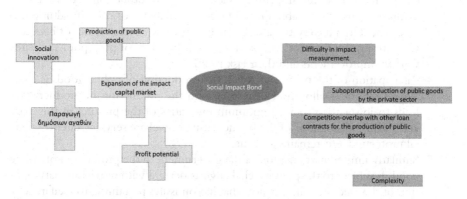

Figure 5.2 Social impact bonds: pros and cons

especially if a large number of investors are involved in funding the project and many institutions are involved in the delivery of the relevant social policy. Thus, to a certain extent, the growth of social impact bonds as a mechanism of financing social policy may be more of a reflection of the political will to materialize partnerships between the private and the public sector, than investment materialized based on positive net present value criteria or a measure that would unambiguously help increase government revenue.[26] For instance, in the case of the Commonwealth of Massachusetts, financial valuation of the project depends on the discount rate used and the income tax rates that the funding parties are subjected to.[27] The choice of specific values for these parameters in the investment valuation process is, to a certain degree, a political decision.

2 Social impact may be simultaneously pursued through other means, for example through the issue of government bonds. In this case, improvement of access to education could be the objective of a government bond issue, whose proceeds will be used for construction of a school complex in a remote area of the country in parallel with a social impact bond issued by the local government aiming to increase the number of students who complete compulsory schooling. Distinguishing which of the two types of finance is to be credited with enhancement of well-being and economic development of the area is not an easy task. The difficulty in matching wealth created from social impact bonds to other forms of funding impact investments constitutes a serious obstacle for raising funds: if the outcome from financing an investment is not evident, investors will lend smaller amounts or demand higher return. Moreover, if the government bond is issued at a lower interest rate than the social impact bond, while addressing similar social needs, there is no reason for the social impact bond to be issued. In general, social impact bonds must target action that does not overlap with the targets of other conventional and well-established means of financing. Focus on social impact reduces uncertainty and attracts investors with clear social priorities and sound business plans.

3 Given that social impact bonds are a relatively recent development, collection and systematic analysis of data for evaluating their performance, as well as comparisons of return and risk characteristics with other competitive investments, may not be feasible due to limited availability of data. In addition, it would be difficult to systematically analyze the key characteristics of investors who are involved in this type of investment in terms of perceptions towards welfare improvements and their risk profile.

4 Participation of the private sector in the production of public goods is challenged by under-allocation of resources to the production of products that leads to lower than socially optimum quantities of the product in the market.[28] Thus, "distortion" of the public nature of welfare services, environmental protection, etc. remains an issue.

5 Similarly, limited participation of the government in the production of public goods is subject to the political challenge associated with restricting participation of the electorate in decision-making on issues pertaining to welfare and,

at the same time, increasing the importance of investors. Essentially, market principles apply and accountability is transferred to "consumers" (the users of social services), who play an important role in the type of products that will be produced. The question is whether welfare decisions are more effective when made by citizens acting as consumers, employees, and entrepreneurs, or when made by citizens acting as voters and elected representatives of the people. While financial risks are transferred from the government to investors, the social uncertainty (about accomplishing the desired impact) is still related to the government's political responsibility about citizen welfare.[29]

6 Contract complexity constitutes an obstacle to wide-scale acceptability of social impact bonds. Inclusion of social impact bonds' terminology in the investors' and policy-makers' jargon is necessary before they become widely accepted as an impact investment tool.

7 Innovation and the transfer of responsibility and financial benefits to private individuals in the context of social impact bonds are expected to increase demand for information in public goods production. In turn, higher demand for information and transparency require systematic organization of information about the economic and societal dimensions of social impact bonds, which may stumble on accounting issues pertaining to recording and measuring impact. To address such challenges, systematic measurement of social impact through systems such as the Impact Reporting and Investment Standards and the Global Impact Investing Rating System is necessary. Setting clear and realistic targets, such as reduction of pollutants in the case of an environmental protection project or bed days in the case of a crime reduction project, or number of startups by young entrepreneurs in the case of a project promoting young entrepreneurship, would help reduce uncertainty and contribute to lowering the cost of financing social investments through social impact bonds.

8 Delivering intended social outcomes by way of launching social impact bonds does not fully replace other types of social policy. Social problems may persist even after expiration of the social impact bond and it is quite important to maintain social impact. As the institutions that deliver social services are non-governmental organizations, it is uncertain they will continue social intervention following termination of the financing period. Of course, continuity in public spending for addressing a certain social issue should not be taken for granted either.

9 It is necessary to develop mechanisms of disinvestment and investors' exit as with conventional investments. This would reduce the risk and increase the liquidity of social investments, thus boosting availability of capital for impact investments. Essentially, what is required is deployment of an organized market for impact investments that would ensure lower transaction costs and increased flow of information to facilitate exit through, for example, sale or liquidation of bonds held.[30]

10 Social impact bonds financing tends to involve a relatively large number of investors and, similarly, delivery of social policy involves many different institutions. This means that success of impact investment depends on effective

amalgamation of institutions with different priorities and ways of operation. Especially insofar as financing is concerned, financial engineering techniques would be extremely useful in merging investors with different profiles in the same investment scheme.

11 Social impact bonds are based on financial and social innovation. To effectively support an organization based on innovation, an outward looking approach is required and, in the case of social policy, adjustment to an ever-changing political, social, and economic environment. More importantly, as social impact bonds constitute social policy, a further challenge is the capability of the mechanism to adjust to changing political contexts that determine the way social policy is exercised and the effectiveness of mechanisms of financing and addressing social problems. In the case of the Peterborough social impact bond, for example, implementation of a new government policy for rehabilitation of former convicts forced the government to limit the number of inmates who would enroll in the program, essentially terminating the services offered in the summer of 2015. Nevertheless, the simplest way through which the government may materialize impact investments is through government spending. The spending side of the government budget specifies the financing needs of social policy from public and private organizations alike and, more importantly, determines the effectiveness of impact investments in the social and economic environment where they are delivered.

12 In the context of social impact bonds, investors often provide funding to an intermediate organization, which also assumes responsibility for organizing operations financed by the social impact bond. Such organizations are often special purpose organizations that are set up for the purposes of a specific social impact bond. On the one hand they provide operational flexibility in project implementation and facilitate collaboration within a diverse set of stakeholders. On the other hand, this intermediation comes at a cost that may include both project management costs and costly contract design that needs to mitigate the challenges of adverse selection, incentive compatibility, and moral hazard. It also needs to tackle all risks that are associated with the operations of a special purpose organization that is set up ad hoc and, therefore, existing laws may not address the concerns of stakeholders that are diverse across the scopes, timing, and societal conditions of different social impact bonds.

CONCLUSION

The Peterborough social impact bond brought into light immense possibilities for partnership between the public and the private sectors to pursue goals of social policy and welfare. Based on measurement of social policy outcomes, social impact bonds transfer the financial risk associated with the impact investment to the private sector, combining the different incentives and special interests of all counterparties to combat successfully social problems. As social impact bonds are a relatively recent phenomenon, implementation is for the moment more of an indication that it is possible to combine different resources and priorities in the context of social and financial innovation, than positive evidence of enhanced savings for governments. Exploiting this new type of institution and confronting successfully the challenges associated with it may transform social impact bonds to a reliable pillar of social policy financing.

The social impact bond market is a rapidly evolving market. Survival of the institution and emergence as a distinct pillar of financing investment for the production of public goods are dependent upon formation of appropriate conditions in the capital market, as well as amendments in the social policy regulatory framework as needed.

MATERIAL FOR DISCUSSION

Issuing bonds to invest in people

Rosenberg, T. 2018. Issuing bonds to invest in people. *New York Times*, March 6. Available at:

www.nytimes.com/2018/03/06/opinion/social-projects-investing-bonds.html.

REVIEW QUESTIONS

1 What are the main characteristics of social impact bonds?
2 Who are the main stakeholders and counterparties in social impact bonds?
3 What is the importance of measurement in social impact bonds?
4 What are the characteristics of the social impact bond for HMP Peterborough?
5 What are the advantages and disadvantages of social impact bonds?
6 What are the main challenges that need to be addressed in the context of social impact bonds as a mechanism of financing social policy?

NOTES

1 Mulgan (2015).
2 See Albertson et al. (2020) for analysis of social impact bonds as social innovations.
3 Olson and Phillips (2013).
4 While this political argument advocated welfare via the inclusion of third-sector capital and initiative in the mitigation of social problems, it also faced criticism on the enterprization of public services (Sepulveda, 2015).
5 Nicholls and Tomkinson (2015).
6 www.sova.org.uk.

7   www.cplsmind.org.uk.

8   www.ormistontrust.org.

9   www.ymca.org.uk.

10   Anders and Dorsett (2017).

11   Disley et al. (2015).

12   www.brookings.edu/blog/education-plus-development/2020/01/06/the-global-impact-bond-market-in-2019-a-year-in-review/.

13   Olson and Phillips (2013).

14   This was a remarkable difference of the Rikers Island social impact bond from its Peterborough counterpart. In the case of Rikers Island, the specific social intervention implemented was group therapy, expanded to include support services to address addiction to substances, housing support, etc. as needed. In contrast, in the case of Peterborough the point was focused to addressing the social problem, with the method being redefined in the process of the intervention. Thus, in Peterborough emphasis was placed on the outcome, rather than commitment to applying a certain model.

15   www.vera.org/publications/rikers-adolescent-behavioral-learning-experi ence-evaluation.

16   https://www.huffingtonpost.com/james-anderson/what-we-learned-from-the-_1_b_7710272.html.

17   Pay-for-success regulatory framework in the USA includes laws such as the Workforce Innovation and Opportunity Act of 2014 and the Social Impact Partnerships to Pay for Results Act of 2018.

18   www.thirdsectorcap.org.

19   Executive Offices in Massachusetts play the role of ministries at the state level.

20   Pay for Success Contract (2014).

21   Established in 1991 in the US, Living Cities is a nonprofit organization whose goal is to improve life in the city for low-income individuals through social innovation. Kresge Foundation is a philanthropic organization established in 1924. Its share capital is 3.6 billion USD. New Profit Inc. is a venture philanthropy and social entrepreneurship organization.

22   Sibalytics and Urban Institute are organizations that specialize in social impact measurement and research.

23   Pay for Success Contract (2014, 2016).

24   See Pandey et al. (2018) on contractual hazards associated with this social impact bond.

25   On the effectiveness of social impact bonds as social intervention compared to non-profit organizations, see the experimental approach of Wong et al. (2017).

26   The net present value is a criterion of evaluating different investments according to which an investment is attractive if the discounted value of expected cash flows exceeds the present value of expenditure associated with the investment.

27   On the importance of the discount rate in social impact bonds valuation in the Commonwealth of Massachusetts, see Pandey et al. (2018). On the importance of the taxation framework for the development of social impact bonds in the US, see Mazur (2017a, 2017b).

28   On the potential problems of public goods production by the private sector, see indicatively Pindyck and Rubinfeld (2018).

29   See Scognamiglio et al. (2019) for a review of social uncertainty in social impact bonds.

30   Shiller (2013) emphasizes the importance of liquidity as a factor behind development of a capital market for social impact bonds.

REFERENCES

Albertson, K., Fox, C., O'Leary, C., and Painter, G., 2020. Towards a theoretical framework of social impact bonds. *Nonprofit Policy Forum*, 11(2). https://doi.org/10.1515/npf-2019-0056.

Anders, J., and Dorsett, R., 2017. *HMP Peterborough social impact bond – Cohort 2 and final cohort impact evaluation*. London: National Institute of Economic and Social Research.

Disley, E., Giacomantonio, C., Kruithof, K., and Sim, M., 2015. *The payment by results social impact bond pilot at HMP Peterborough: Final process evaluation report*. Ministry of Justice. https://assets.publishing.service.gov.uk/government/uploads/system/uploads/attachment_data/file/486512/social-impact-bond-pilot-peterborough-report.pdf.

Disley, E., Rubin, J., Scraggs, E., Burrowes, N., and Culley, D., 2011. *Lessons learned from the planning and early implementation of the social impact bond at HMP Peterborough*. Ministry of Justice. https://assets.publishing.service.gov.uk/government/uploads/system/uploads/attachment_data/file/217375/social-impact-bond-hmp-peterborough.pdf.

Mazur, O., 2017a. Social impact bonds: A tax-favored investment? *Columbia Journal of Tax Law*, 9(1), 141–175. https://doi.org/10.7916/cjtl.v9i1.2861.

Mazur, O., 2017b. Taxing social impact bonds. *Florida Tax Review*, 20(7), 431–494.

Mulgan, G., 2015. Social finance: Does investment add value? In: A. Nicholls, R. Patton, and J. Emerson, eds. *Social finance*. Oxford: Oxford University Press, pp. 45–63.

Nicholls, A., and Tomkinson, E., 2015. The Peterborough pilot social impact bond. In: A. Nicholls, R. Patton, and J. Emerson, eds. *Social finance*. Oxford: Oxford University Press, 335–380.

Olson, J., and Phillips, A., 2013. Rikers Island: The first social impact bond in the United States. *Community Development Investment Review*, 9(1), 97–101.

Pandey, S., Cordes, J.J., Pandey, S.K., and Winfrey, W., 2018. Use of social impact bonds to address social problems: Understanding contractual risks and transaction costs. *Nonprofit Management and Leadership*, 28(4), 511–528. https://doi.org/10.1002/nml.21307.

Pay for Success Contract, 2014. Pay for success contract among the Commonwealth of Massachusetts, Roca, Inc. and Youth Services Inc. www.thirdsectorcap.org/wpcontent/uploads/2015/03/final-pay-for-success-contract-executed-1-7-2013.pdf.

Pay for Success Contract, 2016. Second amended and restated pay for success contract among the Commonwealth of Massachusetts, Roca, Inc. and Youth Services Inc. https://www.thirdsectorcap.org/wp-content/uploads/2016/12/Second-Amended-PFS-Contract-EXECUTION-COPY-11-01-16.pdf.

Pindyck, R.S., and Rubinfeld, D.L., 2018. *Microeconomics*. London: Pearson.

Scognamiglio, E., Di Lorenzo, E., Sibillo, M., and Trotta, A., 2019. Social uncertainty evaluation in social impact bonds: Review and framework. *Research in International Business and Finance*, 47, 40–56. https://doi.org/10.1016/j.ribaf.2018.05.001.

Sepulveda, L., 2015. Social enterprise – A new phenomenon in the field of economic and social welfare? *Social Policy and Administration*, 49(7), 842–861. https://doi.org/10.1111/spol.12106.

Shiller, R.J., 2013. Capitalism and financial innovation. *Financial Analysts Journal*, 69(1), 21–25. https://doi.org/10.2469/faj.v69.n1.4.

Wong, J., Ortmann, A., Motta, A., and Zhang, L., 2017. Understanding social impact bonds and their alternatives: An experimental investigation. *Experiments in Organizational Economics*, 19, 39–83. https://doi.org/10.1108/S0193-230620160000019011.

6

Crowdfunding

After reading this chapter, you will be able to:

1 Outline the characteristics of pay-for-performance/pay-for-success contracts
2 Identify the counterparties, stakeholders, and processes in a social impact bond
3 Assess the diversity of social impact bonds across different social, financial, and institutional frameworks
4 List the advantages and disadvantages of social impact bonds
5 Explain the challenges facing social impact bonds

INTRODUCTION

Crowdfunding is the process of financing social impact or profit-seeking ventures by raising money from a large number of individuals. Crowdfunding relies on relatively small contributions made by each individual investor and the funds are primarily raised over the internet. Crowdfunding is a rapidly expanding mode of social finance. Worldwide funding volume was \$139 billion in 2015 and \$305 billion in 2018,[1] with funding of social ventures constituting a significant part of all projects funded via **crowdfunding platforms**.

> Crowdfunding is the process of financing social impact or profit-seeking ventures by raising money from a large number of individuals.

DOI: 10.4324/9781003230366-8

Crowdfunding is an offshoot of the broader process known as **crowdsourcing**. In crowd-sourcing, the "crowd" contributes resources for attainment of a social, environmental, or entre-

> Crowdfunding is an offshoot of the broader process known as crowdsourcing.

preneurial target. Crowdsourcing is about contributing all kinds of resources (such as labor, material objects, time, money, etc.), while crowdfunding is solely about raising money (see Figure 6.1).

In crowdfunding, individuals or organizations that need to raise capital apply to the crowdfunding platform for funding over the internet. If their application is approved, the funding request is communicated to the "crowd", together with the relevant audiovisual materials ("pitch") that give information regarding the project. The application states the specific amount of money that is targeted through the crowdfunding process. If the required amount fails to be raised through the process, the applicant either returns the money and the project is cancelled (All-or-Nothing) or, less frequently, the applicant keeps the amount raised and proceeds with start-ing the investment project (Keep-It-All). Crowdfunding platforms often finance their operations through commission fees, which correspond to a percentage of the amount contributed to the financed project. For example, Ulule receives commis-sions only for crowdfunding campaigns that attain their funding targets and the commission 6.67% for contributions paid through credit cards and 4.17% for contri-butions paid by check or PayPal (VAT not included).[2]

CROWDFUNDING: TAXONOMY

Based on the particular mode of financing, crowdfunding may be broken down in four categories:

1 **Donation-based crowdfunding**, where there is no commitment to provide compensation to the suppliers of finance in monetary or other material form.

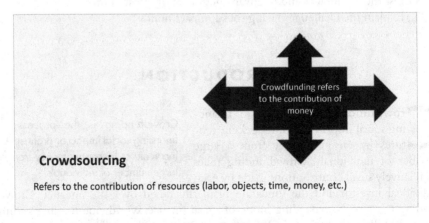

Figure 6.1 Crowdsourcing and crowdfunding

2 **Reward-based crowdfunding**, where suppliers of finance are rewarded in kind. As an example, financing the production of a play may reward each supplier of finance with a free ticket for the theater where the play is staged.

Chuffed.org, presented in Box 6.1, constitutes a typical example of a donation-based and reward-based crowdfunding platform.

Box 6.1 Chuffed.org crowdfunding platform

Chuffed.org is a social enterprise established in Australia in 2013. It operates an internet platform through which money is raised for impact investments. Chuffed. org finances projects in the following areas: social enterprise, international development, refugees, social welfare, animal welfare, community, health and disability, and the environment. It supports crowdfunding campaigns in 32 countries. Religious-related or personal interest-related projects, like automobile purchases, vacations, etc., are not considered for funding by the platform. Evaluation of applications is carried out in less than 24 hours. Approved projects are uploaded on the website of Chuffed.org.[3]

Recipients of finance keep any amount collected through the platform, independently of the degree of coverage of their initial target. Funding does not entail repayment for the donor, who may be rewarded with a "thank you" note sent over social media or a gift, for example, a T-shirt, a mug, or a trip to a place related in some way to the funded project. Payment is carried out through PayPal, Stripe, debit or credit cards. The electronic payment system charges a processing fee between 2% and 2.9% of the amount donated plus 30 cents if the donation is in USD or 20 pence if the donation is in GBP (processing fees vary across countries). Chuffed.org itself does not charge any fee to funded projects, as it finances operations through the contributions of donors, as well as investors and sponsors such as Bevan Clark, Telstra Foundation, and Blackbird Ventures.

---

3 **Equity-based crowdfunding**, where the suppliers of finance have a shareholder relationship with the financed project, in the sense that they share the profits realized by the project proportionately to their monetary contribution. It is worth noting that the idea of anonymous funding by a large number of investors is also present in conventional share capital participation, where a large number of small investors finances large-scale corporations, for a small part of the profit and voting rights. As with conventional financing, expanding the "crowd" of suppliers of finance (outside associates, friends, and relatives) contributes to the viability of the projects funded.[4] What distinguishes crowdfunding from other types of funding is its distinctive way of attracting capital, evaluating investment proposals, allowing for communication between the entrepreneur and the investment community, and accepting special types of projects.[5]

4 **Lending-based crowdfunding**, where suppliers and recipients of finance have a lender–borrower relationship and compensation takes the form of

repayment of the principal borrowed plus interest. In this case, in contrast to conventional bank finance, where commercial banks create money by granting credit, the amounts lent through crowdfunding are equal to the amount provided by the suppliers of finance (who correspond to the depositors of conventional banking. According to UN data, lending-based crowdfunding constitutes 73% of total global crowdfunding.[6] In the European Union, however, lending-based crowdfunding comprises only 21% of the total crowdfunding market.[7] Crowding platform Kiva is a characteristic example of lending-based crowdfunding (Box 6.2).

Box 6.2 Kiva crowdfunding platform

Kiva is a crowdfunding platform operating exclusively lending-based crowdfunding. It was established in San Francisco in 2005 and its goal is to address financial exclusion.[8] So far, 1.9 million lenders have supplied loans worth 1.47 billion USD via Kiva's platform, financing projects in 76 different countries. Kiva has served about 3.6 million borrowers, 81% of whom are women. Moreover, 26% of the loans have been extended to borrowers who are located in developing countries. Repayment rates stand at 95.9%. Every funded project that is uploaded on the platform is given 30 days to collect the requested funding. The minimum amount of lending is 25 USD.

Borrowers may borrow money directly from Kiva or indirectly through Kiva's partners that could be social enterprises, nonprofit organizations, or microfinance institutions. Most projects get a loan from a Kiva field partner before their project is posted on Kiva (and crowdfunding proceeds are employed to repay the loan from the field partner). Depending on contract terms, if the requested amount fails to be collected after completion of the 30 days, the amounts granted are returned to Kiva lenders' accounts (fixed scenario) or any amount that is collected is transferred to the field partner that granted the loan and the borrower must find other means to repay the rest of the loan (flexible scenario).

In the case of direct lending, the money is transferred via PayPal. Most Kiva loans do not bear interest, so Kiva does not receive any interest payments (loans granted by field partners may charge an interest rate though). Instead, it finances its operations based on voluntary donations, 55% from online donations and 27% from corporate ones. Direct lending is conducted following an evaluation process of the proposed project that is carried out by the network of Kiva trustees, whose task is to see that the projects uploaded on the platform for funding are attractive to investors and, more importantly, are fully repaid.

Field partners are classified in credit tiers according to their lending capacity and their credit lines range from 50,000 to 5,000,000 USD. Partners evaluate applications for funding, upload loan requests on Kiva's website, supply capital to the borrowers, and subsequently receive payments, which they forward to the lenders. Unlike Kiva, partners do charge interest on the amounts they provide.

In addition to the basic taxonomy of crowdfunding activities presented earlier, there are **hybrid** forms that combine characteristics of crowdfunding as outlined in Figure 6.2.

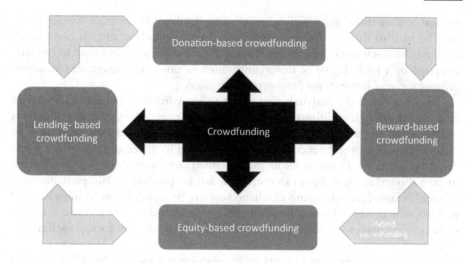

Figure 6.2 Categories of crowdfunding

Depending on the engagement of suppliers of finance in project implementation, crowdfunding may be **passive** or **active**. In contrast to passive crowdfunding, in the case of active crowdfunding, suppliers of capital actively take part in decisions pertaining to the project. It should be noted, however, that the dividing line between passive and active crowdfunding is not perfectly clear, as even in the case of passive crowdfunding, suppliers of finance may influence the management of the investment through their presence on their internet. For example, they can communicate with other suppliers of finance through the platform and form teams with common investment and/or social interests.

Crowdfunding goes well beyond the relationship between suppliers and recipients of finance. It involves a plexus of relationships, where other suppliers of finance (outside the

> Crowdfunding goes well beyond the relationship between suppliers and recipients of finance.

platform), such as investors, donors, lenders, and organizations that supply services to the platform, such as evaluation of the creditworthiness of loan applicants, are involved. Thus, participation in an internet platform brings about complete transformation in the corporate governance of the social enterprises that seek finance through crowdfunding.

To the extent that the capital market is a market of buying and selling **corporate control**,[9] the dispersion of sources of finance and the distinct technology needed to diffuse capital to social enterprises redefine the enterprise as a network of relationships between providers of resources, especially capital. As far as the market for corporate control is concerned, crowdfunding platforms introduce a dimension of geographical dispersion that is different from that of shares in the case of a corporation.

The taxonomy of crowdfunding channels could also be based on the objective of the funded activity as the criterion. For example, in real estate crowdfunding, suppliers of finance participate in real estate investment. Business proposals that seek to raise money through crowdfunding tend to involve activities that would otherwise be hard to finance through conventional capital markets, such as commercial banking, the stock market, or venture capital. This is so because they tend to be characterized by a high degree of uncertainty, often in uncharted investment areas and unknown credit histories for prospective borrowers.

So, what could the activities that resort to crowdfunding because they cannot raise capital through traditional capital markets be? It could be young entrepreneurs whose novel business ideas cannot convince conventional suppliers of finance to provide them with the financial resources they need to materialize their idea. Or it could be artists who seek an anonymous "crowd" of suppliers of finance in order to raise money to help them carry on their artistic projects. In the particular case of social finance, crowdfunding platforms support financing of social purposes and projects, which extend beyond standard risk–return analysis for the investor, pursuing social welfare outcomes. Social projects constitute about 20% of total crowdfunding activities.[10]

In developing countries, projects financed through crowdfunding tend to target economic development. For example, the United Nations Food Programme is running ShareTheMeal, a donation-based crowdfunding application which finances food assistance in more than 80 countries, thereby contributing to the achievement of SDG 2 on ending hunger.[11] The major obstacle in exploiting the immense capabilities of crowdfunding in developing countries is financial and technological illiteracy. Moreover, although poor countries receive a large fraction of the global impact investment pie, their undeveloped regulatory framework prevents them from reaping the full benefits stemming from such activities, but also deal with pertinent risks. In East Africa, for example, there is no specific legislation on crowdfunding, thus the laws that govern lending and donations also regulate operation of crowdfunding platforms.[12]

In general, as crowdfunding involves a large number of individuals financing a given project, its main advantage lies in that it can offer individual investors a kind of social legitimacy, in the sense of acceptance of the investor's targets and ideological aspirations by the general public.[13] Attaining legitimacy through crowdfunding is also supported by ongoing communication between suppliers of finance and between suppliers of finance and investors through the crowdfunding platform. Thus, crowdfunding puts in place a process that supports **social capital**, providing the basis for the transformation of social capital to financial capital for the owners of the funded project.[14] For example, the financing of an enterprise that produces and sells jewelry manufactured by women who live in war zones shows that a large number of individuals (the "crowd" of suppliers of finance) understand the need to support people who live in those areas and to support entrepreneurship as a basic pillar of economic development.

CROWDFUNDING: ADVANTAGES

Crowdfunding is a mechanism of providing resources for the materialization of projects that are typically excluded from organized capital markets. As such, they make

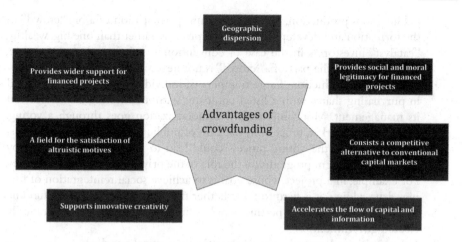

Figure 6.3 Advantages of crowdfunding

remarkable contributions in many respects. Figure 6.3 gives a schematic representation of the main advantages associated with crowdfunding.

1 **Wide geographical dispersion**

In principle, due to the electronic nature of the platform used in crowdfunding, the suppliers of finance for a certain project could be located all over the globe. This causes a complete transformation of the geographic characteristics of conventional financing (for example, the customers–borrowers of a bank in a certain area are typically people who live nearby).

It is worth stressing, however, that according to EU data, only 8% of crowdfunding represents cross-border transactions.[15] Similarly, in the case of the Sellaband crowdfunding platform that financed music artists, a significant part of finance for the production of music albums came from friends and relations who live in the neighborhood of the funded artist.[16]

2 **Broad evaluation and legitimization of the entrepreneurial idea, artistic work, or social project**

Wide participation and feedback, along with external evaluation of the proposed project by the suppliers of finance, offer the social entrepreneur the opportunity to test the attractiveness of the business idea among the community and identify areas for improvement. In this sense, crowdfunding also plays the role of a marketing platform for the goods and services offered by the proposed investment.[17] Likewise, both the social media and the social networks that emerge through each platform transform the reproduction mechanisms of the principles that govern a social project that is financed through crowdfunding.[18] For example, the values of a project whose goal is protection of the natural environment are becoming even more legitimate and valid when they are filtered through a social network of suppliers of capital who give resources and political priority to the specific project. Moreover, under certain conditions, crowdfunding constitutes a method of "democratization" of public goods production, because it permits participation of a big "crowd" in the formation and development of social projects, rather than one big, wealthy, "catalyst" investor as in the case of conventional capital markets. Of course, participation on the part of a "crowd" is not necessarily sufficient for democratization of production. Large numbers of individuals may also be involved in purchasing shares with a listed company, without exerting any impact on its management. More importantly, democratization goes through a voting, rather than a market, process. In the case of public goods production by private individuals, the voting process could lead to common resource use by approving pertinent programs on the role of the private sector in the economy. For example, in a project whose goal is to achieve social reintegration of former drug addicts, it is hard to tell whether the "democracy" of crowdfunding is more effective than a pertinent policy implemented by a democratically elected government.

3   Competitive alternative to conventional capital markets

Crowdfunding may be considered as a substitute to conventional mechanisms of supplying capital, such as banking, the stock market, or venture capital financing.[19] The resulting intensification of competition may force conventional mechanisms of supply of capital to reduce the interest rate charged and the return they demand for project financing. In addition, operating in a complementary fashion to conventional capital markets, crowdfunding platforms may secure capital for individuals and organizations that tend to be excluded from conventional capital markets due to their nationality, location, gender, financial condition, or specific type of business. Especially in the case of social enterprises, emphasis on social impact at the expense of profit reduces access to bank lending and investment funds. Nevertheless, activities with social impact are more attractive in the highly outgoing environment of the internet in a discourse framework that promotes social and environmental goals through crowdfunding platforms. Furthermore, enhanced legitimization offered by crowdfunding platforms contributes to the reduction of financial risk as perceived by both suppliers and recipients of finance.

4   Higher speed in the flow of capital and information

The evaluation process performed by a crowdfunding platform for a candidate investment is a lot simpler and thus less time consuming than the respective evaluation process carried out by conventional banks, investors, or regulatory bodies. Therefore, crowdfunding permits immediate flow of funds into the projects funded. However, increased speed comes at a price: while crowdfunding platforms may apply due diligence and screening criteria for posted projects, evaluation of the investment project is essentially managed by the suppliers of capital, that is by the "crowd" that takes the risk and responsibility of processing the information provided.[20]

5   Satisfies the need for innovative creativity

Especially in the case of financing cultural or artistic projects, suppliers of finance acquire a sense of contributing to a creativity through crowdfunding.[21] Many pioneer projects that would have been rejected by conventional "down to earth" evaluation on the conventional market find the gestation space they need through crowdfunding.

6 **Satisfies the need for social and altruistic giving**

   Often people are interested in the good of society and the environment they live in. This runs counter to some narrow utilitarian assumptions of economic analysis and incorporates satisfaction of deeper needs of human beings in "optimal solutions" to economic problems that relate to the scarcity of resources.[22] Independently of the economics propositions, the humans are diachronically motivated to give. In the case of crowdfunding for the purposes of public goods production, this motive is fulfilled by donation-based crowdfunding. Even outside donations, reward-based crowdfunding constitutes a kind of offering that goes beyond the typical altruism-self-interest dipole.[23]

7 **Wider support for funded projects**

   Passing along the message of a social project may attract more individuals who are willing to offer non-monetary support (crowdsourcing). Raising money on the part of some may prompt others to offer volunteer work or donate material objects that are necessary for the production of public goods.

CROWDFUNDING: DISADVANTAGES

Although crowdfunding constitutes a conduit for financing projects that would have found it extremely hard to raise money through conventional capital markets or through the government budget, financing the production of public goods through crowdfunding is confronted by certain severe weaknesses (see Figure 6.4).

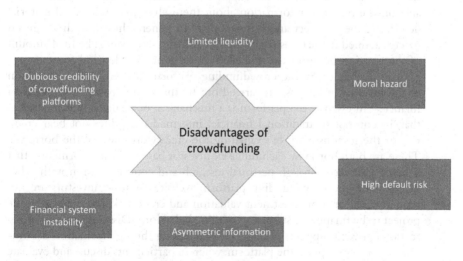

Figure 6.4 Disadvantages of crowdfunding

1 High default risk for suppliers of finance

Like other financial decisions, financing investments through crowdfunding is subject to default risk and failure of the investment to yield any benefit to the lender. Unsuccessful investment implies failure of the recipient of finance to repay suppliers of finance in money or in kind. This is especially important in the case of crowdfunding, where the information investors have about the borrower is generally limited. High default risk increases the yield demanded by suppliers of finance, thus reducing the amount they are willing to supply.

Default risk is not the only kind of risk that financial backers undertake in lending-based crowdfunding. Especially in the case of financing projects that involve production of public goods, failure goes beyond non-recovered amounts of money. It is about failure to deliver a welfare goal. Given that public goods are at stake, the issue is not merely financial, but also one of social impact. Failure to deliver the public good means that the social or environmental priorities of the suppliers of finance remain unsatisfied. Furthermore, outside profitability, performance evaluation of impact investments faces challenges associated with the actual measurement of effectiveness of social entrepreneurship. These are taken up in Chapter 8.

2 Adverse selection

Most of the times recipients of finance possess more information than the suppliers of finance about both the investment project and their skills in managing the resources needed to deliver it. This asymmetry in information constitutes a challenge for suppliers of finance, as it may lead them to inferior choices that they would not have made had they been better informed. This is the problem of **adverse selection**, which precedes the financial transaction. Adverse selection is important because it implies that resources in general and capital in particular are not utilized in the most efficient way possible.

In crowdfunding, a large number of candidate projects compete for resources that are made available by the suppliers of finance. Candidates make available on the platform information about themselves and audiovisual material describing their project and business plan. In general, however, there are no strictly defined regulations regarding information disclosure. The final amount of information being made available is determined by demand for and supply of information in the crowdfunding platform. Moreover, the evaluation of the investment proposal is carried out by the entire crowd of suppliers of finance.[24] In essence, the platform is a mechanism of financial intermediation that, in contrast to traditional financial intermediaries, does not bear credit risk or the responsibility of evaluating the creditworthiness of the borrower. These are both borne by each different investor based on the information that is being collected through personal research and communication with other investors on the crowdfunding platform website. As most investors are not trained in the area of investment valuation and credit risk, risk analysis of the project to be financed is subject to herding behavior.[25] Dissemination of information between suppliers of finance is carried out through formation of common interest groups on the platform, wherein participants discuss and evaluate candidate investments in a discussion forum. Occasionally, interest groups have group leaders, who have a special role in the management of information and the evaluation of investment proposals. Group leaders may be remunerated for their services, thus having a personal interest in getting a project approved for funding. This practice may imply that group leaders develop incentives outside mere protection of interests of group members.[26] Thus disclosure of information from the recipients of finance to the potential suppliers must be, to the extent possible, seamless and free from any intermediation.

Addressing asymmetric information with enhanced flow of information to all interested parties has a downside. The main medium of communication between the recipient of finance and the suppliers of finance is the audiovisual materials uploaded on the crowdfunding platform, which presents the orientation of the project and aspects of the business plan for its materialization. However, communicating the business plan essentially means revealing it to rivals, risking loss of the pioneering position or competitive advantage associated with delivering a unique investment project. This is particularly important in crowdfunding platforms, where a large number of social entrepreneurs compete for access to capital funds that are offered by a crowd of investors, each of whom contributes a small amount.

3 Moral hazard

Moral hazard is incurred when the risk the recipients of capital expose the suppliers of capital to is far higher than the risk recipients of capital would undertake if they financed the investment project themselves. In conditions of asymmetric information and unclear regulatory framework, moral hazard is likely to occur after the financial transaction, that is, after the funding is received by the borrowers. In donation-based crowdfunding for impact investments, as the recipient of finance is typically not required to repay suppliers of finance, there is room for taking riskier social entrepreneurship decisions when using the suppliers' resources. This is important in financing social impact investments, where the motivation has to do with solidarity and trust in the social project to be financed.

Naturally, the main control mechanism in crowdfunding platforms – as with social media – is the public voice and opinion expressed through the communities or interest groups formed by prospective suppliers of finance who focus on a specific project. Both the project and the entrepreneur who propose it are evaluated there through credit score mechanisms generated for the purposes of the platform. Nevertheless, as information is often incomplete and investors are not trained economists, evaluation of an investment by a "crowd" is always subject to herding.[27]

4 Instability of the financial system

Crowdfunding platforms constitute a vehicle of providing investment capital, donations, and loans. Like conventional organizations of capital management, crowdfunding is subject to fluctuations of the financial system. Financial markets instability affects the availability of capital, with financial crisis increasing credit risk for suppliers of finance and reducing money contributions for crowdfunding purposes. In addition, financial challenges tend to pass on to the real economy, restricting entrepreneurial opportunities in most sectors, including those that typically seek finance through crowdfunding. In contrast, economic crises may also generate new areas for social entrepreneurship and, by implication, for social finance. Contraction of the welfare state and the reduction in availability of government resources for development policies in times of crises makes it both possible and desirable to expand production of public goods through the private sector and social economy. Such productive activity is often financed through crowdfunding platforms, as well as though other mechanisms of social finance, such as microfinance and venture philanthropy.

5 Crowdfunding platforms of dubious credibility

Electronic financing through the internet is confronted by a special plexus of challenges pertaining to dubious transparency and credibility. This is typical in the case of crowdfunding, where the reputation of the platform and the quality of its operations are critical for attracting both projects that seek finance and suppliers of finance. Ezubao, the Chinese crowdfunding platform, is a case in point. Ezubao, which had raised 7.6 billion USD through crowdfunding, collapsed at the beginning of 2016 when it was revealed that it was just fraud and most of its financed projects were simply nonexistent. Thus, credibility of all stakeholders is critical to mitigate investment and credit risk, as well as to enhance **liquidity** in the crowdfunding market.

6 Limited liquidity

Liquidity (that is, convertibility into cash) constitutes a challenge for the crowdfunding market, mainly due to the lack of an organized secondary market for loan securities and assets of enterprises that are financed through crowdfunding. This implies that, in contrast to the shares of listed firms or the corporate bonds issued by big corporations that are being traded in capital markets, in the case of crowdfunding suppliers of finance cannot easily sell their participation in the financed project and get out. For instance, if impact investors finance a social enterprise that sells works of art created by former prisoner-artists, each contributing 20 EUR through the crowdfunding platform, it is not easy to sell their participation in the project (unlike stocks that trade in the stock market). Limited liquidity increases the financial risk of being trapped into an investment, reducing the supply of capital, which in turn increases the required yield for investors and lowers the present value of the investment project.

REGULATORY FRAMEWORK

As the institution of crowdfunding is a relatively novel mechanism of social finance, legislation on the operation of crowdfunding platforms is scant. In most countries, crowdfunding is regulated through legislation that pertains to the capital markets, bank lending, entrepreneurial finance, and philanthropy. However, in fall 2020 the European Parliament and the Council of the European Union adopted Regulation (EU) 2020/1503 to establish a unified framework on crowdfunding across the EU single market.[28] According to the regulation, the maximum amount that can be raised by project owners via crowdfunding platforms should be 5,000,000 euros per project. The adopted legislation highlights the risk of regulatory arbitrage due to fragmented regulatory framework across member-states. The same regulatory framework calls for the establishment of a public register of crowdfunding platforms in the EU (the register is to be established by the European Securities and Markets Authority [ESMA], which is to supervise and monitor crowdfunding platforms in the EU). This legislation also lays out transparency requirements, according to which each crowdfunding service provider should provide investors a "key investment information sheet" about project characteristics and risk warnings, so that investors can make informed decisions. In terms of prudential requirements, crowdfunding service providers should always have 25,000 euros in place or an amount equal to 25% of the previous year's fixed overheads (the higher of the two alternatives).

In the US, regulation of crowdfunding was materialized through the Jumpstart Our Business Startups Act (JOBS), on supporting innovative entrepreneurship. The JOBS Act was issued in 2012 and was incorporated in the US Securities and Exchange Commission (SEC) regulations in 2015. According to JOBS Act, the maximum capital to be accumulated through crowdfunding is USD 1,000,000 annually. For investors with wealth or annual income level up to USD 100,000, the maximum amount to be invested is USD 2,000 or 5% of their income or level of wealth (whichever – income or wealth – is lesser). For higher income investors, the maximum amount to be invested is 10% of annual income or level of wealth.[29] Among other things, recipients of finance through crowdfunding are required to disclose investors who own more than 20% of the investment project, as well as to upload their financial statements on their website.

Crowdfunding evolves in congruence with the needs of the real economy. Thus, investment opportunities offered through crowdfunding and the accompanying regulations are also evolving. The relevant regulatory framework is a plexus of rules that must confront the main challenge that bugs crowdfunding, namely asymmetric information (adverse selection and moral hazard), in order to give investors, social entrepreneurs, and suppliers of finance the opportunity to provide support for production of goods and services that would otherwise not be funded through conventional money and capital markets. From a practical point of view, construction of an effective regulatory framework as a mechanism of enhancing participation, mitigating obstacles, and limiting threats associated with relevant investments is critical for the future of crowdfunding as a sustainable mode of social finance (Figure 6.5).

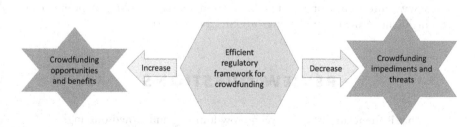

Figure 6.5 Crowdfunding regulation

CONCLUSION

In conclusion, as with every money and capital market, crowdfunding needs to be structured in order to contribute to economic development and welfare. The crowdfunding market needs to ensure that the capital needed for production purposes will be allocated to the use that exploits it in the most effective manner to bring about visible improve impact on living standards and society. Especially in the case of projects that have social and environmental goals, the question that arises is whether the flow of money to such projects through crowdfunding platforms is more effective in attaining those goals compared to other modes of finance, for example through conventional capital markets (e.g., banks, stock markets) or through the government budget or through other supranational development financing mechanisms like the World Bank. Crowdfunding markets could be designed to effectively complement or substitute organized capital markets.

Nevertheless, effectiveness of crowdfunding in attaining social or private goals should not be taken for granted. First, there is a need to support research in this area in order to bring into light the determining factors of the emergence of crowdfunding, ways of exploiting the opportunities offered through crowdfunding, and ways to address the risks entailed for suppliers of finance, recipients of finance, and society as a whole. Research findings, along with market experience, are expected to help form a set of regulations that will effectively address the special characteristics of crowdfunding in relation to conventional loans, investment capital, and donations.

In that direction, the training in economics and finance of the individuals who wish to make use of crowdfunding platforms would constitute an important step. Financial literacy is a necessary and sufficient condition for attaining economic growth and, more importantly, for ensuring that capital markets will play a positive role in the process, thus boosting overall welfare.

MATERIAL FOR DISCUSSION

China's $7.6 billion Ponzi scam highlights growing online risks
Miller, M., and Zhang, S. 2016. China's $7.6 billion Ponzi scam highlights growing online risks. *Reuters*, February 3.
Available at:
www.reuters.com/article/us-china-fraud/chinas-7-6-billion-ponzi-scam-highlights-growing-online-risks-idUSKCN0VB2O1.

REVIEW QUESTIONS

1 What is the relationship between crowdfunding and crowdsourcing?
2 What are the major types of crowdfunding platforms?

3 What are the opportunities offered by crowdfunding platforms to the financing of projects that would not otherwise have access to conventional capital markets?
4 What are the difficulties that confront crowdfunding platforms?
5 How does the Kiva crowdfunding platform operate?
6 What are the challenges pertaining to the regulatory framework on crowdfunding platforms?

NOTES

1 https://p2pmarketdata.com/crowdfunding-statistics-worldwide/.

2 https://support.ulule.com/hc/en-us/articles/211812409-What-is-Ulule-s-commission-.

3 https://Chuffed.org/eu.

4 Davidson and Poor (2016).

5 Mochkabadi and Volkmann (2020).

6 http://undp.org/content/sfinace/en/home/solutions/template-fich12.html.

7 www.europarl.europa.eu/RegData/etudes/BRIE/2017/595882/EPRS_BRI(2017)595882_EN.pdf.

8 www.kiva.org.

9 Jensen and Ruback (1983), Pitelis (1987).

10 www.undp.org/content/sdfinance/en/home/solutions/template-fiche12.html.

11 www.wfp.org/zero-hunger.

12 www.jbs.cam.ac.uk/fileadmin/user_upload/research/centres/alternative-finance/downloads/2017-05-eastafrica-crowdfunding-report.pdf.

13 See, for example, Lehner and Nicholls (2014).

14 Lehner (2014).

15 European Commission (2016).

16 Agrawal et al. (2015). The authors report similar findings on geographical boundaries in their study on the Kickstarter crowdfunding platform (Agrawal et al. 2014). For an economic geography approach, see Langley (2016) on the emergence, boundaries setting, and diversity of crowdfunding mechanisms.

17 See, for example, Lehner et al. (2015), Gabossy (2016).

18 On the importance of social media, Mollick (2014) shows that success of a funded project is positively related to the number of Facebook friends of the entrepreneur who seeks crowdfunding. Hong et al. (2018) show that the network structure of project backers (embeddedness) is associated with the success of crowdfunding campaigns for social ventures.

19 For the complementary or substitute nature of the relationship between crowdfunding and conventional capital markets, see Ellman and Hurkens (2019).

20 See Cumming et al. (2019) on the importance of platform due diligence for the success of crowdfunding campaigns.

21 Schwarz (2015).

22 See, for example, Bergstrom (2006).

23 André et al. (2017).

24   For a discussion of asymmetric information issues on financing through crowdfunding platforms, see Yum et al. (2012).

25   However, signaling and information disclosed on the platform may lead to sound choices. For example, Kim and Viswanathan (2019) showed that in the case of Appbackr crowdfunding platform for financing mobile phone applications, the "crowd" on the platform depicted the most experienced investors and the latter tend to earn higher financial returns.

26   Hildebrand et al. (2016) studied crowdfunding platforms in relation to the role of group leaders in lending. They found that when group leaders are remunerated for their services they recommended loans that involve higher credit risk compared to those recommended when they do not receive any remuneration.

27   Belleflamme et al. (2015).

28   Regulation (EU) 2020/1053 of the European Parliament and the Council of 7 October 2020 on European crowdfunding service providers for business, and amending Regulation (EU) 2017/1129 and Directive (EU) 2019/1937 (OJ L347, 20.10.2020).

29   These amounts were determined in the JOBS Act. The Securities and Exchange Commission of the US has included adjustment of these amounts for inflation: the maximum amount that may be raised through crowdfunding is USD 1,070,000. If the investor's annual income or net worth is less than USD 107,000, then the investor can invest the greater of either USD 2,200 or 5% of the lesser between her annual income and net worth.

REFERENCES

André, K., Bureau, S., Gautier, A., and Rubel, O., 2017. Beyond the opposition between altruism and self-interest: Reciprocal giving in reward-based crowdfunding. *Journal of Business Ethics*, 146(2), 313–332. https://doi.org/10.1007/s10551-017-3652-x.

Agrawal, A., Catalini, C., and Goldfarb, A., 2014. Some simple economics of crowdfunding. *Innovation Policy and the Economy*, 14, 63–97. https://doi.org/10.1086/674021.

Agrawal, A., Catalini, C., and Goldfarb, A., 2015. Crowdfunding: Geography, social networks and the timing of investment decisions. *Journal of Economics and Management Strategy*, 24(2), 253–274. https://doi.org/10.1111/jems.12093.

Belleflamme, P., Omrani, N., and Peitz, M., 2015. The economics of crowdfunding platforms. *Information Economics and Policy*, 33, 11–28. https://doi.org/10.1016/j.infoecopol.2015.08.003.

Bergstrom, T.C., 2006. Benefit-cost in a benevolent society. *American Economic Review*, 96(1), 339–351. https://doi.org/10.1257/000282806776157623.

Cumming, D., Johan, S.A., and Zhang, Y., 2019. The role of due diligence in crowdfunding platforms. *Journal of Banking and Finance*, 108. https://doi.org/10.1016/j.jbankfin.2019.105661.

Davidson, R., and Poor, N., 2016. Factors for success in repeat crowdfunding: Why sugar daddies are only good for bar-mitzvahs. *Information, Communication and Society*, 19(1), 127–139. https://doi.org/10.1080/1369118X.2015.1093533.

Ellman, M., and Hurkens, S., 2016. Optimal crowdfunding design. *Journal of Economic Theory*, 184. https://doi.org/10.1016/j.jet.2019.104939.

European Commission, 2016. *Crowdfunding in the EU capital markets union*. Commission Staff Working Document, 3/5/2016. Brussels: European Commission.

Gabossy, A., 2016. New directions in crowdfunding. *Public Finance Quarterly*, 2016(4), 533–544.

Hildebrand, T., Puri, M., and Rocholl, J., 2016. Adverse incentives in crowdfunding. *Management Science*, 63(3), 587–608. https://doi.org/10.1287/mnsc.2015.2339.

Hong, Y., Hu, Y., and Burtch, G., 2018. Embeddedness, prosociality, and social influence: Evidence from online crowdfunding. *MIS Quarterly*, 42(4), 1211–1224. https://doi.org/10.25300/MISQ/2018/14105.

Jensen, M.C., and Ruback, R.S., 1983. The market for corporate control: The scientific evidence. *Journal of Financial Economics*, 11(1–4), 5–50. https://doi.org/10.1016/0304-405X(83)90004-1.

Kim, K., and Viswanathan, S., 2019. The "experts" in the crowd: The role of experienced investors in a crowdfunding market. *MIS Quarterly*, 43(2), 347–372. https://doi.org/10.25300/MISQ/2019/13758.

Langley, P., 2016. Crowdfunding in the United Kingdom: A cultural economy. *Economic Geography*, 92(3), 301–321. https://doi.org/10.1080/00130095.2015.1133233.

Lehner, O.M., 2014. The formation and interplay of social capital in crowdfunded social ventures. *Entrepreneurship and Regional Development*, 26(5–6), 478–499. https://doi.org/10.1080/08985626.2014.922623.

Lehner, O.M., Grabmann, E., and Ennsbarger, C., 2015. Entrepreneurial implications of crowdfunding as alternative funding source for innovations. *Venture Capital*, 17(1–2), 171–189. https://doi.org/10.1080/13691066.2015.1037132.

Lehner, O.M., and Nicholls, A., 2014. Social finance and crowdfunding for social enterprises: A public-private case study providing legitimacy and leverage. *Venture Capital*, 16(3), 271–286. https://doi.org/10.1080/13691066.2014.925305.

Mochkabadi, K., and Volkmann, C.K., 2020. Equity crowdfunding: A systematic review of the literature. *Small Business Economics*, 54, 75–118. https://doi.org/10.1007/s11187-018-0081-x.

Mollick, E., 2014. The dynamics of crowdfunding: An exploratory study. *Journal of Business Venturing*, 29(1), 1–16. https://doi.org/10.1016/j.jbusvent.2013.06.005.

Pitelis, C., 1987. *Corporate capital: Control, ownership, saving and crisis*. Cambridge: Cambridge University Press.

Schwarz, A.A., 2015. The nonfinancial returns of crowdfunding. *Review of Banking and Financial Law*, 34, 565–580.

Yum, H., Lee, B., and Chae, M., 2012. From the wisdom of crowds to my own judgement in microfinance through online peer-to-peer lending platforms. *Electronic Commerce Research and Applications*, 11(5), 469–483. http://dx.doi.org/10.1016/j.elerap.2012.05.003.

7

Islamic finance

After reading this chapter, you will be able to:

1 Explain the fundamental principles of Islamic finance
2 Identify the main Islamic financial services
3 Assess the regulatory framework of Islamic financial institutions
4 Evaluate the major challenges facing Islamic financial institutions
5 Demonstrate understanding of the intersection of Islamic finance with social finance

INTRODUCTION

Islamic finance is an emblematic case of money and capital markets formation through the ages within a specific social and cultural context.[1] Islam is a monotheistic religion that originates in the Middle East and the 7th century AD. Islam literally means peace, but also submission to God, Allah, and Muhammad is the messenger of God. The plexus of Islamic principles is imprinted in Akhlak, Aqidah, and **Shariah**. Akhlak is a code of ethics and conduct. The principles of Islamic faith are contained in Aqidah, while Shariah regulates the practical matters of Muslim life. The part of Shariah that regulates every dimension of economic and social life and

DOI: 10.4324/9781003230366-9

applies in the courts of justice is the Muamalat. Religious life is regulated by Ibadat. Shariah rules pertain to all economic activities and enforcement of the rules guarantees the morality that governs financial transactions. Very often implementation of Shariah is required by law. Shariah rules sum up principles found in the Qur'an and the Sunnah, the holy books of Islam. The Qur'an is the revelation of the word of God to Muhammad, while Sunnah includes the sayings, deeds, and teachings of Prophet Muhammad. Shariah also includes consensus views of theologists and scientists of law on issues of interpretation of the Qur'an and the Sunnah.[2] In the context of Shariah, the actions of a Muslim are divided in forbidden action (haram) and permissible action (halal). In particular, action can be classified as mandatory, recommended, neutral, disapproved, or forbidden. An action may or may not carry punishment and may or may not be rewarded. Assessment of action and classification as haram or halal is often a matter of interpretation of the Shariah, as well as a matter of jurisprudence.[3]

Islamic finance is a plexus of financial and risk management institutions that is based on the principles of Shariah. The major tenets of Shariah include prohibition of interest and excessive borrowing, as well as risk sharing

> Islamic finance is a plexus of financial and risk management institutions that is based on the principles of Shariah.

between the suppliers and recipients of finance. Islamic finance is a form of social finance, because in the course of capital flow and materialization of investment, the profit motive is not the sole target of the investor. Instead, there is clear orientation and support for a specific cultural framework. In a way, Islamic finance could be considered a kind of "ethical banking" in conventional banking terms.[4] Although the emergence of Islamic finance as a distinct system of values, practices, and rules in the fields of investments and business finance dates back to the 1960s, the basic principles are a lot older, preceding in a way the appearance of Islam.

Islamic finance is a widespread phenomenon, whose full coverage goes beyond the scope of the present chapter. The purpose of this chapter is to present the major tenets of Islamic finance, along with major financial services. Special emphasis is placed on the concept of the interest rate, which is forbidden by Shariah, as well as on the impact of rules on social responsibility of business organizations and enterprises that constitute an important link between social and Islamic finance.

ISLAMIC FINANCE: MAJOR TENETS

Up until the Middle Ages, commerce in the Middle East was governed by Shariah, which imposed rules similar to those imposed on European merchants (who were trading extensively with the Middle East) by Christianity, including the prohibition of interest. The rules had to do primarily with trade: in the first years of Islam, Medina – the second holiest Muslim city – was a commercial center. Several Shariah principles on economic life were associated with the need to regulate commercial activity in a way that would provide an armor against moral risks often accompanying commerce. In the place of interest, commercial transactions were based on commercial credit and participation in the profit or loss of financed activities (what we would nowadays call investment). Muhammad himself was a merchant: while profit from commercial activities is encouraged, lending at interest is forbidden.[5]

This type of financing commercial activities developed enormously, supporting effectively commerce from the 8th to the 14th century, also known as the Islamic Golden Age, not only because of the economic development attained, but also because of the cultural, political, and geographical expansion of Islam. Taking a big leap in time, we realize that the beginnings of development of financial institutions in the field of Islamic finance is to be found in the 1960s, while implementation of Islamic finance principles contributed immensely to the expansion of the Islamic financial system.[6] Nowadays, total assets of Islamic financial institutions globally exceed 2 trillion US dollars. The deployment of financial institutions in this area attracted an international regulatory framework and, perhaps more importantly, academic interest on the principles of Islamic finance, primarily of course on prohibition of interest.

Shariah shapes business ethics, prohibiting certain types of conduct and determining the principles to which enterprises must abide. Especially in the case of financial enterprises, similar to conventional banks,[7] implementation of principles that are beyond the pursuit of profit have a positive impact upon Islamic banks' profitability.[8] The primary principle that governs economic activity is devoutness: all economic agents need to be devout and must apply the principles of Shariah in their personal and public life. Beyond devoutness, honesty and transparency are also important principles in the conduct of economic activities. Both transparency and honesty in transitions imply that it is strictly forbidden to purchase a product at a very low price from a needy producer/seller or to deceive the buyer by giving false information about the characteristics of the products, their value, as well as the method of repaying financial obligations. In addition, similar to Christian principles, the mission of human beings in Islam is to care for God's creations on earth. While private property is permissible under Islamic law, it is considered transient, because the presence of human beings on earth is also ephemeral. During that period, humans' responsibility is to protect God's creation. Thus, enhancing wealth and property possessions are permissible if they are in congruence with the appropriate way of life of humans (the owners), their families, and society.

In many places, prohibition of **interest** was for years the outcome of the belief that interest is either immoral or harmful for welfare. This belief preceded Islam. In *Politics*, Aristotle argues that money is a medium of exchange, thus its use is confined to its immediate consumption. Aristotle stresses that, as a medium of exchange, money has no intrinsic value. It follows that money cannot be produced out of money. Aristotle, therefore, defines **usury** as production of money out of money. For Aristotle, usury is an unnatural way of creating wealth, because money has no property of reproduction by itself. At around about the same period, interpretation of Deuteronomy allowed the extension of interest-bearing loans from Israelites to non-Israelites, prohibiting interest-bearing lending to fellow Israelites (essentially banning all lending between Israelites), thus stipulating prohibition of interest-bearing lending on any loan, whether that was extended to Christians or other religions, during the first centuries of the Common Era.[9] Prohibition of interest-bearing lending is also found in the Old Testament, in the 22nd chapter of Exodus (22:25). Moreover, the 15th Psalm of David praises non-interest-bearing lending. Later on with the prevalence of Christianity in Europe, interest-bearing loans were dramatically reduced. In the New Testament, in the Gospel of Luke (6:34), Jesus says that lending in the hope of repayment of amount lent is the act of a sinner. During the centuries that followed, even though interest-bearing debt often emerged out of lack of capital and liquidity in politics and the economy – wars in continental Europe, international trade, and crusade are some of the cases in point – prohibitions of interest persisted and some even survived until the 19th century.

In Islamic finance, **riba** means "increase" or surplus". Secondarily, riba also means usury. Any predetermined, fixed interest rate that is independent of the yield of a financed investment project is prohibited. There is wide diversity in the views regarding the types of transactions that fall under the category of riba, regarding whether responsibility for punishment lies with God or with human justice, as well as whether riba constitutes a sin. Thus, since capital is a factor of production, a reward (profit) for the supplier of capital is allowed, but not as a predetermined compensation for the owner of capital that would be independent of the investment outcome. A guaranteed return (interest) reduces risk and restricts productivity incentives, thus leading to inefficient allocation of resources in the economy. In contrast, the owner of capital must undertake the risk and share any losses or any profits incurred as a result of the investment, effectively becoming more of a partner in business than a creditor. In the event that no profits are realized, the principal to be repaid can be reduced by the amount of the realized loss. Additionally, (predetermined) interest is considered inequitable, because it implies that risk is borne by just one of the two parties (the borrower). In this line of reasoning, corporate bonds are prohibited because in effect they are interest-bearing loans. Similarly, preferred stock is prohibited, as it discriminates between shareholders with respect to participation in the management of the company (which is against the basic Islamic principles of justice and equality) and involves riskless profit in the form of a guaranteed dividend.[10,11]

Except for interest-bearing credit, Shariah also prohibits economic activities related to tobacco, weaponry, pork meat, sex, and alcoholic beverages (production of surgical spirit for medical purposes is allowed). Other prohibitions include hoarding, superfluous uncertainty (gharar), and gambling (maysir). Given that uncertainty is inherent in economic life, Shariah does not completely prevent engagement in economic activities that involve uncertainty, but sets specific boundaries to it.

Although the notion of gharar implies uncertainty, in practice uncertainty is inevitable. Therefore, there are different interpretations of the uncertain outcomes associated with economic activity to incorporate the necessity of taking risks. For example, fluctuations of the prices of real or financial assets, as well as investors' preferences constitute sources of uncertainty. Gharar refers to uncertainty due to insufficient information about the characteristics of the investment that the supplier of finance provides capital for. Because part of the value is affected by factors that are beyond the investor's control or knowledge, lack of information relates to what is known in conventional financing as due diligence, that is the need for financial transactions in general and investments in particular to be carried out as a result of thorough analysis. In this line of reasoning, the sale of assets that are not in one's possession (as in the case of futures markets for agricultural commodities) – and, therefore, one does not have knowledge of their characteristics – is forbidden. Similarly, Shariah forbids gambling because gambling is a situation where one of the two parties loses their entire capital, while the other party gains it. This implies a return of –100% for one party, plus 100% for the other party. This is against the Shariah principle, according to which risk along with resulting profits or losses must be shared.

Islamic finance generally implies that entrepreneurial and financial risk must be shared between suppliers and recipients of finance. Thus, a reasonable level of uncertainly in economic activity is permissible. First, entrepreneurial risk is inherent in every entrepreneurial endeavor. In Islam, it is acceptable that the entrepreneur and the merchant will function in anticipation of profit, which is indispensable in the pursuit of entrepreneurship. Because entrepreneurship constitutes a vital part of economic life, the uncertainty associated with it is permissible by Shariah. An additional type of uncertainty that is compatible with Shariah is uncertainty that is owed to natural disasters or generally "force majeure". Such risks are acceptable and, alongside them, insurance contracts issued for their management are permissible. Furthermore, risks associated with human conduct are also acceptable. For example, if the partners, employees, or customers of entrepreneurs behave in a certain manner, the entrepreneurs could be exposed to uncertainty that is beyond their control: the owner of a medical center would be exposed by the human error of a medical doctor who works for the center.

> It is acceptable that the entrepreneur and the merchant will function in anticipation of profit, which is indispensable in the pursuit of entrepreneurship.

ISLAMIC FINANCIAL SERVICES

In Islam, prohibition of interest-bearing lending is absolute and there are no exceptions to the rule. However, even where interest is strictly forbidden, the credit risk undertaken by the lender, along with the expenses the lender has incurred to have a presence in the market, are fully acknowledged. This explains the influx and expansion of a wide range of financial services that, although non-interest bearing, they compensate the lender with an amount higher than the principal lent. Thus, just like in conventional finance, taxation and transaction costs are determining factors in the design of Islamic financial services.

The main transactions in Islamic financing are **murabaha** and **tawarruq**, which involve the sale of an asset (merchandise, agricultural commodities, metals, or real estate) to a bank for cash and repurchase of the asset from the bank at a higher price. The price difference resembles the interest rate earned in the case of conventional financing. Especially when the repurchase is made in installments, the murabaha contract has the characteristics of a conventional loan that is paid off in installments. In any event, the sale of an asset presupposes that the asset is in the possession of the seller. Such forms of credit are used in the context of commercial loans, as well as working capital loans, interbank loans, and mortgages. In this line of reasoning, a number of financial products have been developed as illustrated in Figure 7.1.

Bai al-Sarf: A contract for buying or selling foreign exchange in the spot market.

Conventional finance	Islamic finance
	Murabaha
	Tawarruq
Interest-bearing credit and insurance	Bai al-Sarf
	Qard al-Hasan
	Wadiah
	Mudharabah
	Musarakah
	Ijarah
	Sukuk
	Hawala
	Takaful

Figure 7.1 Conventional and Islamic financing

Qard al-Hasan: A non-interest-bearing loan that must be fully repaid by the borrower. It resembles a current account that earns no interest.

Wadiah: A type of financial service whereby an Islamic bank offers custodial services to customers' material objects or money. As a safekeeping service, it involves a fee charged by the bank. The bank may decide to invest the deposit. In that case, the terms of splitting the proceeds between the bank and the depositor are specified in a mutually agreed contract.

Mudharabah: A contractual agreement between an investor (supplier of finance, usually an Islamic bank) and an entrepreneur (recipient of finance). The entrepreneur is known as mudarib. Through a mutually agreed contract, profits are shared between the two parties proportionately, as stated in the contract. Losses are borne by the owner of capital, except in cases of mismanagement on the part of the entrepreneur, where the latter bears part of the loss. Depending on contract terms, the entrepreneur may be subjected to limitations in terms of type of investment, components of the portfolio, and risk management techniques. The entrepreneur may invest the capital to yield a regular flow of income, resembling earning interest. For the most part, Mudharabah resembles venture capital, although in some cases it is similar to asset management.

Musharakah: A financing mechanism that mainly serves the purposes of buying fixed assets. Proceeds from the use of fixed assets are shared between the suppliers of finance (investors) based on the relevant contract terms. Depending on contract specifications, it resembles joint ventures and leasing contracts.

Ijarah: A leasing contract, which permits transfer of ownership of an asset from the lessor to the lessee upon expiration of the contract (in some contracts, it is possible to transfer the asset to the lessee before contract expiration, provided that the lessee pays the lessor the full price of the asset). No interest is charged, although rental payments are determined in such a way to incorporate a kind of return similar to an interest rate. The asset belongs to the lessor throughout the leasing period. At the end of the leasing period, transfer of ownership is materialized either through the leasing contract or through a separate exchange agreement.

Sukuk: A loan contract with some of the characteristics of the interest-bearing securities of conventional financing. In a way, sukuk constitutes the Islamic equivalent of fixed income or discount bonds. However, as interest is forbidden, sukuk is more of a cash flow management technique. It is possible that the supplier of finance will own part of the investment project in order to be entitled to receiving part of the profit (in the place of interest). In addition, as with conventional bond contracts, the principal borrowed is repaid over a specific period at the end of which, along with repayment of the face value, the borrower buys out the share of the lender in the investment project. A very limited number of sukuk trade in the secondary market. Naturally, only investments that are Shariah-compliant may be financed. In spite of the restrictive Shariah framework, there is a wide variety of sukuk contracts. Furthermore, as sukuk contracts have certain similarities with conventional bonds, they experienced several credit events during the global financial crisis of the late 2000s.

Hawala: An informal mechanism of payment that does not involve a contract. If individual A wants to transfer an amount of money to individual B, who lives in a different place or even in a different country than A, A may pay that amount to individual X, who communicates accordingly with an individual Y who is located in the area of B. The intermediators, X and Y, profit from the commission charged for the service offered, as well as from the exchange rate differential in the case of cross-border transactions. The intermediators need to exchange money amounts between them only if their balance is different from zero. Communication is password-protected and determined by individuals A and B. Obviously, hawala transactions are often associated with the informal sector and are, therefore, banned by law in many Islamic countries.

Takaful: An insurance mechanism. Part of the insurance proceeds is invested, producing profits or losses that are shared between the insured and the insurance company. For the most part, however, insurance payments are not invested; they are available for covering indemnities. Conventional insurance is forbidden in Islam because it entails both gharar and riba. Depending on the type of takaful contract, the insurance company may receive either compensation for the services provided or a share of the profits realized or both.

Conventional derivative products are forbidden in Islamic finance, because Shariah prohibits the sale of products not yet produced or not owned by the seller. In general, there are different interpretations of the boundaries of transactions with the characteristics of derivative products that are Shariah-compatible. Nevertheless, certain Islamic banking products do have financial derivatives characteristics as illustrated in Figure 7.2.

> Conventional derivative products are forbidden in Islamic finance, because Shariah prohibits the sale of products not yet produced or not owned by the seller.

Salam: The buyer (usually an Islamic bank) makes a payment in advance to purchase a product. The seller agrees to deliver a specific quantity and quality of the product at a predetermined future date. The buyer usually buys the product at a lower than the spot cash price. As a rule, the bank sells the good to a third party upon delivery by the seller. If the sale is carried out through a promissory note issued by the bank, it is a sale on credit. The goal of this financial service is to supply liquidity to farmers for production support and subsistence until the harvest period. Likewise, salam is an essential instrument for the conduct of international trade (exports and imports).

Conventional finance	Islamic finance
Financial derivatives	Salam
	Istisna
	Urbun
	Khiyar al-Shart

Figure 7.2 Financial derivative products in Islamic finance

Istisna: A contract where one party agrees to deliver an asset at a future time and prespecified time. This type of financing often applies to real estate. The customer of the Islamic bank agrees to purchase a newly built property at a certain price. The price is higher than that paid by the bank to the construction company that built the property. If the payment by the customer of the bank is carried out in installments, istisna resembles the conventional mortgage.

Urbun: A premium is paid up front in order to purchase an asset at a predetermined point in time in the future (the premium is considered a down payment for the purchase of the asset). The counterparty has the right to cancel the transaction over a period specified in the contract, in which case the premium is forgone. Urbun resembles the conventional call option.

Khiyar al-Shart: A financial contract with a predetermined maturity period and price for the asset to be delivered at the end of the maturity period, with no premium to be paid up front. The counterparty has the right to cancel the transaction.

The prohibition of earning interest determines the choices available to private investors and portfolio construction. Highly indebted companies and enterprises that extend interest-bearing credit are not included in the range of available investment choices. Depending on the regulator, there are many ways to assess the total debt burden of a company, and by implication its compliance with Shariah and appropriateness for investment. Indicatively, according to the **Accounting and Auditing Organization for Islamic Financial Institutions:**[12]

1   Short-term and long-term interest-bearing debt must not exceed 30% of a company's market capitalization.
2   Interest-taking deposits should not exceed 30% of market value of equity.

Similarly, Islamic portfolios preclude securities issued by corporations that have revenues from business involving gambling, sex, pork meat, or alcoholic beverages. Obviously, the dividing lines are thin and vary depending on different interpretations of the Shariah. For example, the stock of a hotel company is a potential investment choice, even though part of the hotel's revenue comes for the sale of alcoholic beverages at the hotel's bar, which is forbidden. In such cases, profit **purification** practices are applied. In general, purification is applied to the portion of corporate profit that is distributed to shareholders as a dividend, rather than the total increase in company value due to higher profits. For example, to purify profits, a portion of dividends may be donated to charity.

Despite implementation of Shariah principles that gives Islamic financial systems a distinct flavor, conventional finance and Islamic finance bear substantial similarities in practice. This creates some skepticism with regard to the degree of commitment of Islamic financial institutions to Shariah values. In the first place, Islamic financial intermediaries often need to apply conventional banking practices to comply with international financial regulations and/or carry out transactions between different banking systems in a more efficient manner (see Box 7.1 on the publicly traded sukuk that was issued by the Islamic Development Bank in response to Covid-19). In addition, the short history of organized Islamic capital and money markets generates the need to "mimic" conventional markets.

Box 7.1 Islamic development bank: sukuk issuance in response to Covid-19

The Islamic Development Bank (IsDB) is a financial institution that finances economic development and focuses on Islamic finance. It is owned by member-countries of the Organisation for Islamic Cooperation, which are 57 member-countries, most of them being Muslim-majority. Saudi Arabia holds approximately one-fourth of the bank's equity. In June 2020, IsDB issued a five-year sukuk, with nominal value of 1.5 billion USD, semi-annual periodic payments, and 0.908% annual rate of return. The issue was successful and attracted international investor interest.[13]

The proceeds from the sukuk will finance Covid-19-relief initiatives. It is part of IsDB's Sustainable Finance Framework and its Respond-Restore-Restart approach to Covid-19, incorporating short-term (Respond), medium-term (Restore), and long-term (Restart) responses to the economic effects of the pandemic – short-term responses addressing healthcare and food emergency challenges, long-term responses involving infrastructure projects for economic development.

The issuance of a sukuk in response to Covid-19 constitutes an example of the link between social finance and Islamic finance, as it relies upon solidarity and the ethics of financing contracts according to Shariah. It also constitutes an example of bridging Islamic finance with conventional capital markets:

♦ The sukuk is rated AAA from credit rating agencies (that otherwise assess interest-bearing credit). Similar to conventional bond contracts, the sukuk pro-spectus contained information about IsDB's capital adequacy, liquidity, and financial performance.
♦ The sukuk is traded in the Irish Stock Exchange, Bursa Malaysia, and Nasdaq Dubai, alongside securities beyond the realm of Islamic finance such as interest-bearing debt securities.

- The sukuk was distributed by a blend of non-Islamic and Islamic financial institutions, such as Citigroup, Credit Agricole, Emirates NBD Bank, and Kuwait International Bank.
- Being part of a global capital marketplace, the sukuk attracted geographically dispersed investor interest, 53% of investments coming from the Middle East and North Africa, 37% from Asia, and 8 % from Europe.
- IsDB is sharing some sustainability values in common with the global financial system: IsDB classifies this sukuk as part of its contribution to the attainment of SDG 3 (Good health and well-being) and 8 (Decent work and economic growth). Moreover, the sukuk is evidence of convergence between Islamic finance and environmental, social, and governance concerns (ESG) in conventional financial institutions. Hamed Ali, Chief Executive Officer of Nasdaq Dubai, said,

IsDB is playing an important role in the expansion of Nasdaq Dubai as a listing venue of choice for capital markets issuances that meet Environmental, Social and Governance (ESG) criteria. We are preparing further initiatives to support the ESG sector and look forward to welcoming many more such issuances from a range of public and private sector institutions.[14]

Even though entrepreneurship and transparency are favored in the Shariah context and are being encouraged through pertinent rules established by Islamic capital market and entrepreneurship regulatory bodies, prohibition of interest and transactions at low prices pose severe limitations on the operation of capital markets. These limitations may prevent derailing at times of extreme volatility, but also act as a deterrent for capital market growth and, by implication, for growth of the economies that deploy this type of finance (see Box 7.2 on regulation of Islamic financial services). As with every regulatory framework, the question that arises for the Shariah rules is whether restrictions on trade and capital markets are more conducive to welfare than deregulation. In this instance too, evaluation of welfare gains is of course political and ideological.

Box 7.2 The Islamic Financial Services Board (IFSB)

Adapted from the website of the Islamic Financial Services Board (www.ifsb.org)
Based in Kuala Lumpur, the Islamic Financial Services Board (IFSB) was officially inaugurated in November 2002 and started operations in March 2003. It serves as an international standard-setting body of regulatory and supervisory agencies that have an interest in ensuring the soundness and stability of the Islamic financial services industry, which is defined to include banking, capital markets, and insurance.

In advancing this mission, the IFSB promotes the development of a prudent and transparent Islamic financial services industry through introducing new, or adapting existing international standards consistent with Shariah principles, and recommending them for adoption.

To this end, the work of the IFSB complements that of the Basel Committee on Banking Supervision, International Organisation of Securities Commissions, and the International Association of Insurance Supervisors.

As of June 2020, the 187 members of the IFSB comprise 79 regulatory and supervisory authorities, nine international intergovernmental organizations, and 99 market players (financial institutions, professional firms, industry associations, and stock exchanges) operating in 57 jurisdictions.

Since its inception, the IFSB has issued 32 Standards, Guidance Notes, and Technical Notes, which regulate the conduct of business of Islamic financial institutions in the areas of operation including risk management, capital adequacy, corporate governance, transparency and market discipline, Islamic insurance (takaful) liquidity risk management, stress testing, ratings on Shariah-compliant financial instruments, commodity murabaha transactions, etc.

ISLAMIC ENTREPRENEURSHIP AND SOCIAL IMPACT

Independently of the special nature of Islamic financial services or their impact on welfare in Islamic countries, implementation of Shariah principles in entrepreneurship and in financing entrepreneurship constitutes social impact, because social entrepreneurship is defined as systematically pursuing social targets in addition to profit. Thus, development of enterprises and mechanisms of finance that fundamentally target implementation of Islamic principles implies that Islamic finance qualifies as social finance.

A characteristic example of the connection between Shariah and the social impact of economic activity is **zakat**, one of the main pillars of Islam that is directly associated with social finance. Zakat is the regular (usually annual) payment of a certain proportion of a devout Muslim's wealth for charity or social benefit purposes. Zakat is not compulsory when the individual's level of wealth is below the subsistence level (nisab). Instead, zakat is not estimated for levels of wealth below nisab. Each devout Muslim calculates zakat differently based on their own needs (e.g., health condition, marital status, etc.). In general, zakat implies giving away 2.5% of one's wealth. In some countries, zakat is optional, while in others it is required (e.g., Saudi Arabia, Sudan, Yemen). The exact zakat payment time varies for different individuals, but for agricultural producers payment always coincides with the harvest period. Beneficiaries of zakat are determined by the Qur'an: the poor, zakat committee members who may represent needy groups or the government, those in debt, those who have migrated abroad and cannot afford to return home, and those who participate in a Jihad, one of the duties of Muslims according to Ibadat. Zakat funding may also be aligned with the attainment of SDGs, especially those related to mitigating inequality and eradicating poverty and hunger. In 2017 Indonesia's National Board of Zakat contributed 350,000 USD to the United Nations Development Programme to be invested in renewable energy-related SDGs and in 2019 the United Nations Development Programme partnered with the World Zakat Forum to channel zakat funds to the attainment of SDGs.[15,16]

Zakat and nisab are determined according to the form one's wealth is held in. For example, in the case of metals, the nisab level is 85 grams of gold (or the monetary equivalent). In the case of agricultural production, the nisab level is about 650 kilograms of edible produce that can be preserved without refrigeration (e.g., wheat, coffee, rice, and dates). The level of zakat is 10% in the event that no labor and irrigation expenses are involved or 5% if labor and irrigation expenses are involved in production. Zakat also includes transactions in merchandise and real assets (automobiles, land, textiles), excluding products for personal use, as well as livestock (camels, sheep, goats) provided that it is raised for commercial or production purposes. In this case, nisab is five camels or 40 goats (or sheep) and varies according to livestock kind and age. For example, ownership of 25–35 camels corresponds to zakat of one camel that is older than one year of age; 36–45 camels correspond to zakat of one camel that is older than two years of age; 46–60 camels correspond to zakat of one camel that is older than three years of age; 61–75 camels correspond to zakat of one camel that is older than four years of age.

Beyond zakat, the general emphasis placed by Islamic finance on social impact and welfare is in line with similar developments in the conventional financial system. For example, conventional **socially responsible investments** preclude businesses active in gambling, alcoholic beverages, tobacco, and weaponry, just like the portfolios of Islamic financial institutions.[17] Furthermore, emphasis on social solidarity, which constitutes a fundamental principle of Islam, justifies adoption of social finance mechanisms like social impact bonds and microfinance.[18]

CHALLENGES CONFRONTING ISLAMIC FINANCE

As part of the global financial system, Islamic finance organizations compete directly with conventional financial organizations for resources and market share. At the same time, they need to combine the principles of Shariah with international developments. The dynamic environment of international capital markets poses several challenges for Islamic finance (see Figure 7.3).

1 Financial innovation in **risk management**, along with the expanding terrain of **fintech**, intensify the need for creation of novel institutions to take advantage of the capabilities offered by contemporary financial engineering, while at the same time remaining compliant with Shariah principles. Purification is critical in this respect, because it allows carrying out certain transactions that are not Shariah-compatible, as long as the investor donates part of the profit for a social cause.

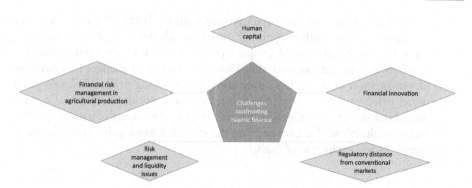

Figure 7.3 The main challenges confronting Islamic finance

2   Human capital: Expertise in Islamic banking is scarce, thus Shariah coun-
    cils and the expanding organizations of Islamic intermediation lack access to
    appropriately educated personnel.[19]
3   Risk management and liquidity issues: Islamic banking is rather restrictive
    when it comes to risk management and interbank lending; therefore the inter-
    bank market is very small and undeveloped.
4   Regulatory framework: Legislators of conventional capital markets must pro-
    vide for the presence of Islamic banks in Western markets and, at the same
    time, Islamic regulatory bodies must provide for the interaction of Islamic
    banks with conventional banks in international capital markets. A character-
    istic example of regulatory differences between the two systems is the dif-
    ferentiation of Islamic financial practices by the Accounting and Auditing
    Organization for Islamic Financial Institutions, as well as the implementation
    of internal control by the **Shariah Supervisory Board**.
5   In general, since the sense of risk is accentuated by the lack of information and
    the lack of understanding about the investment environment, there is a need
    for greater transparency and easy-to-use conversion and reading mechanisms
    of Islamic financial institutions data by conventional investors and vice versa.
    This is important for both banking regulation matters (capital adequacy rules)
    and integrated, or at least comparable, accounting standards.
6   With many Muslim areas facing severe subsistence challenges, the develop-
    ment of financing tools to support agriculture and farming, as well as regional
    economic development in general, is important from the point of view of
    Shariah too, which emphasizes community welfare through taking up pro-
    ductive activities. The development of financial tools for agricultural products
    can help agricultural production, although focus on the purely productive ori-
    entation of such financing implies financial risks for the financial institution
    that supplies these tools and the management of such risk requires investments
    in commodities that have little to do with production. Furthermore, financial
    contracts must be designed in a way to account for the periods of sowing and
    harvesting. Given that these periods cannot be accurately defined and may

vary from year to year, linking repayment with the harvesting date is a source of increasing uncertainty. Another financing challenge is the management of volatility of agricultural product prices. In Shariah-compliant countries markets are not standardized, thus leading to serious challenges pertaining to determination of prices (e.g., purchasing price, selling price, wholesale price, retail price, etc.). Moreover, Shariah-related restrictions on financial derivatives limit the choices of producers in managing the impact of natural disasters on agricultural produce, magnifying the risks that need to be shared between suppliers and recipients of capital.

CONCLUSION

Prohibition of interest is considered to be the most important difference between Islamic and conventional finance. This, however, is not perfectly accurate because on the one hand, the prohibitions about interest and usury are not a purely Islamic phenomenon while, on the other hand, there are a number of other major features that distinguish the principles and practices of Islamic finance. The prohibition of lending at interest – initially defined as usury irrespectively of the level of the interest rate – was based on the argument that interest constitutes unearned income and it was commonplace in many Christian countries for most of the historical trajectory of Christianity.[20] In addition, philosophical and ethical arguments against charging interest had already been put forward in pre-Christian and pre-Islam times, with Aristotelian arguments constituting a major example.

Beyond prohibition of interest, Shariah is a plexus of rules that together orient entrepreneurship and financing to a specific direction. In the first place, undertaking risk in the context of entrepreneurship is permissible, as risk is associated with the uncertainty that stems from interaction of the enterprise with the external and the internal environment. What is not permissible is superfluous uncertainty (uncertainty that stems from improper or defective understanding of the business environment). Of course, uncertainty associated with gambling is forbidden. Furthermore, the principle of transparency is of utmost importance, along with honesty and justice in economic life. Moreover, in congruence with conventional corporate social responsibility, Islamic finance focuses on the contribution of economic activity in regional development and welfare, supporting in this way the expansion of cooperatives in general and (to a lesser extent) cooperative financial institutions in particular. Finally, Islamic finance deters investments in gambling, alcoholic beverages, tobacco products, weaponry, and sex.

In a globalized economic environment, businesses and financial organizations of the Islamic world often find themselves operating under the same regulatory framework and carrying out similar functions with the conventional businesses and banks they work with, adapting their activities to global economic conditions. This forces them to strike a balance between conventional finance practices and the demands of Shariah.

In general, Islamic finance constitutes social finance insofar as, beyond risk and return, investments, credit, and financial intermediation are evaluated based on their impact on welfare. In the context of Islamic finance, welfare provisions made by financial institutions imply adoption of Shariah principles, precluding interest-bearing lending, limiting the exposure of the economy to risks and orienting portfolio management to choices that do not include investments in tobacco, pork, weaponry, gambling, sex, and alcoholic beverages.

MATERIAL FOR DISCUSSION

Growth of Islamic finance drives demand for degrees

Murray, S. 2018. Growth of Islamic finance drives demand for degrees. *Financial Times*, June 17.

Available at:

www.ft.com/content/7fe86024-699c-11e8-aee1-39f3459514fd.

REVIEW QUESTIONS

1 What is Islamic finance? What are the principles that govern Islamic financial institutions?
2 What are the main Islamic financial services?
3 What is the association between Islamic finance and social finance?
4 What are the main reasons for convergence between Islamic and conventional financial institutions?
5 What are the main challenges Islamic finance needs to address?
6 In what way(s) could Islamic finance affect the teaching of finance?

NOTES

1 The tile of this chapter, "Islamic finance", denotes both the set of financial institutions that operate in the context of the Shariah and the academic analysis of Islamic financing.

2 The main Sunni schools of thought are Hanafi, Maliki, Hanbali, and Shafi'i. The main Shi'ite branches (and schools of jurisprudence) are Jafari, Zaidiyyah, and Isma' ilism.

3 Alexakis and Tsikouras (2010).

4 Pappas et al. (2017). On ethical banking, see Chapter 2.

5 On the difference between commercial credit and interest-bearing lending in Islam, see Graeber (2011).

6 Gheeraert (2014).

7 For the purposes of this chapter, the term "conventional" refers to all financing mechanisms that are not part of the Islamic financial system.

8   Platonova et al. (2016).

9   In the 23rd chapter of Deuteronomy, verse (23:19), it is stated that interest-bearing lending is forbidden, whether in cash or in edible goods. However, verse (23:20) states that lending foreigners is permissible.

10   Mohamad et al. (2017) suggest ways of designing share capital contracts with preferred stock characteristics to secure compliance with Shariah.

11   In general, interest-bearing lending can be justified on the basis of the credit risk incurred by the lender, the opportunity cost of lending, liquidity risk, and inflation risk. Nevertheless, the financial crisis of the late 2000s showed that lending and interest rate changes are critical for economic growth and welfare and, therefore, need to be addressed through pertinent regulatory interventions in a political environment that supports welfare. In that sense, limitations in interest-bearing credit expansion do not merely constitute a concern for specific religious principles but for any plexus of institutions that aim at economic development.

12   AAOIFI (2015).

13   www.isdb.org/news/islamic-development-bank-issues-us-15-billion-debut-sustainability-sukuk-in-response-to-covid-19.

14   www.isdb.org/news/nasdaq-dubai-welcomes-listing-of-usd-15-billion-sukuk-by-islamic-development-bank-to-support-covid-19-interventions.

15   www.id.undp.org/content/indonesia/en/home/presscenter/pressreleases/2017/07/19/indonesia-s-national-zakat-body-extends-first-contribution-to-support-sdgs/.

16   www.undp.org/content/undp/en/home/news-centre/news/2019/UNDP_and_World_Zakat_Forum_launch_new_partnership_for_the_SDGs.html.

17   Nevertheless, implementation of socially responsible investments is not sufficient for full compliance with the investment rules of Islamic finance – Erragraguy and Revelli (2015). Having said that, there is empirical evidence that country-level Shariah compliance is associated with good bank performance in terms of environmental, social, and governance criteria (Paltrinieri et al. 2020).

18   On Shariah-compliant microfinance, see Zada and Saba (2013). On social impact bonds in the context of Islamic finance, see Mohamad et al. (2017).

19   Basov and Bhatti (2014) claim that hiring low-quality human capital is largely responsible for the lower returns realized by Islamic portfolios compared to conventional portfolios (as opposed to Shariah-related restrictions imposed on investors' choices).

20   Visser and MacIntosh (1988).

REFERENCES

AAOIFI, 2015. *Shari'ah standards*. Manama: Accounting and Auditing Organization for Islamic Financial Institutions.

Alexakis, C., and Tsikouras, A., 2010. *Islamic finance and banking*. Athens: Stamoulis.

Basov, S., and Bhatti, M.I., 2014. On Sharia's compliance, positive assortative matching, and return to investment banking. *Journal of International Financial Markets Institutions and Money*, 30, 191–195. https://doi.org/10.1016/j.intfin.2013.12.010.

Erragraguy, E., and Revelli, C., 2015. Should Islamic investors consider SRI criteria in their investment strategies? *Finance Research Letters*, 14, 11–19. https://doi.org/10.1016/j.frl.2015.07.003.

Gheeraert, L., 2014. Does Islamic finance spur banking sector development? *Journal of Economic Behavior and Organization*, 103, S4–S20. https://doi.org/10.1016/j.jebo.2014.02.013.

Graeber, D., 2011. *Debt: The first 5000 years*. Brooklyn, NY: Melville House.

Mohamad, S., Ahmed, M.U., and Badri, M.B., 2017. Preference shares: Analysis of Shariah issues. *ISRA International Journal of Islamic Finance*, 9(2), 185–189. https://doi.org/10.1108/IJIF-07-2017-0008.

Mohamad, S., Othman, J., Lehner, O., and Muda, R., 2017. Social sukuk: A new mechanism to fund social services. *Journal of Emerging Economies and Islamic Research*, 5(1), 69–81.

Paltrinieri, A., Dreassi, A., Migliavacca, M., and Piserà, S., 2020. Islamic finance development and banking ESG scores: Evidence from a cross-country analysis. *Research in International Business and Finance*, 51. https://doi.org/10.1016/j.ribaf.2019.101100.

Pappas, V., Ongena, S., Izzeldin, M., and Fuertes, A.-M., 2017. A survival analysis of Islamic and conventional banks. *Journal of Financial Services Research*, 51(2), 221–256. https://doi.org/10.1007/s10693-016-0239-0.

Platonova, E., Asutay, M., Dixon, R., and Sabri, M., 2016. The impact of corporate social responsibility disclosure on financial performance: Evidence from the GCC Islamic banking sector. *Journal of Business Ethics*, 151(2), 451–471. https://doi.org/10.1007/s10551-016-3229-0.

Visser, W.A.M., and MacIntosh, A., 1988. A short review of the historical critique of usury. *Accounting, Business and Financial History*, 8(2), 175–189. https://doi.org/10.1080/095852098330503.

Zada, N., and Saba, I., 2013. The potential use of Qard Hasan in Islamic microfinance. *ISRA International Journal of Islamic Finance*, 5(2), 153–162.

8

Quantitative evaluation of impact investments

After reading this chapter, you will be able to:

1 Employ the fundamental principles and techniques of impact measurement to evaluate impact investments
2 Assess the information that impact measurement systems offer
3 Evaluate the challenges facing the measurement of impact
4 Explain the structure, the operation and the limitations of major impact measurement systems
5 Illustrate the importance of qualitative aspects in impact assessment

INTRODUCTION

Historically, production of public goods with participation of the private sector has developed in the absence of an organized system of **impact measurement**. For example, in the past, the decision of a donor to finance the construction of a public library was not typically accompanied by a quantitative estimate of the reduction of illiteracy or the increase in the number of

> Historically, production of public goods with participation of the private sector has developed in the absence of an organized system of impact measurement.

DOI: 10.4324/9781003230366-10

readers in the local community because of library use. Similarly, in ancient Greece, sponsorship of a theatrical performance was not accompanied by an estimate on the cultural advancement of Athenian citizens because of attending tragedy and learning from it. Things have changed however and, nowadays, significant emphasis is placed on measurable outcomes. The rationale is that impact measurement improves the organizational structure and the planning process of social ventures. In addition, measurement helps improve the allocation of finance amongst alternative uses that tend to compete for capital resources, the owners of which seek ways to get involved in the production of public goods while simultaneously pursuing profit. Thus, those on the demand side of capital for impact investments face pressing requirements for collecting specific and measurable evidence on the effectiveness of impact investment they are about to undertake. Nevertheless, while impact measurement is important in sustaining investment readiness in impact ventures, social finance is still far from having a fully developed, widely accepted, and synthetic enough mechanism of measurement that could support investment evaluation processes effectively.

Systematic quantification is necessary to address some of the key challenges confronted by social finance. In the first place, systematic measurement helps distinguish between realistic and materializable investment choices with tangible results, vis-à-vis action that is merely based on abstract expectations about resolving social problems. From the microeconomic point of view, systematic measurement contributes to the efficient allocation of resources in the process of production of public goods financed by impact investors. Thanks to systematic measurement, investors and society can follow the extent to which the intended social impact is attained. Moreover, recording social impact brings into light the degree to which blending social finance with organized capital markets could limit social impact to realization of financial returns only. For example, measurement of the proportion of non-performing loans, the return on equity, or the percentage of low-income citizens who receive financing may contribute to depicting potential deviation of the social finance mechanism used for that purpose from its developmental orientation.

CAPTURING SOCIAL IMPACT: STRUCTURE AND ISSUES OF MEASUREMENT

Measuring social impact and, where possible, its economic value may help develop an integrated reference framework, in which outcomes of impact investments are documented, both in terms of history and estimates for the future. Measurement covers the entire spectrum of public goods production by a social enterprise. Naturally, measuring the performance of an organization is subject to challenges.[1] In the case of an organization that blends the production of public goods with the pursuit of financial viability, performance measurement must combine financial results that are measurable in

> In the case of an organization that blends the production of public goods with the pursuit of financial viability, performance measurement must combine financial results that are measurable in monetary terms, with social impact on welfare that is not.

monetary terms, with social impact on welfare that is not. Systems of measurement face several issues.

1 Different approaches to the operation and the mission of a social enterprise may lead to measurement of different indicators.
2 Different ways of measurement may lead to different conclusions and investment choices.
3 Different approaches to defining the mission of social enterprises and the ways of measuring their impact tend to be based on different political aspirations and personal interests.
4 A large part of the anticipated impact on social activities is not measurable (e.g., the sense of security amongst citizens in an area experiencing reduction in crime).
5 Public goods are often produced through deployment of several different activities and utilization of infrastructures. Thus, it is hard for a system of measurement to capture positive changes that are associated with production of a specific public good. For example, it is difficult to tell whether the reduction in the crime rate in a certain area is attributable to the number of youngsters who are supported by a social enterprise not dropping out of school, or to increased police presence.
6 A system of measuring impact investments that cover a broad spectrum of social, economic, and environmental challenges may inevitably be appropriate for certain impact investments more than others. For example, a system of measuring benefits from environmental protection would focus on different areas of outcomes than a system of measuring benefits from the reduction of illiteracy.
7 As with most efforts to measure the performance of an organization, quantification gives only partial information on the qualitative picture of a productive process. Thus, adoption of a specific system of measurement is associated with accepting certain qualitative dimensions as being more important than others are that are not so easily quantifiable.
8 Another challenge in the performance measurement of impact investments is the fact that some investments have more of a preventive effect, deterring the occurrence of a certain social problem, rather than a suppressing effect, treating the social problem after it has occurred.

> Some investments have more of a preventive effect, deterring the occurrence of a certain social problem, rather than a suppressing effect, treating the social problem after it has occurred.

For example, a social purpose organization is more likely to engage in activities discouraging the use of drugs by youngsters rather than taking action to support drug users. In this case, it may be more difficult to determine the time horizon for the purposes of investment evaluation and, even more so, for determining the investment impact. One way of impact measurement is to compare the rate of change of registered users in the years following implementation of the impact investment with the rate of change in the number of users before materialization of the impact investment. Nevertheless, the problem of linking improvement or deterioration of a social problem with a specific social investment remains (e.g., how clear is it whether the improvement is due to the social investment and not to other reasons, such as the pertinent action of other organizations or government policy?). In these cases, one measurement approach is the so-called counter-factual analysis, which seeks to ascertain what would have happened had the impact investment not been materialized. Counter-factual analysis requires finding one area with similar social characteristics and issues, where a similar social investment was not implemented. Of course, as two areas are never quite the same, such a comparison could never be accurate. Thus, it would be up to the analyst to define the degree of similarity (or difference) of the two cases and arrive at an evaluation of the investment that would be feasible and meaningful.

In any case, difficulties in measurement do not render systematic recording of action and impact of social investments impossible to deliver. On the contrary, since all economic activity aims at achieving a certain goal in the future, the target is to identify ways to address the needs for forecasting and measurement. Suppose that an impact investor is considering supporting a medical organization providing assistance in war zones (or more generally in areas excluded from care). If there are two organizations to be funded (e.g., Doctors Without Borders and Doctors of the World), choosing one of them could be based on the effectiveness of each organization in dealing with medical problems. It is not possible to make the financing decision without assessing which one of the two options would be superior. Essentially, though often implicitly, this means that one of the two options will yield *more* outcomes. In this line of reasoning, a quantitative approach to social impact is necessary. The investor in our example would need information on the number of cases treated by each medical body, the number of countries served, the number of doctors employed, the number of surgery operations performed and would generally need to be informed about various data expressing aspects of action of such an organization. Undoubtedly, data do not fully portray the work conducted by a medical organization nor the entirety of the investor's priorities. Nevertheless, the need for measurement is there: the decision to finance a social venture can never be made in an environment of certainty and perfect information but can certainly be made more effectively when there is some kind of quantification available that captures the potential for social impact.

Deployment of measurement systems occurs in three main ways. First, through institutionalization of measurement rules by a regulatory body that has some authority to enforce the proposed rules.[2] Second, through emergence of measurement techniques relevant to the specific needs of each transaction and each impact investment, thus leading to a measurement method that is established in a gradual manner. The third way is a combination of the first two methods: institutionalization of certain rules does not arise from identification of a gap, but as a result of a synthesis of the main stakeholders involved with rules (including regulatory authorities that institutionalize the frameworks of measurement).

Measurement of social prosperity and economic growth does not only occur as a consequence of the emergence of the terrain of social economy, social entrepreneurship, and social finance. In addition to the rich literature in the field of measuring the performance of organizations, measurement of welfare is considered to be a central component of applied research in the field of welfare economics, economics of happiness, and development economics.[3] This rich literature also includes a wide range of governmental and intergovernmental policies for economic development (e.g., the policy changes proposed by the Organization for Economic Cooperation and Development). Furthermore, other than the bodies of policy design and implementation, measurement also concerns the plethora of social enterprises and charities interested in capturing the effectiveness of their activities. As the social economy is integrated into organized capital markets, its necessity, orientation, and practices increasingly incorporate the financial criteria of social investors. Thus, theory, policy, and social entrepreneurship provide a wide variety of ways of measuring social impact, as well of the constraints to be addressed by quantifying quality criteria related to improving people's quality of life. Especially in the case of entrepreneurship, with more and more companies taking on the responsibility to go beyond production of (competitive and exclusive) products, measurement of their performance in the field of social and environmental responsibility has provided a wide range of estimates and has contributed to a rich discourse that incorporates both the opportunities and the limitations of measuring social impact.[4] Thus, although social and environmental responsibility differ from social entrepreneurship, some measurement methodologies are applicable to both.

Measuring social impact presupposes formulation of a definition for it. A definition can shed light on all different aspects of social investments and the changes induced on the environment and society as a result. For the purposes of creating one recording and evaluation system of effectiveness of investments, social impact may be defined as improvement in prosperity that is directly linked to an impact investment and that produces outcomes beyond what is expected from other factors that affect social well-being.[5]

> Social impact may be defined as improvement in prosperity that is directly linked to an impact investment and that produces outcomes beyond what is expected from other factors that affect social well-being.

Quantitative analysis of impact investments has several distinctive features. There are two main differences in the analysis of impact investments from conventional financial analysis. First, the typical case of investing is a framework in which the supplier of capital is also the party that expects to receive the benefit. For example, the main shareholder of a private hospital supplies the capital and expects profit as reward for the investment. Conversely, in the case of a medical infrastructure that is financed to serve people who cannot afford, or do not have access to, healthcare, the supplier of capital is not the primary stakeholder when it comes to economic benefit: direct orientation of the medical infrastructure is towards the supported social group. Of course, in the case of the private hospital, patients, too, benefit from the investment in infrastructure. However, the structure of **accountability** and, consequently, the need for measurement differ. In the case of the private hospital, corporate governance primarily examines whether the use of shareholders' capital was in the direction of enhancing their wealth. In contrast, accountability to the patients is based on the fact that patients pay for services in their capacity as clients, which gives them specific rights. In impact investment (e.g., a social clinic) things are different: neither the supplier of finance requires accountability on a profit basis as a priority nor do patients have the rights that come with being a client.

A second key difference in analyzing the effectiveness of impact investments is that the field of public goods is not competitive, as far as the relationship between producers is concerned. Definitely, production of public goods by social economy organizations is not free of problems pertaining to the scarcity of resources and, frequently, users of public goods have to choose between different producers who have similar goals in the field of social well-being. However, the relationship between these producers in terms of social impact is not competitive. If, for example, an organization that aims at reducing the incidence of sexually transmitted diseases in an area is established, its aim will be to reduce incidents beyond the extent to which reductions would be attained by the action of other organizations with similar targeting or in the context of government policy in this area. This does not necessarily imply that the relationship of different public benefit organizations is cooperative, but it does indicate that the effectiveness of the investment does not arise from competition for a finite market share, as the boundaries of improving social welfare can always be shifted upwards. In contrast, the pursuit of prosperity by strengthening entrepreneurship (e.g., through supporting entrepreneurship efforts of recently released prisoners for the purpose of their smooth reintegration into society) faces the competition that is typical of entrepreneurship (the enterprises that employ recently released prisoners compete with other similar companies in this area).

The uniqueness of impact investment places restrictions on the development of an accountability framework, where it is necessary to include every kind of social impact that is directly related to the evaluated impact investment. Another peculiar characteristic of reports that capture the performance of impact investments is that – in contrast to conventional financial investments – their authors and their readers themselves are often nodes of the network (e.g., employees of non-governmental organizations and beneficiaries of community action). In the evolving landscape of quantifying social investments and their impact, development of a framework for measurement would be a function of the level of risk the investor is willing to undertake (which could be mitigated by a complete framework of analysis that reduces uncertainty), the level of **transaction costs** (which could be reduced in an environment of increased information and transparency), and the level of **accuracy** of measurement that would be required by the investor in order to commit capital to a specific impact investment.

INFORMATION OFFERED BY AN IMPACT MEASUREMENT SYSTEM

A system for measuring – and, where possible, valuing – the performance of social investment must define the object of measurement, its user, the organization that performs it, its purpose, the way of measurement, and the timing of measurement. These issues are interrelated: the definition of one determines the content of others, as illustrated in Figure 8.1.

The expediency of measurement concerns accountability to stakeholders, such as suppliers of finance or citizens who make use of the investment, as well as the effectiveness of the internal operation of a social purpose organization (resource depletion and decision-making are based on the evaluation of measurable outcomes).

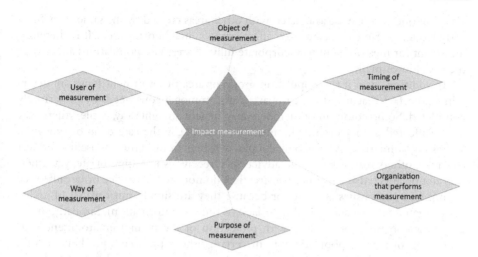

Figure 8.1 Information in a measurement system

More importantly, expediency of measurement concerns the effectiveness of a social investment as a whole, its impact on affected social groups, areas, as well as stakeholders in general.

Beyond expediency, development of a measurement system is based on determining the object of measurement. Such determination may take several directions. For example, a measurement system could assess direct or indirect impact. Alternatively, it could focus on the processes of the organization or on the ultimate outcome for society. For instance, a system measuring the performance of an organization combatting drug addiction could measure: a) the number of addicted people who asked for and received help from support centers or b) the number of registered drug addicts in the area, the reduction of which is an indication of a positive result. Furthermore, measurement can be applied at different levels, for example at the individual, family, the community, the region, society level or a combination of these levels. The number of families who have asked for and received help could be used as a measure of effectiveness of an organization that supports people with addiction. In the case of an organization operating in several areas or addressing many types of addiction, it is possible to distinguish measurement among different areas or types of addiction. Of course, depending on the object of measurement, different methods and different measures are proposed, thus expressing different perceptions of social problems and ways of dealing with them.

Determining the object of measurement starts from impact investment objectives themselves. Measurement should focus on the social group to be assisted or in the geographical area where the social investment will be delivered. This is a subtle issue, as social groups or areas often tend to extend beyond the original target of the investment. An organization dealing with the protection of the natural environment in an area can also affect the well-being in other areas. For example, the protection of a river in one area may be associated with other areas crossed by the same river. Similarly, reducing crime in an area may affect crime in neighboring areas. It is, therefore, important for measurement to incorporate fully all areas and populations affected by the social investment.

In addition, even if the population group or area of investment focus are determined, the fact that investment impact is not homogeneous needs to be seriously considered. Some community members may benefit straightaway, while others may not be affected or may even be harmed. For example, in the case of an organization addressing domestic violence, some couples may benefit from the counseling services provided, others may suffer if the advice they receive is not appropriate, yet others may not be affected at all, either because they do not use the service or because they do not face such issues at home or because they are simply not capable of taking advantage of the service (e.g., due to lack of time or information). Similarly, in the case of an organization dealing with protection of the natural environment (e.g., protection of marine populations from certain fishery practices), the benefit for a community may involve a direct loss for some of its members (fishermen and fishmongers). In general, by measuring the performance of social purpose organizations, it is possible to address the inherent difficulties in the economic analysis of public goods: in contrast to private goods, where the buyer and the seller interact directly through a transaction, public goods are neither exclusive nor rivalrous and, therefore, their impact cannot be generally confined in a strict framework.

To accommodate the different dimensions of social investments and arrive at the best possible measurement of its impact, it is necessary to incorporate the estimates of as many **stakeholders** as possible.[6] In an investment with multidimensional impact – often beyond the scope of its initial targeting – collaboration with different stakeholders gives a more complete picture of the impact of the social investment. **Engagement** of stakeholders in measurement affects the outcome of measurement. As different sides have different needs and priorities, the end result reflects the synthesis of different positions, with the beliefs of the strongest group of stakeholders prevailing and ultimately determining the outcome of measurement. For example, in evaluating an investment aiming at crime reduction through a social impact bond, creditors would focus on the financial performance of the bond, the local government would focus on reducing crime in the area, and each of the beneficiaries (e.g., released prisoners who expect to be reintegrated in society) would focus on their personal story.

> As different sides have different needs and priorities, the end result reflects the synthesis of different positions, with the beliefs of the strongest group of stakeholders prevailing and ultimately determining the outcome of measurement.

Thus, as the management of a social purpose organization or an impact investment involves stakeholders in the process of measuring impact, how measurement affects each stakeholder and how impact can be measured in accordance with the importance it has for each shareholder also need to be taken into account. For example, in the case of a social pharmacy, patients benefit from receiving treatment, as well as from the overall improvement in the level of health in the community they live in, as their fellow citizens also enjoy the services of the social pharmacy. However, the first, more tangible, dimension is the one that the patient perceives immediately. This is an indispensable component of measuring the impact on the specific stakeholder group (the patients in this example).

In addition, engagement of a stakeholder in the measurement process reinforces the impact investment, especially when its goal is to serve citizens. For example, the involvement of refugees into the evaluation process of an impact investment aimed at their integration into society acts in their support, because through measurement processes their views end up influencing the very functioning of the organization that has been set up to support them. Similarly, interviewing a drug user about how a nonprofit organization helps one escape addiction can further enhance the positive outcome stemming from the relevant impact investment.

However, engagement of stakeholders affected by an impact investment needs to be carried out cautiously. Contact with stakeholders requires research and evaluation in order to reach out to those stakeholders who are more likely to offer useful information. For example, in the hypothetical case of a social clinic dealing with pediatric cases it would be necessary to consider whether questionnaires and interviews are to be addressed to doctors, parents, or to the children themselves.

Another question that needs to be addressed about measuring impact measurement is the timing of measurement. For example, in the case of investments aimed at tackling the use of narcotic substances or reducing crime, both of which tend to bear fruit years after materialization of the investment, assuming that reduction in the numbers of addicts or reduction in life-threatening crime incidents is a proxy for project success, what should be the elapsing period before measurement starts? This is an important question, as it has a decisive effect on the financial dimension of the evaluation process. The time horizon of an investment determines the period over which the cost-benefit analysis of the investment will be carried out, discounting both costs and benefits at an interest rate that expresses the perception of investors, society, and all stakeholders regarding the level of risk associated with the investment. Extending the investment horizon also entails accountability risks regarding managers of investment projects, as well as the reliability of mechanisms used to evaluate their performance. For example, if an organization raises capital to deliver action for prevention of climate change, successful exploitation of these resources may help prevent temperature rise by 1 degree Celsius in 50 years' time. It is highly unlikely that after 50 years current investors will be able to meet current managers of the respective projects to assess whether they were successful in managing the capital invested (in addition to the difficulty of attributing, even partly, global climate change to a specific environmental conservation initiative). This is an issue that requires special caution, as the exact opposite practice leads to **investment myopia**: while the investment horizon is long, management of funds is carried out aiming at the immediate future.[7] In the case of environmental action, inability to measure what the impact would be several decades later means that evaluation must be carried out with emphasis on intermediate objectives, such as public information campaigns or preparation of pertinent proposals submitted to policy-makers, even though there is no certainty that intermediate objectives contribute positively to achieving long-term goals.

In summary, evaluation of impact investments requires incorporation of the needs of as many stakeholders as possible. Moreover, it should not be limited to the priorities of investors, but incorporate all required resources in order to assess the impact on the social groups intended to be served, emphasizing the way in which each group evaluates the specific social venture. In addition, in evaluating impact investments, it is useful to consider any unintended effects on individuals who are not involved in the specific welfare service. As with any investment analysis, what matters is the attitude of impact investors towards risk and the resources they are willing to utilize in order to reduce uncertainty through thorough analysis of the impact investment in question.

EVALUATION OF IMPACT INVESTMENTS: QUANTITATIVE APPROACHES

Methodology of measuring returns on impact investments relies primarily on accounting, with three key approaches dominating **impact investment evaluation**.[8] First, in **positivism**, the accounting approach is considered to express in monetary terms a reality that exists objectively and independently of the analysts and the methods they use to evaluate social investments. The second approach is based on **critical theory** and treats the accounting depiction of economic reality as a result of and as a part of power relations. The structure and dynamics of power relations determine what is to be measured and how it is to be measured, as well as the audience to be addressed and integration of measurement in the decision-making of different nodes of a financial network.[9] The third approach deals with social economy accounting **interpretatively**, examining the way in which those involved in the preparation, distribution, and use of accounting information perceive symbols, such as codes and accounting contracts, and the institutional areas of accounting as these are articulated in accounting practices and facts. The interpretative approach is based on systematic observation of the social venture by analysts and analysts' collaboration with stakeholders, in order to map the impact of a social investment and/or modify the social venture accordingly.

These three approaches are quite distinct from each other. Each one of them employs different assumptions about the nature of economic phenomena and society. Differences in assumptions lead to different measurement methods and, ultimately, to different ways of making decisions. The positivist approach is compatible with naturalism in the social sciences in general and in neoclassical economics in particular, notably the belief that social phenomena can be treated as natural phenomena. Thus, in this approach, natural sciences methods are considered to be applicable in the analysis of social and economic phenomena, including impact investments. The explanation of social phenomena takes the form "If X ... then Y" and the emergence of social phenomena can be illustrated via mathematical functions.[10] The main advantage of this approach is the use of methods that are based on the "purity" of mathematical reasoning and have been successfully tested in other, non-social, contexts of scientific analysis. Analysis of impact investments in such a context may be highly quantitative and complex in processing. Such methods require a substantial amount of data, which can be drawn from official statistical databases, archives of nonprofit organizations, questionnaire surveys, even mere observation. Key approaches in the context of positivist methods include cost-benefit analysis, experimental methods used in the social sciences, models based on randomized controlled trials, microeconomic models that study the disclosure of individuals' preferences and their willingness to pay for access to a certain public good,[11] welfare economics models that measure the individual's satisfaction in life, models of measuring value-added, life expectancy weighted by the individual's health (Quality Adjusted Life Years – QALY[12]), etc.

The positivist approach offers a rich toolbox of quantitative methods in the analysis of impact investment, answering key questions for investors and stakeholders. At the same time, however, it faces several challenges. In the first place, analysts and stakeholders of an impact investment are often more interested in the evaluation of individual dimensions of the investment than in a single number that evaluates, albeit comprehensively, impact investment as a whole. Frequently, individuals and entities involved in the investment also need to know the reasons why the investment did not meet their expectations, or the different ways in which it impacted the social groups involved. Therefore, abstract quantification that results in numerical evaluation may serve the purpose of saving time at the expense of oversimplification of the particularly complex process of impact investment.

> Analysts and stakeholders of an impact investment are often more interested in the evaluation of individual dimensions of the investment than in a single number that evaluates, albeit comprehensively, impact investment as a whole.

In general, the problem with applying neoclassical financial analysis on evaluation of social phenomena is that the uniqueness of these phenomena makes it inappropriate for a statistical analysis based on a big sample of similar phenomena. Impact investments constitute a typical example in this regard. For example, if an investor decides to invest in an organization whose goal is the integration of refugees into the local communities in a specific area, it may be hard to find a large sample comprising similar investments (and valuations) in the area. Moreover, in contrast to the analysis of natural phenomena, a mechanistic approach is not always the most appropriate method to illustrate the will of the people who – in historically unique conditions – decide to take action and end up transforming or reproducing the social structures that support and surround them.[13] Quite often, in the case of unique social phenomena, like a crisis or – on a much smaller scale – an impact investment, abstract quantification is not feasible.

> Quite often, in the case of unique social phenomena, like a crisis or – on a much smaller scale – an impact investment, abstract quantification is not feasible.

Of course, even in the context of these objections to the positivist approach, quantitative methods may be helpful, complementing analysis and being useful in examining the frequency of occurrence of historical data that may constitute the beginning of thorough study of a social problem, as well as help draw conclusions about the social structures produced by social phenomena. For example, repetitive attributes of older impact investments attributes, although

> The goal of scientific methods is to satisfy the requirements of those who shape them and those who use them.

not identical to the investment under evaluation, may belong to broader related categories of investments and social phenomena. Additionally, despite its weaknesses, the positivist approach answers mainly questions posed by investors and impact investment stakeholders. If an investor asks, "Is it worth allocating 1 million euros for an impact investment?" the single-word answer can only come from a positivist approach that will work in a simplistic and abstract way: the answer can be summarized in one and only one number. Surely, there is much more than a number to impact investment. However, the goal of scientific methods is to satisfy the requirements of those who shape them and those who use them. In this specific case, if the citizens and the organizations that provide the resources for the implementation of an impact investment require from scientific analysis just one figure, then scientific analysis – to the extent that there will be adjustment and accountability to those who supply the funds – needs to adjust accordingly and investors get what they ask for: just one figure. Similar issues are faced by financial analysis in general: financial evaluation of constructing a motorway or a hotel, for example, can only be properly carried out to the extent that it will take into account the particular social and economic conditions that go together with any investment in private and public goods. However, if at the end of the day investment evaluation ends up being a simple cost-benefit comparison question, it may also need to be described through a single figure.

The concerns regarding the necessity and appropriateness of quantitative methods during the impact investment evaluation process delineated earlier may lead to integration of more dimensions of the evaluated projects. In that direction, the influence of critical theory, albeit not a social theory based on quantitative models, is important for both accounting and business strategy, because it provides guiding principles for quantitative analysis in the direction of prioritization of the costs and benefits borne by the parties involved in the impact investment. As stated earlier, involvement of groups benefiting from an impact investment in the process of evaluating it empowers these groups and enhances the benefits incurred to them through this process. Just like the content of an impact investment is the outcome of a dynamic synthesis of resources, forces, and power relations linking all parties involved, evaluation should incorporate impact on all those involved in the investment. It should be borne in mind, however, that measurement is not objective, but expresses the balance of power between stakeholders. For example, an investment in a social impact bond may involve more or less emphasis on profit or social impact, depending on the stakeholder who influences the measurement mechanism. This line of reasoning includes methodologies such as the **Social Return on Investment** (SROI), as well as multidimensional measures such as **balanced scorecards** that combine monetary and non-monetary performance measures in each of the dimensions that define specific impact investment outcomes.

Each measurement approach has advantages and disadvantages, which are evaluated based on the specific context of each impact investment and the priorities of the individuals who provide resources for implementation of the impact investment and are, therefore, entitled to know whether their resources are

> Each measurement approach has advantages and disadvantages, which are evaluated based on the specific context of each social investment and the priorities of the individuals who provide resources for implementation of the social investment.

being utilized in the best possible manner. In this process, an important decision concerns the institutional body that carries out impact investment evaluation, assesses the effectiveness of utilization of resources in the context of the impact investment and whether the expectations of those who designed and support the social investment are met. This decision concerns the conduct of audit by members inside or outside the social purpose organization. Taking advantage of the significance of **external audit** for the effectiveness of social purpose organizations,[14] the evaluation process could be based on delegation of control to another organization that will study the outcomes of the impact investment and compare them with best practices from the broader field of impact investments. However, a key difficulty to be taken into account and tackled with regard to this approach is the absence of established best practices and generally accepted standards for impact investment. Impact measurement is gaining traction but seems to lack consensus.

MEASUREMENT SYSTEMS

Over the past two decades, several mechanisms of capturing social and financial outcomes of impact investments have been developed.[15] Among the most important ones are the Impact Reporting and Investment Standards (IRIS), the Global Impact Investing Rating System (GIIRS), EngagedX, and the scoreboard Outcomes Matrix.

Impact Reporting and Investment Standards (IRIS)
Established in 2008, IRIS was the product of the collaboration of the Rockefeller Foundation with Acumen and B-Lab.[16] In 2009, IRIS joined the Global Impact Investing Network (GIIN), constituting a decision-making toolkit for the GIIN investment community. IRIS is primarily designed to meet the needs of investors and portfolio managers. While including many non-monetary measurements, the purpose of the measures it entails is to support decisions that do not fully sacrifice financial return for the sake of social impact, but seek to achieve a mixed impact, with both financial and social characteristics. Precisely because social impact has non–quantitative dimensions, IRIS standards include qualitative variables, such as the mission statement or the social and environmental goals of a social purpose organization.

IRIS is not a reporting system, in the sense that it does not guide organizations in the preparation of indicators and reports, nor does it require calculation of certain indicators for the purposes of certification, as IRIS is not a certification mechanism. In fact, IRIS entails a list of over 600 measures, which gives each investor the opportunity to choose those measures that illustrate best effectiveness of their investment. Thus, the use of indicators is a personal matter for the user and the results must be evaluated against the objectives that each organization has set for itself and against the performance of similar organizations. For example, in the case of an organization that seeks to address issues of illiteracy or dropping out of school at an early age, one of the relevant standards is PI4279. PI4279 is called "Educational Resource to students Ratio" and counts the number of textbooks and digital education resources offered to each students as a result of the impact investment.

GIIN and IRIS encourage investors to create their own metrics, supplementing IRIS measurements with their own. The measurement system does not only include measurements but also a method of analyzing indicators in the form of a navigator. The navigator is a way of analyzing indicators in a way that demonstrates the overall performance of the organization in its effort to fulfill its goals and support its stakeholders in the market where it operates. In that direction, GIIN created the *Impact Toolkit* and *Navigating Impact*.[17] *Impact Toolkit* is used to classify measurement methods, indicators, and data that can be processed in order to help investors to choose their own mix of measurements for evaluating their social impact. *Navigating Impact* is a guide for impact investors on the development of strategy. The guide specializes in various fields of entrepreneurship, such as access of socially and economically excluded groups to finance and housing, access to environmentally sustainable energy, etc. Strategic planning on the part of impact investors in each of these areas is linked to specific business objectives, while evaluation of results in terms of objectives is linked to a grid of GIIN and IRIS measurements. IRIS metrics cover five dimensions of impact assessment (Figure 8.2).[18]

1 **WHAT:** Prospective outcomes and their importance for stakeholders
2 **WHO:** Stakeholders whose welfare is affected by the impact investment
3 **HOW MUCH:** Number of stakeholders who are experiencing impact, depth, and duration of impact experience
4 **CONTRIBUTION:** Does investment accomplish impact that would not have been realized if the investment had not been undertaken?
5 **RISK:** Likelihood that realized investment impact will not be as expected.

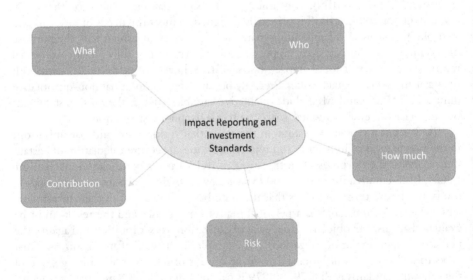

Figure 8.2 Impact Reporting and Investment Standards: dimensions of measurement

IRIS measurement is determined through different components. For example, in the case of PD9364:

1 **ID** – "PD9364".
2 **Metric name** – "Percent Recycled Materials".
3 **Definition** – "Percentage of recycled materials used to manufacture the organization's product (including packaging)/services during the reporting period".
4 **Footnote** – "Organizations should footnote all assumptions used".
5 **Calculation** –

$$\frac{\text{Recycled Materials (OI4328)}}{\text{Total weight or volume of materials used in products}}$$

or

$$\frac{\text{Weight or volume of recycled materials used in products}}{\text{Total weight or volume of materials used in products}}$$

6 **User guidance** – "Recycled materials are those comprised of processed recovered waste. Recycled materials may include glass, paper, metal, plastic, textiles, and electronics. Composted or other processed biodegradable waste is also considered recycled material".

In general, IRIS does not create standards from scratch. It collaborates with organizations specializing in standardization (GRI, IASB, etc.) and organizations that are active in the fields in which IRIS offers measurements (e.g., the World Health Organization), as well as with investors who systematically use measurement to obtain the best possible results. As a result, many IRIS metrics are aligned with other standards (for example, the metrics of the Alliance for Water Stewardship are aligned with IRIS metrics such as OI7680, "Wastewater Treatment Compliance", and OI7365, "Water Quality Practices").

Global Impact Investing Ratings System (GIIRS)

GIIRS was created by the nonprofit organization B-Lab. Its goal is to create a set of standards for the quantitative evaluation of social investments. The organizations that are evaluated through GIIRS are for-profit: they pursue profitability in parallel with social impact. GIIRS is part of B Analytics, the quantitative methods toolbox of B-Lab, which comprises indices and grids of quantitative analysis similar to Morningstar and Capital IQ. In this context, GIIRS constitutes a mechanism of evaluating organizations that deliver investments aimed at social impact. While GIIRS is not a for-profit mechanism, the reports offered by B Analytics are available at a price, while a more generic part of measurements is available to the general public free of charge.

GIIRS measurements are divided into five categories:[19]

1 **Governance:** Measurements in this category rate organizations according to their mission, their ethics, their accountability, and the quality of transparency in communication with all stakeholders.

2 **Workers:** These measurements assess the working environment of the organization, emphasizing features such as remuneration of employees, employee participation in ownership of the organization, training opportunities within the organization, as well as respect for human rights.

3 **Consumers:** Measurements in this category concern the users of products and services of the organization, including whether the products and services offered benefit the organization's customers beyond the boundaries of private benefit of a conventional production process, resulting in positive social impact. The extent to which action by the social purpose organization is aimed at social groups that are in greater need of this type of help and are more affected by the impact investment is also taken into account (special emphasis is placed on the protection of social groups whose financial means are limited and/or are socially excluded).

4 **Community:** These measurements reflect the extent to which the organization is integrated in the local community and how it provides service to it. For example, they reflect whether the organization donates to community service activities or encourages its employees to spend time on volunteer work, whether it supports employment in the local community focusing on socially excluded individuals, etc.

5 **Environment:** These measurements evaluate the way in which the operation, infrastructure, and services provided by the organization affect the natural environment. They also specialize according to the activity performed by each evaluated organization (e.g., an agricultural enterprise is evaluated in such a way that evaluation captures sustainable use of the natural environment).

One of the challenges faced by measurements of this sort – and of efforts to measure social impact in general – is that they focus more on the social purpose organizations' actions than on the impact of these actions upon society and the environment, which may be long term and difficult to link with a certain welfare initiative more than with another. For example, it is very easy to count the number of trees planted in an area hit by wildfires. However, it would be less straightforward to measure (in this restrictive context) the impact of this initiative upon sustainability of the natural environment in the area, as this would require long-term assessment of the situation and separation of the impact of the welfare activity from the impact of other factors affecting the natural environment of the specific area.

EngagedX

EngagedX was established in 2012 in the United Kingdom by Karl Richter and Rupert Evenett.[20] It is an organization that offers private and government agencies consulting services on impact investment.[21] Part of its services is a platform for systematic presentation of a wide range of information and measurements. It is an expanding database aspiring to provide impact investing data and information in an organized fashion following the model of Reuters and Bloomberg. EngagedX maintains investor anonymity and offers information on variables such as amount of capital invested, interest rate, area of focus of social investors' action, and impact of welfare activities in tackling social problems. In addition, similar to GIIRS, a small part of the data is available for free to the general public, while other data is sold to members of the investment community and policy-makers. Prices are charged in the form of subscriptions, as in the case of Bloomberg and Reuters.

Outcomes Matrix

The Outcomes Matrix is a measurement system created by Investing for Good and Big Society Capital, two social financial institutions based in the United Kingdom. Like other measurement systems, Outcomes Matrix tries to capture the ways in which welfare action results in tangible outcomes that improve the well-being of the population it aims to support. The fields of evaluation for impact investments are as follows:

♦ Employment, training, and education.
♦ Income and financial inclusion.
♦ Housing and local facilities.
♦ Physical health.
♦ Mental health and well-being.
♦ Family, friends, and relationships.
♦ Citizenship and community.
♦ Arts, heritage, sports, and faith.
♦ Conservation of the natural environment.

Each of these categories includes a variety of indicators and measurements, facilitating evaluation of impact investment and decision-making not only for the social purpose organization as a whole, but also for each sub-category of action. In this measurement context, social impact is assessed at two levels: a) impact on individuals, and b) impact on the population or field of action. Thus, Outcomes Matrix is a mechanism of analysis that supports the holistic approach of evaluating impact investments, while maintaining flexibility by focusing on individual aspects of the social purpose organization.[22]

Measurement systems: commentary

In general, to date, measurement systems tend to interpret data in a static way. This has to do mainly with the fact that most databases have been created relatively recently, while social purpose organizations also change very often, merging with other organizations, being re-established, or simply closing down. However, if the impact investment community manages to set up a rudimentary measurement system, it will also manage to support gradual transformation of this system into a framework of analysis that will keep up with dynamic changes incurred in social purpose organizations. Expanding the social economy and documenting social enterprises in databases and social impact measurement systems are, therefore, necessary.

In addition, analysts' efforts to create a functional framework for evaluating impact investments is influenced by their own personal judgment and principles on the issue of impact investing. Thus, quantitative measurement is never "objective". It is always based on the aspirations of those who conduct the measurement and those who use it and can never free them from the responsibility of making personal decisions in evaluating an impact investment. The personal judgment of the analyst and everyone else involved (government, investor, citizen) highlights the way the specific context of an impact investment is combined with the characteristics of social or environmental problems and the personal aspirations of the analyst. Expression of these aspirations and their involvement in the evaluation of impact investment complement the measurement and quantification of operations of a social purpose organization and, consequently, its social impact. In addition, the analyst's relationship with the social purpose organization – in terms of trust and involvement with the people and processes of the impact investment – shapes the quality and quantity of information reflected in an evaluation procedure.

In this context, the analyst's personal contact with the organization renders data collection essential and gives content to its outcome. In addition, the needs of the analysis regarding the quality and quantity of information depend on the scale and complexity of the impact investment, as well as on the uncertainty those who provide resources in general and investors in particular are willing to accept. Reducing uncertainty implies enhancement of measurement, but also more substantial involvement of analysts in the implementation and outcome of social investments.

MEASURING IMPACT ON A GLOBAL SCALE: SUSTAINABLE DEVELOPMENT GOALS INDICATORS

Adoption of the 2030 Sustainable Development Agenda by the United Nations shapes the pursuit of welfare and development globally. In the context of the Agenda, each Sustainable Development Goal (SDG) is associated with a set of targets and each target is associated with a set of indicators (see Box 8.1 for the set indicators in the implementation of SDG 7). Although this chapter discusses mostly impact measurement systems for third-sector investors rather than governments, SDGs and the respective indicators are essential for third-sector investors because they affect the ways in which impact is pursued all over the globe and, therefore, rearrange the terrain of social finance. For example, the GIIN has documented the correspondence between IRIS metrics and the SDGs.[23]

As with third-sector investments, performance measurement of government policies for sustainable development is necessary in assessing chosen strategies and use of employed resources. SDG indicators are not immune to the fundamental challenges facing impact measurement. First, impact data may be missing and/or hard to come by.[24] Furthermore, construction and interpretation of SDG indicators is inevitably subjective and, therefore, interest- and ideology-laden. For example, definition of the desirable magnitude of change in the proportion of the population with primary reliance on clean fuels and technology (Indicator 7.1.2) or determination of the acceptable level of investments in clean energy research and development (Indicator 7.a.1) may vary in different developed and/or developing countries. Expectedly, there is evidence that the outcome of international comparisons of government policies on the SDGs is sensitive to the choice of measurement approach; for example, in the context of SDG 1 ("end poverty in all its forms everywhere"), assessment of policy effectiveness depends on whether performance is measured with the percentage of population that lives on less than $1.90 per day or the rate of change in poverty over the last two decades.[25] Additionally, the familiar causality problems associated with impact investments are also pertinent in the case of government policies; for example, which national policies can claim full responsibility for a change in the suicide mortality rate (SDG Indicator 3.4.2)?

Perhaps the most important challenge facing impact assessment in the framework of SDG indicators lies in potential tradeoffs and complementarities in the achievement of different SDGs.[26] For instance, increasing the share of renewable energy in total final energy consumption (Indicator 7.2.1) can help reduce the material footprint per capita (Indicator 12.2.1). However, achievement of 7% annual growth in least developed countries (Target 8.1) may run counter to reducing greenhouse gas emissions in the context of the United Nations Framework Convention on Climate Change (Target 13.2), if production technology does not make a remarkable shift towards sustainability.[27]

Box 8.1 Sustainable Development Goal 7: ensure access to affordable, reliable, sustainable, and modern energy for all.

7.1 By 2030, ensure universal access to affordable, reliable and modern energy services	7.1.1 Proportion of population with access to electricity
	7.1.2 Proportion of population with primary reliance on clean fuels and technology
7.2 By 2030, increase substantially the share of renewable energy in the global energy mix	7.2.1 Renewable energy share in the total final energy consumption
7.3 By 2030, double the global rate of improvement in energy efficiency	7.3.1 Energy intensity measured in terms of primary energy and GDP
7.a By 2030, enhance international cooperation to facilitate access to clean energy research and technology, including renewable energy, energy efficiency and advanced and cleaner fossil-fuel technology, and promote investment in energy infrastructure and clean energy technology	7.a.1 International financial flows to developing countries in support of clean energy research and development and renewable energy production, including in hybrid systems
7.b By 2030, expand infrastructure and upgrade technology for supplying modern and sustainable energy services for all in developing countries, in particular least developed countries, small island developing States and landlocked developing countries, in accordance with their respective programmes of support	7.b.1 Installed renewable energy-generating capacity in developing countries (in watts per capita)

Source: https://sdgs.un.org/goals

EVALUATING IMPACT INVESTMENTS: BEYOND MEASUREMENT

Evaluation of impact investments is entangled with the need of the investor to justify allocation of resources to a social venture.[28] However, as evaluation is always personal and often fails to capture with precision the social impact that is diffused in uncharted ways in space and time, the first explanation why a social investment is materialized is **faith**: the investor will provide funds, the volunteer will offer labor, and society will support a social venture because its members believe in it. Frequently, faith as a justification for undertaking a social venture is partly quantitative, as for example in certain cases of state funding (tied to achieving specific goals) and social impact bonds. In general, volunteer work, allocation of capital in spite of negative expectations for returns (donations), production of public goods by private individuals, provision of services free of charge (an organization offering training to the unemployed) are based on priorities that redefine the analysis of operation of an economic system, altering the roles played by economic actors, the basic function of markets for goods and services and for factors of production.

However, an impact investment does not always have features that are easily quantifiable. Although faith is not independent of numerical accounts and promises related to community service, it is closely linked with engagement of the analyst or impact investor. This engagement means that the investor monitors closely the social venture, meets the people who manage the pertinent resources, as well as those who benefit from the impact investment, and observes the way the physical characteristics and the strategic orientation of the impact investment are being formed. Direct contact of the investor (or the analyst in general) with the investment gives measurement content, reinforces personal views in decision-making, and ultimately determines faith in the purpose of a certain social venture. Evaluation of complex and historically distinct ventures in the field of impact investment cannot be carried out without **qualitative evaluation**. The latter necessitates engagement of the analyst with the investment. Engagement and necessity of measurement are, therefore, complementary: requirements for detailed and accurate measurement of impact decline to some degree when confidence increases in the people who run a social organization and in the capacity of the organization to bring about positive social change.

Faith is also strengthened when the metrics used are included in an established standardization framework (which is the main reason why it is necessary to deploy quantification frameworks along the lines of GIIRS, IRIS, etc.). In general, the role of trust in the evaluation of impact investments and in the signaling of their measurements varies widely, depending on the organizational characteristics of each investment and the particular characteristics of those who finance social investments, those who work for them, and those who benefit from them.

CONCLUSION

This chapter presented the main methodologies and issues of measurement pertaining to the impact of social ventures. Impact assessment in social investment is very important, as it is in any investment decision in conventional financial analysis. In line with conventional financial analysis and political economy, in addition to values resulting from a valuation mechanism, the role of individuals who materialize social investments, as well as the role of those who benefit from them, are equally valuable.[29]

As data availability is necessary for the deployment of investment and further deployment of investment contributes more data to analysis mechanisms, the establishment of systems of measurement is interrelated with expansion of impact investment. The growth of the third sector of the economy, which lies between the public and the private sector, creates demand for data on the part of every single stakeholder, which drives the development of quantitative measurement systems for social ventures and their impact.

Even though it is widely accepted that transparency and clarity should be key features of a measurement system designed for evaluating impact investments, the fact that there are different perceptions about what is socially beneficial and that different interests and different roles in social economy lead to different beliefs about what is an appropriate social investment evaluation measure, must not be overlooked. Donors, employees, the government, and beneficiaries evaluate social investments differently. The way of measurement that is ultimately selected results from a synthesis of all these different views and stakes. Nevertheless, as impact investments address social problems, the synthesis of different interests in the field of social investments should be structured in such a way to best reflect those who would benefit most from these investments, namely the citizens. In the absence of a regulatory framework, it is by no means certain that competition between different perceptions and respective measurement mechanisms will represent in a transparent manner those who need to be supported by social entrepreneurship mechanisms and flows of social financing.

In addition, as the quantification of an organization's performance and its accounting image carry a special weight, quantitative evaluation is likely to enhance the effectiveness of impact investment. The faith of all stakeholders in the value of the process of measurement, combined with emergence of more and richer systems of measurement, may end up convincing people that something positive is happening, reinforcing support for social investments and increasing positive outcomes. Moreover, development of a measurement system highlights the importance of both methods that are used in the evaluation of impact investment, namely measurement resulting in a single, usually expressed in monetary terms, figure and multidimensional measurement that emphasizes the diverse dimensions of value creation and social prosperity. However, it should always be borne in mind that each impact investment is a unique social phenomenon and that measurement cannot draw sufficient reliability from computational complexity and successful implementation of similar impact investments, precisely because similar investments usually do not exist.

Measurement would acquire essential content and the evaluation of a social venture would be more complete if those who support and benefit from impact investment were fully involved in measurement. The study of impact investment mechanisms and of the social problems that impact investment tries to address, the contact with people who manage the delivery of impact investments, and the contact with beneficiaries of impact investments constitute necessary components of any essential process of evaluating social entrepreneurship.

MATERIAL FOR DISCUSSION

The next frontier in social impact measurement isn't measurement at all

Ruff, K., and Olsen, S. 2016. The next frontier in social impact measurement isn't measurement at all. *Stanford Social Innovation Review*.

Available at:

https://ssir.org/articles/entry/next_frontier_in_social_impact_measurement.

REVIEW QUESTIONS

1　Why do we need to measure the impact of social investments?
2　What kind of information is provided by an impact measurement system?
3　What are the main challenges facing the development of a system measuring the impact of social investments?
4　What are the characteristics of the Impact Reporting and Investment Standards?
5　What are the main factors that underlie the subjective nature of quantitative measures of social impact?
6　What are the qualitative aspects of impact measurement?

NOTES

1　See, for example, Andrikopoulos (2010).
2　Nicholls et al. (2015).
3　See, for example, Blanchflower and Oswald (2011).
4　On the financial significance of corporate social responsibility, see, for example, Liang and Renneboog (2017), Becchetti et al. (2015), Krüger (2015).
5　Nicholls et al. (2015).
6　For example, according to Maas and Liket (2011), most systems of social impact measurement incorporate the priorities of different stakeholders of the social investment.
7　The main issue in pension fund management, where the goal is to secure pensions several decades later, managers are usually evaluated by administration based on earlier portfolio yields, for example, annually (Benartzi and Thaler (1995).
8　Nicholls et al. (2015).
9　Nicholls (2018).
10　See, for example, Lawson (1997).
11　On the willingness of Cambodian citizens to pay for improvement of the environmental conditions and the hygienic conditions in agricultural areas (as a mean to evaluate pertinent social investments) combined with social finance impact through microfinancing, see Yishay et al. (2017).
12　The Quality Adjusted Life Years (QALY) index weights each individuals' age with the quality of their health each year. In the reasoning of this metric, one year during which the

individual is healthy corresponds to 1 QALY, while one year with weak health corresponds to less than 1 QALY. Analyzing impact investments in the healthcare sector, impact can be measured in QALYs offered to individuals who make use of the medical services offered. See, for example, Whitehead and Ali (2010).

13   See, for example, Andrikopoulos (2013).

14   See, for example, Greenlee et al. (2007), Garven (2012).

15   A number of systems of standards depict the social and environmental impact of enterprises and organizations, with those proposed by the Global Reporting Initiative consti-tuting, perhaps, the most characteristic example. This section focuses on systems of standards that have been developed primarily to cover the needs of social investors for information and decision-making.

16   https://iris.thegiin.org.

17   https://impacttoolkit.thegiin.org, https://navigatingimpact.thegiin.org.

18   https://iris.thegiin.org/document/iris-and-the-five-dimensions/.

19   http:///b-analytics.net/content/standards-navigator. B Analytics issues social impact certificates to organizations that are evaluated. Certificates involve payment of a price. B Analytics is financed through donations and subscription fees for the services it offers to its members.

20   www.engagedx.com.

21   EngagedX has offered services to the UK government, the European Commission, and the G8.

22   www.bigsocietycapital.com.

23   Global Impact Investing Network (2019).

24   PwC (2016), Dang and Serajuddin (2020).

25   Dang and Serajuddin (2020).

26   Pham-Truffert et al. (2020).

27   Hickel (2019).

28   Nicholls et al. (2015).

29   See, for example, Tsakalotos (2005).

REFERENCES

Andrikopoulos, A., 2010. Intellectual capital accounting: On the elusive path from theory to practice. *Knowledge and Process Management*, 17(4), 180–187. https://doi.org/10.1002/kpm.355.

Andrikopoulos, A., 2013. Finance: An essay on objects and methods of science. *Cambridge Journal of Economics*, 37(1), 35–55. https://doi.org/10.1093/cje/bes027.

Becchetti, L., Ciciretti, R., and Hasan, I., 2015. Corporate social responsibility, stakeholder risk and idiosyncratic volatility. *Journal of Corporate Finance*, 35, 297–309. https://doi.org/10.1016/j.jcorpfin.2015.09.007.

Benartzi, S., and Thaler, R., 1995. Myopic loss aversion and the equity premium puzzle. *Quarterly Journal of Economics*, 110(1), 73–92. https://doi.org/10.2307/2118511.

Blanchflower, D.G., and Oswald, A.J., 2011. International happiness: A new view on the measure of performance. *Academy of Management Perspectives*, 25(1), 6–22. https://doi.org/10.5465/amp.25.1.6.

Dang, H.-A.H., and Serajuddin, U., 2020. Tracking the sustainable development goals: Emerging measurement challenges and further reflections. *World Development*, 127. https://doi.org/10.1016/j.worlddev.2019.05.024.

Garven, S.A., 2012. Are audit-related factors associated with financial reporting quality in nonprofit organizations? PhD Thesis. University of Alabama, Alabama.

Global Impact Investing Network, 2019. Iris+ and the SDGs. https://s3.amazonaws.com/giin-web-assets/iris/assets/files/guidance/IRIS-SDGs_20190515.pdf.pdf.

Greenlee, J., Fischer, M., Gordon, T., and Keating, E., 2007. An investigation of fraud in nonprofit organizations: Occurrences and deterrents. *Nonprofit and Voluntary Sector Quarterly*, 36(4), 676–694. https://doi.org/10.1177%2F0899764007300407.

Hickel, J., 2019. The contradiction of the sustainable development goals: Growth versus ecology on a finite planet. *Sustainable Development*, 27, 873–884. https://doi.org/10.1002/sd.1947.

Krüger, P., 2015 Corporate goodness and shareholder wealth. *Journal of Financial Economics*, 115(2), 304–329. https://doi.org/10.1016/j.jfineco.2014.09.008.

Lawson, T., 1997. *Economics and reality*. London: Routledge.

Liang, H., and Renneboog, L., 2017. On the foundations of corporate social responsibility. *Journal of Finance*, 72(2), 853–910. https://doi.org/10.1111/jofi.12487.

Maas, K., and Liket, K., 2011. Social impact measurement: Classification of methods. *In*: R. Burritt, S. Schaltegger, M. Bennett, T. Pohjola, and M. Csutora, eds. *Environmental management accounting and supply chain management. Eco-efficiency in industry and science, 27*. Dordrecht: Springer, 171–202. https://doi.org/10.1007/978-94-007-1390-1.

Nicholls, A., 2018. A general theory of social impact accounting: Materiality, uncertainty and empowerment. *Journal of Social Entrepreneurship*, 9(2), 132–153. https://doi.org/10.1080/19420676.2018.1452785.

Nicholls, A., Nicholls, J., and Paton, R., 2015. Measuring social impact. *In*: A. Nicholls, R. Patton, and J. Emerson, eds. *Social finance*. Oxford: Oxford University Press, 253–281.

Pham-Truffert, M., Metz, F., Fischer, M., Rueff, H., and Messerli, P., 2020. Interactions among Sustainable development goals: Knowledge for identifying multipliers and virtuous cycles. *Sustainable Development*, 28(5), 1226–1250. https://doi.org/10.1002/sd.2073.

PwC, 2016. Navigating the SDGs: A business guide to engaging with the UN global goals. www.pwc.com/gx/en/sustainability/publications/PwC-sdg-guide.pdf.

Tsakalotos, E., 2005. Homo economicus and the reconstruction of political economy: Six theses on the roles of values in economics. *Cambridge Journal of Economics*, 29(6), 893–908. https://doi.org/10.1093/cje/bei075.

Whitehead, S.J., and Ali, S., 2010. Health outcomes in economic evaluation: The QALY and utilities. *British Medical Bulletin*, 96(1), 5–21. https://doi.org/10.1093/bmb/ldq033.

Yishay, A.B., Fraker, A., Guiteras, R., Palloni, G., Shah, N.B., Shirrell, S., and Wang, P., 2017. Microcredit and willingness to pay for environmental quality: Evidence from a randomized-controlled trial of finance for sanitation in rural Cambodia. *Journal of Environmental Economics and Management*, 86, 121–140. https://doi.org/10.1016/j.jeem.2016.11.004.

Appendix

Financial economics: eight introductory points

FINANCIAL ECONOMICS

Different areas of science assume content and orientation based on the social groups that comprise them and use scientific knowledge in practice. Thus, it would be hard to arrive at a meaningful definition of finance, identifying strict boundaries for it and detaching it from its historical, social, and political context. Nevertheless, even if inevitably incomplete, a definition is necessary for the beginning of scientific discourse:

Financial economics is the economics of decision-making of individuals, businesses, and governments about the use of capital and money, in conditions of uncertainty and risk. Some clarifications regarding the implications of this definition are necessary:

> Financial economics is the economics of decision-making of individuals, businesses, and governments about the use of capital and money, in conditions of uncertainty and risk.

♦ Financial economics is part of **economics** in general and **microeconomics** in particular. However, complete analysis of financial phenomena would only be possible with integration of analytical mechanisms from other scientific fields, such as business administration, sociology, political science, law, history, and psychology. For example, analysis of investors' herding behavior necessarily encompasses theoretical principles and empirical findings from the field of psychology. For the same reason, analysis of implementation of monetary policy by the European Central Bank, commercial banks supervision, or regulation of capital markets is based on the political science discourse about international relations, notably European integration. Correspondingly, analysis of the importance of the cost of borrowing of the government or stock market dynamics would be more comprehensive if encompassing inferences stemmed from law and political science.

♦ Finance is about making decisions in conditions of **uncertainty** and **risk**. While risk and uncertainty are concepts that are used interchangeably in everyday language, their meaning in microeconomics is quite distinct. Compared to risk, uncertainty is broader as a concept. Uncertainty denotes a condition whose outcome is unknown, while in the case of **risk** although the outcome is unknown, different outcomes are assigned some probability of occurrence. For example, although the level of the euro/dollar exchange rate tomorrow is unknown, one may assign a 40% probability that it will go higher than today's level and a 60% probability that it will go lower.

♦ Finance is about money and capital.

Knowledge of finance is essential to comprehend developments in money and capital markets, such as changes in interest rates and stock market indices. It is also useful in the conduct of everyday life decision-making. For example, knowledge of finance can help evaluate practical issues such as the decision to purchase goods on credit, the decision to buy a home, get a loan, or place money in a time deposit. In addition, knowledge of finance helps entrepreneurs and professionals in either private or public companies to evaluate investment decisions such as purchases of equipment, buying or selling of a business, refinancing of loans, etc. Beyond financial decisions pertaining to one's personal and/or professional life though, financial knowledge can help evaluate available policy options on issues such as the regulatory framework of financial enterprises, the issue of government bonds as a way of financing government expenditure, government default risk management, as well as valuation and sale of public-sector property. The most convincing arguments for such practical matters are expressed in the **language** of finance.

If language is a system of rules about perception of reality and communication, the language of finance may be used to express one's position regarding changes in government borrowing rates, the nominal value of public debt, interest rates charged on credit cards, or terms of getting a mortgage. Thus, the language of finance is a key way of communication, regardless of the actual accuracy of proposals expressed. For example, the purchase of a property based on the discounted value of cash flows to be received upon renting that property is usually founded upon arguments that tend to prevail over others, such as the content of a prayer or a dream about this property, which are likely to be less convincing to investors.

Evolution of the language of finance is ongoing, as finance itself evolves to respond to the needs of the individuals and the social groups that use it. Thus, the most important criterion to evaluate finance is its ability to improve the lives of those who apply it.

FINANCIAL MANAGEMENT DECISIONS

Financial decisions in context of entrepreneurship depend on whether they are made from the standpoint of employees, owners, customers, or creditors of a business. For example, acquisition of one firm by another may be eyed differently by employees who gauge changes in their working environment as a result of the acquisition, compared to owners who care about the price the acquisition will fetch. Consequently, the financial approach entails a nexus of contracts,[1] whereby contracts denote the relationships between different stakeholders associated with the business. Thus, business is a network of relationships that integrates employees, own and external capital, the state, customers, suppliers, rivals, supervisory mechanisms, and regulatory authorities.[2] On first reading, firm financial decision-making (e.g., financing, investments, or distribution of profits) is conducted by the individuals and/or the groups responsible for making the respective decisions. For example, the decision to sell on credit to customers is made by the Chief Financial Officer; the decision to buy out another firm using borrowed funds is made by the board of directors, in consultation with a bank and the board of directors of the target company. On second reading, however, decision-making mechanisms arise from the dynamics of the nexus of contracts that define the firm: rules, procedures, and roles are constantly being redefined, shaping the ever-changing internal and external environment of the firm. For example, the decision to sell on credit may not concern the Chief Financial Officer alone, but also the commercial bank that lends the company. If the bank is reluctant to extend credit to the company, the ability of the company to sell on credit to its customers will also be adversely affected. Correspondingly, the decision to conduct a buy-out also depends on the degree to which the organizational culture of the buying firm fits that of the buy-out target.

In short, the main business decisions in the context of financial management relate to two key questions: "Is it worth placing the firm's capital in a certain investment?" "How to raise capital in order to undertake an investment?" According to financial analysis, the answer to the first question is that the value of an investment is the **present value** of the future cash flows stemming from the capital placed in that investment. Present value is the value that expected future cash flows from the investment would have if collected at present. For example, the value of a piece of property constructed with own and external capital for commercial purposes is the present value of the sum of rentals to be collected, after deducting maintenance, insurance, and repair costs. The part of the property value that corresponds to owners is the present value of the sum of rentals, after interest, taxes, and other expenses are paid. Similarly, the amount of the loan granted to the construction firm that builds this property is equal to the present value of the sum of the installments to be paid back. Because the concept of the present value relates to the fact that an amount of cash today is worth more than that same amount in the future, cash flows received in the future are discounted by applying a rate that reflects the risk borne by the lender to never get their money back. Thus, the amount of a loan granted for a given investment is inversely related to the estimate of the risk undertaken by the lender: the higher the risk, the higher the interest rate and, correspondingly, the lower the amount of the loan. To put it differently, for a given amount, the higher the interest rate, the higher the cash flow required to repay the loan. Precisely because future cash flows received by the lender include interest, their sum is higher than the principal amount that was initially granted.

Firm value is estimated in a similar manner. Stock valuation has a special place in financial theory. **Stock** or **share** refers to ownership or participation in the capital of a special legal form of business, the corporation. Ownership of shares entitles the holder to vote in the general assembly meetings of the corporation, as well as the right to receive part of the corporation's profits based on the number of shares held. Large companies whose shares trade in organized stock exchanges are corporations and are quite important, as the shares of large companies tend to be part of pension fund portfolios worldwide. Because shares represent ownership, their time horizon generally spans over a large number of years with the life span of the company. As with other investments, the price of a share is the present value of the cash flows that the shareholder will receive in the future (namely, the share of future profits for the holder of the shares).

In practice, however, shares are often bought and sold with a short-term investment horizon, rather than constituting strategic stakes in a business. Nevertheless, even in that case, both the short-term subjectivity of investors and market trends are based on the present value of future earnings (see Box A.1 on the subjectivity of valuation proposals). For example, one can buy a stock today and sell it a week later upon announcement that the company lost an important customer. It is possible that during that week neither announcement of financial results nor other announcement pertinent to the firm's profitability took place. At first glance, the decision to sell the stock appears to be associated solely with the very short-term flow of information. However, the change in investors' sentiment in this case is attributable to the perceived reduction in the firm's future profitability, since the firm lost a customer (or, more often, to investors' perception about the anticipated reaction of other investors to the negative news about the firm's prospects). While this methodology is primarily relevant for the shares of large-scale listed companies, its basic principles (valuation of an investment based on the present value of the revenue it will generate in the future) are applicable to other forms of business.

At this point, it is worth noting that this specific way of calculating value, although in principle capital-oriented, also concerns other stakeholders, including the state and company employees. For example, for the state the expediency of an investment can be evaluated (among other things) by estimating the present value of taxes to be collected, while for company employees the value of a business may relate to the present value of their remuneration for as long as they work in the company.

Box A.1 Valuation and truth

Valuation is an investment decision-making mechanism. If, for example, the value of a share is calculated at €15 and the current market price is €18, the share is considered to be **overvalued** by the market. Investors are expected to realize this and to gradually engage in transactions that will lead to a reduction in the share price. Thus, one does not choose to purchase this stock or, if they own it, they sell it at once, expecting its value to fall. Conversely, if the market price is lower, for example €12, this implies that the share is **undervalued** by the market and, if the market is gradually convinced about this valuation "error", the price of the stock is expected to increase.

The terms "undervalued" and "overvalued" do not refer to the true value of a share. Instead, the estimated value depends on the valuation method and the time horizon over which investors estimate that they will realize profits. In financial theory and practice, a market price that never yields profit to any investor is not considered a fair or just or true share price. For example, an investor with a six-month investment horizon (at the end of which the investor intends to liquidate the investment), is only interested in the market price at that point of liquidation of the investment.

It should also be noted that propositions on valuation of securities – for example, "the value of the share is €16" – are not refutable.[3] This practically means that it is not possible to distinguish whether the proposition is true or false, as we cannot compare it with an "external" reality to find out whether it is valid or not. In contrast, the statement "there are eight chapters in this book" can usually be ascertained by counting the book chapters. The number of book chapters is generally independent of subjective opinions. This is not true in the case of stock valuation.

Regarding the second key financial management question pertaining to investment financing, the financial criterion mainly concerns the value, either in whole or in part, of the capital invested for the owners and their owners' creditors. This decision is vital, because if the value of the firm (of the capital invested) is affected by the composition of capital (i.e., the capital structure), then a firm can increase its value without increasing sales or improving its strategy, simply by changing the mix of its capital structure. This constitutes an oxymoron: if this were not the case, we would expect businesses to be indifferent as to capital formation with own or external funds.[4] Although in practice they are not, they do not seem to adopt a systematic method of choosing to finance new investments with external or own funds. The main advantage of external (e.g., loan) financing is tax savings, which stems from the fact that interest payments reduce taxable corporate profits. If, for example, the borrowing cost is 9% and the corporate income tax is 40%, then the real borrowing cost is 9% − (40% × 9%) = 5.4%. The reason is that any monetary reward to external capital − in contrast to the reward to own capital, which is profit − is an expense and, as such, it is calculated and paid for before taxes are paid. Thus, it helps reduce tax payments of the firm. If profits before interest and taxes are €40 and the loans of the company are €50, then interest payments are €4.5 (€50 × 9%) and profits before taxes are €35.5 (€40 − €4.5). Thus, profits after taxes are €21.3 = 35.5 − 40% x 35.5. If the company did not pay any interest, it would have expenses reduced by €4.5, but also reduced profits by €2.7. Profits would be €24 = €40 − (€40 × 40%). The difference, €1.8 = €4.5 − €2.7, would be precisely due to the effect of interest (0.4 × 4.5 = €1.8). If the €4.5 were not paid in the form of interest to the lender for the loan granted, but were distributed to a shareholder for a contribution to share capital of €50, there would be no tax savings.

In this line of reasoning, a first thought would be to finance all investment projects through external funds. However, this approach is confronted by obvious obstacles. The cost of both own (equity) capital and external finance is not fixed. As the firm replaces increasing amounts of equity with external capital, the cost of borrowing will increase and so will the burden for the firm, thus raising default risk and reinforcing further increases in the cost of capital. Moreover, a highly indebted firm is likely to also face increased cost of equity, as potential shareholders will require higher yield for offering lower amounts to the firm's own capital. Thus, while increased borrowing brings forth a tax advantage in relation to raising equity capital, after a certain point this advantage is entirely offset. More borrowing can be beneficial up to a point, to the extent that this is feasible for the firm (e.g., businesses with high value real estate, equipment, and transport vehicles find it easier to borrow than businesses that do not have sufficient fixed assets to place as collateral against loans).

However, as the firm constitutes a network of relationships, the decision to raise new capital by selling debt (borrowing) or selling equity (inviting more co-owners) is determined by the individual priorities of the firm's management that makes funding decisions, **asymmetric information**, and capital market dynamics. Starting with the first component, namely management priorities, the financing decision determines control of the firm, as well as of its resources, procedures, and orientation. Thus, changes in financing decisions involving fresh borrowing or co-owners imply changes in power relations and positions of authority for some individuals who will therefore risk losing both tangible and intangible benefits related to their current positions (e.g., prestige and/or social network). For this reason, management tends to prefer financing new investment through own-capital reserves and, as a second option, external funding, because in loan financing intervention of suppliers of finance is limited to the terms and maturity period of the loan contract. In contrast, the third option of financing investments through share capital increases, suppliers of finance stay with the business and maintain control of the company's resources potentially "forever".[5]

> The financing decision determines control of the firm, as well as of its resources, procedures, and orientation.

It should also be noted that organization of production in the company that seeks financing is better known to company insiders than to company outsiders. This means increased uncertainty for suppliers of capital (own or external) and correspondingly lower funding and higher required return. Thus, the funding decision depends on the distribution of information between suppliers of capital and recipients of capital.[6] Finally, the choice of financing between own and external funds has also to do with capital market dynamics.[7] Businesses tend to prefer the form of finance that is more favorable depending on market dynamics. When the stock market is on the rise and the sentiment is optimistic, investors tend to position themselves more easily in businesses, thus rendering investment financing through share capital increase the most preferable option. Regardless of capital market dynamics, however, the fact is that companies are increasingly relying on borrowing over the past few decades, although only a few of them systematically choose to do so.[8]

In general, the analysis presented here shows that financing decisions, dynamics, and diversity from business to business mainly depend on:

1   The specific characteristics of each company in terms of management and structure of assets. For example, airlines have high-value fixed assets, thus ending up being heavily in debt, with aircraft installment payments extending over decades. In general, companies in the same industry tend to have similar capital structure choices.
2   Taxation, which makes certain forms of financing more attractive than others.
3   The regulatory framework on corporate governance in general and disclosure in particular, as it is critical for the apparent asymmetry of information and decision-making in many types of businesses, as well as in representation and power relations between capital owners and firm management.
4   Capital market dynamics, which highlight the financing choice that involves the lowest cost of capital.

Another key financial management choice and, by implication, investment valuation decision is the **distribution of corporate profits**. The part of the profits of a corporation that is distributed to shareholders is called **dividend**. If the profits of a business are not distributed to shareholders but are retained for generating reserves to finance future investments, then the debt burden of the company, as well as the need to seek new financing sources is being reduced. Thus, the decision of distributing corporate profits is linked to the financing decision and the decision to materialize investment projects, linking distribution of profit to firm value. In this case, another oxymoron occurs: the firm could determine its value by altering the distribution of dividends instead of, for example, enhancing efficiency of operations. Although increasing firm value through changes in dividend policy is not straightforward in practice, empirical evidence supports the hypothesis that the decision of distribution of profits to investors is affected by capital market dynamics, availability of information to investors, as well as company-specific characteristics such as profitability, size, and liquidity.[9]

RISK AND OTHER DETERMINANTS OF RETURN

In making an investment or extending a loan, the supplier of capital expects in the future a higher amount than the principal invested or lent at present. This expectation affects the amount of money to be provided and determined by four main factors as follows:

Risk

The basic premise of financial theory is that individuals make financial decisions based on two criteria, **risk** and **expected return**. A higher return is expected from investments

A higher return is expected from investments that involve higher risk, because they expose the investor to a wider range of probable outcomes about the future value of the capital invested.

that involve higher risk, because they expose the investor to a wider range of probable outcomes about the future value of the capital invested. Both risk and expected return are determined based on the probability and the monetary value associated with each possible outcome of a specific investment. Box A.2 gives a simple example of financial theory assumptions regarding investment decisions based on expected return and risk.

Box A.2 Expected return and risk in investments

Return is calculated as a percentage change in investment value. For example, purchasing a plot of land at €48,000 today and selling it a year later at €54,000, return is 12.5% (€6,000).

If the future value of the investment is uncertain, valuation incorporates probability estimates.

Scenario 1: The land will be worth €52,000 with a probability of 50% and €56,000 with a probability of 50%.

Scenario 2: The land will be worth €48,000 with a probability of 50% and €60,000 with a probability of 50%.

The two scenarios have the same expected return (12.5%), but different risk. It is assumed that most investors would prefer the first scenario over the second.

It is important to emphasize that both risk and expected return refer to the future, reflecting investors' perceptions about something that has not yet been realized and, therefore, are inevitably subjective. In fact, the subjective nature of risk and expected return are intensified by the uniqueness of individual financial phenomena, which may hinder perception of potential outcomes in the form of frequencies. In more general terms, recurrence of a natural phenomenon implies that probability of occurrence may be expressed as frequency, as opposed to unique social phenomena, such as an economic crisis, formation of a hung parliament, a referendum on the autonomy of a region, or adoption of a certain currency. In addition, the way each investor evaluates decisions in the return-risk context is inevitably distinct and contingent on the investor's personal attitudes towards risk or, simply put, how much risk the investor is willing to take.

The level of return required as compensation for taking risk depends on the investor's degree of risk aversion. Buying a property of questionable value, participating in a business with unknown prospects or granting a loan to a borrower with poor credit history, are realized only with expectation of higher return compared to other, safer investment options. The expectation of higher returns in the future is the flip side of paying a lower amount for an investment at present. Assume, for example, payment of €1,000 (on a deposit, loan, or investment) today with the understanding of receiving with certainty €1,050 in the future. If the investor has less confidence about the prospect of getting their money back, the investor would require €1,200 in a year's time. Correspondingly, for €1,000 to be received a year from today, the investor would be willing to pay €950 if the investor were confident that the €1,000 would be paid back next year. However, if the investor has less confidence about repayment of €1,000 in a year, the investor would be willing to pay only €800 today.

Risk may originate from many sources and there are several ways of classifying it.[10] In the case of businesses, risk may be distinguished into **entrepreneurial** and **financial**. Entrepreneurial risk is related to uncertainty about efficient operation of the firm and its ability to meet customer demand. Financial risk is related to the probability of failure to meet payment obligations. Another type of risk, namely **credit risk**, is directly related to financial risk. Credit risk is associated with the probability of failure to pay back. This type of risk relates to firms in two ways, as it denotes both failure of the firm to collect revenues when selling products on credit and failure of the firm to repay a bank loan. In the case of companies that are directly exposed to the global economic environment, an additional category of risk is **foreign exchange risk**, which stems from changes in the exchange rate. For example, an exporting company faces foreign exchange risk in terms of the sales revenue collected in the event that the exchange rate between the domestic currency and the currency of the country in which sells its products changes. Similarly, a Japanese bank that lends the Norwegian government is exposed to the changes in the exchange rate between the Norwegian Krone and the Japanese Yen, which affects the value of both interest payments and the principal that will be paid back. In this case, the Japanese bank is confronted by another type of risk, namely **interest rate risk**: daily changes in the interest rate required in the market to lend the Norwegian government, changes the value of the Norwegian government's promise to repay its creditors, thus, affecting the value of assets of the Japanese bank. Especially with regard to sovereign lending and the decision to invest in a national capital market, a special category of risk is the **political risk**, which relates to political stability that, in turn, is linked to the stability of the regulatory framework for economic activity and general stability of social and economic life in a certain country (**country risk**).

The main **risk management** technique in investment analysis, especially in the case of stocks and bonds, is **diversification**: through investing in different assets (various shares, bonds, real estate, etc.), the range of fluctuations in the value of the total amount invested becomes significantly narrower. The collection of assets in which capital has been invested is called a **portfolio**. Effective portfolio management meets the needs of the investor (rather than those of the portfolio manager), which tend to be defined in the risk-return context.

In essence, risk is investors' exposure to change, be that change in the economic environment, information, or available options. Change is, of course, inevitable. Thus, risk occurs with certainty and, therefore, the management of risk boils down to the management of change. The challenge for investors is to manage risk in a way that would be beneficial for them (Box A.3).

> Risk is investors' exposure to change. Thus, risk occurs with certainty and, therefore, the management of risk boils down to the management of change.

Box A.3 Uncertainty and change

Change of some kind is prerequisite to the existence of uncertainty; in an absolutely unchanging world the future would be accurately foreknown, since it would be exactly like the past. Change in some sense is a condition of the existence of any problem whatever in connection with life or conduct, and is the actual condition of most of the problems of pure thought, since these are after all more or less related to practical requirements. We live in a world full of contradiction and paradox, a fact of which perhaps the most fundamental illustration is this: that the existence of a problem of knowledge depends on the future being different from the past, while the possibility of the solution of the problem depends on the future being like the past.

(Knight, 1921: 313)

Inflation

One euro today will probably not have the same purchasing power in a year's time, primarily because the prices of goods and services tend to increase over time. There are many reasons for this, including increases in prices of raw materials and the rewards to labor and capital used in production, as well as increases in demand (accompanied by smaller increases in production) in an economy that experiences growth of output, income, and aggregate demand for goods and services. Especially in the event that price increases are unanticipated or prices rise more than expected, inflation benefits borrowers and harms lenders, because any amounts repaid in the future have lower purchasing power. Uncertainty about the future price level constitutes an additional source of financial risk and, as such, it tends to increase the required return on an investment. This means that suppliers of capital (investors, lenders, depositors) granting one euro expect to get back more than one euro in the future, and that extra amount is part of the required return on the investment. Conversely, the higher the inflation rate the lower the amount investors would give up today for a given (fixed) promise of payment in the future.

The negative effects of inflation on economic activity – mainly through the resulting uncertainty and difficulty in planning – is one of the reasons why price stability consti tutes the mandate of European Central Bank, which safeguards that eurozone inflation is contained up to 2% per annum. At the other extreme, systematic reduction of prices (**deflation**) is not a good sign for the outlook of economic activity. For example, in cases of economic crisis, deflation is the sign of an economy experiencing ongoing decline in income and, consequently, lower aggregate demand leading to falling prices.

Liquidity

Liquidity denotes convertibility of an asset into cash, but also ability to meet one's short-term financial obligations. When an investor gives up one euro, lending, depositing, or investing it, the investor is deprived of liquidity. Loss of liquidity is one explanation behind demanding to be rewarded through interest for lending an amount of money. In this sense, the higher the estimated loss of liquidity, the greater the compensation required. If a property and a share have the same risk according to the investor's estimate, the required rate of return in the case of the share will be lower than the required rate of return in the case of property, because the latter exhibits greater difficulty in being converted into cash. If the investor urgently needs the amount invested, it is harder to sell a building than a stock that trades in an organized stock market.

Opportunity cost

Opportunity cost is probably the most important component of expected return. Placing a certain amount of capital in a certain type of investment precludes any other investment possibilities. For example, an investor wishing to invest €100,000 could buy an apartment. Alternatively, the investor could buy shares in the stock market, government bonds, or pay for a postgraduate Business Administration degree from a leading university. Choosing to buy property, the opportunity cost of the investment is the value of the best foregone alternative. Comparison between different options implies comparable frameworks for risk, liquidity, and inflation (the other interest rate determinants). For example, the opportunity cost of purchasing a €10 lottery ticket cannot be a €10 bank deposit, as the two options have completely different risk and liquidity characteristics (we can withdraw our money from the bank, but we cannot just as easily sell a lottery ticket at the price we bought it).

Funding costs are important to both suppliers and recipients of capital. On the one hand, recipients of capital have an interest in demonstrating that cost of capital increases are insignificant, so that they can finance their activities in favorable terms. On the other hand, suppliers of capital have an interest in demonstrating that cost of capital increases are quite significant in order to justify higher required returns. Thus, the seller of a piece of property has all the reasons to argue that future inflation will be low, property will be easy to sell, and fluctuations in property value will be limited. Thus, the required rate of return for investors should be low, while the present value of rentals and the price of the property should be high. In contrast, the buyer of the property has all the reasons to argue that rentals are uncertain, inflation is expected to be high, and the resale potential of the property is limited. Based on these arguments, the prospective buyer will try to claim a higher rate of return and a lower price for the property. Similar reasoning applies to sovereign debt. The government has an interest in convincing its creditors that interest payments and repayment of the principal borrowed through the issue of bonds are assured, that inflation will be low and that demand for government bonds will remain robust, thus ensuring a high degree of liquidity for sovereign debt in the secondary market. Thus, the rate of return required by lenders would be low and the value of the capital they will be willing to provide would be high. In other words, the interest rate at which lenders would be willing to lend the government would be low.

MARKET EFFICIENCY

The analysis of security valuation is based on the hypothesis of efficient markets. The capital market is considered to be efficient if security prices reflect all available

information and opinion on the value of securities. Security prices reflect relevant information through the **price mechanism**.
A security transaction carried out at price X
integrates all available information on the part
of the seller, including the seller's opinion that
the value of the security is lower than or equal
to X, as well as all available information on the
part of the buyer, including the buyer's opinion that the value of the security is equal to or

> The capital market is considered to be efficient if security prices reflect all available information and opinion on the value of securities. Security prices reflect relevant information through the price mechanism. If security prices embody all relevant information, seeking information outside prices makes no sense.

higher than X. The fact that all available information is (supposedly) incorporated in
security prices is of utmost importance for portfolio management and articulation
of investment options. If security prices embody all relevant information, seeking
information outside prices makes no sense, meaning that it is impossible to attain
profits beyond the "normal" level dictated by a capital market equilibrium model.

Market efficiency comes in three forms.
In **weak-form efficiency**, prices incorporate
all information available in historical security
prices. This means that any information or
assessment that could be extracted from statistical processing of past prices has already
emerged and is already embodied in security
prices. If the market is weak-form efficient,
technical analysis, which attempts to identify
patterns of systematic price changes in order to

> Technical analysis attempts to identify patterns of systematic price changes in order to arrive at profitable trading rules and anticipate price changes. Fundamental analysis estimates the value of the firm based on publicly available information, such as announcements about company financial statements, the annual report, etc.

arrive at profitable trading rules and anticipate price changes, is not useful. In **semi-
strong form efficiency**, prices incorporate not only the information contained
in historical prices, but also all publicly available information on a security, such as
announcements about company financial statements, the annual report, etc. Thus, if
the market is semi-strong form efficient, it is impossible to earn supra-normal profits
(profits higher than expected) through **fundamental analysis**, which estimates the
value of a firm based on publicly available information. Finally, in **strong-form efficiency** prices incorporate not only information contained in historical prices and
published financial statements, but also private information held by "insiders" of the
company that has issued the security. In strong-form of efficiency, even information
held by the Chief Executive Officer of the company is somehow known to the public
and is already embodied into security prices. Thus, supra-normal profits cannot be
realized even if inside information is possessed. As this form of efficiency is difficult to
apply in practice, trading based on inside information is illegal for companies whose
shares are listed on the stock exchange.

PORTFOLIO MANAGEMENT

As stated earlier, the portfolio is a set of securities comprising investments in money
and capital markets. **Portfolio theory** denotes a set of proposals that determine the

composition of portfolios, based on assumptions about the operation of markets and the preferences of investors.[11] One of the cornerstones of modern financial theory, portfolio analysis was the first step in the process of "secession" of finance from fundamental analysis.[12] Portfolio theory may also be seen as the terrain where economics (science) meets finance (practice). The professional field of risk management and the scientific field of portfolio theory evolve together, with science supplying scientists and methods of risk management to the market and the market posing some of the research questions for science and, occasionally, sponsoring scientific research.

The main portfolio property is that the total risk exposure of investors is different than the sum of the risks of individual components of the portfolio. Therefore, with appropriate construction, the portfolio can attain lower risk for a given level of expected return. The portfolio construction problem is associated with the choice of weights of the investor's wealth to be placed in each security available for investment.

The portfolio construction problem is associated with the choice of weights of the investor's wealth to be placed in each security available for investment. Portfolio construction exploits the correlation of security returns in order to achieve the best possible relationship between expected return and risk (see Box A.4 on the importance of correlation in portfolio management). This practice is called **portfolio diversification**.

Box A.4 The correlation of security returns

Like most economic quantities, the returns of securities tend to move up and down together. This correlation is not perfect: individual securities and entire industries have at times moved against the general flow of prosperity. On the whole, however, economic good and ill tend to spread, causing periods of generally high or generally low economic activity.

If security returns were not correlated, diversification could eliminate risk. It would like flipping a large number of coins: we cannot predict with confidence the outcome of a single flip; but if a great many coins are flipped we can be virtually sure that heads will appear on approximately one-half of them. Such cancelling out of chance events provides stability to the disbursements of insurance companies. Correlations among security returns, however, prevent a similar cancelling out of highs and lows within the security market. It is somewhat as if 100 coins, about to be flipped, agreed among themselves to fall, heads or tails, exactly as the first coin falls. In this case there is perfect correlation among outcomes. The average outcome of the 100 flips is no more certain than the outcome of a single flip. If correlation among security returns were "perfect" – if returns on all securities moved up and down together in perfect unison – diversification could do nothing to eliminate risk. The fact that security returns are highly correlated but not perfectly correlated implies that diversification can reduce risk but not eliminate it.

(Markowitz, 1959: 5)

Efficient portfolios

Portfolios that attain the best possible return for a given level of risk are called **efficient portfolios**. All efficient portfolios lie on a curve called **efficient portfolio frontier** (Figure A.1).

If the assumptions of portfolio theory hold, the only "meaningful" portfolios are those lying on the efficient frontier.[13] Portfolios that lie to the left of the curve are not feasible given the securities that are available in the market. Portfolios that lie to the right of the curve are inferior, as they are dominated by portfolios that involve superior risk-return combinations that lie on the efficient frontier. All efficient portfolios are equivalent in terms of risk and return. At this point, it is worth stressing the difference between portfolio efficiency and market efficiency. Efficient portfolios offer investors an optimal risk-return combination, while market efficiency denotes that prices of securities incorporate all available information and opinion that affect security prices.

In fact, as it often happens with scientific theory, portfolio reality is somewhat different than assumed in portfolio theory. Not all investors are risk averse, there are transaction costs, trading of securities is not continuous, and information available to investors is not evenly distributed. In addition, stocks are rarely if ever

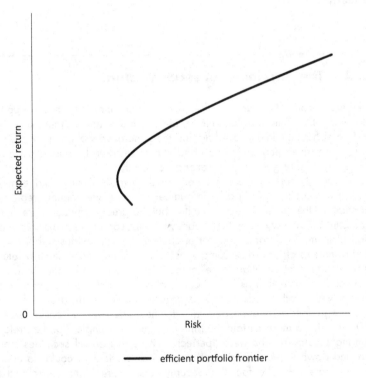

Figure A.1 The efficient portfolio frontier

perfectly negatively correlated. Most of the times the correlation of returns of two shares trading in the same stock exchange is higher than +0.3. This is attributable to the fact that all shares are exposed to pretty much the same macroeconomic and capital market dynamics. Also, the benefits of diversification are exhausted with a relatively small number of securities (less than 30). Once including this relatively small number of securities in the portfolio, reduction in the volatility of returns from adding more securities is negligible, taking into account respective transaction costs and portfolio management costs associated with construction of the portfolio.

Nevertheless, portfolio theory is widely used, which implies that in practice it appears to "work" quite well. The main reason for this is that portfolio theory gives specific, quantitative answers to portfolio management questions. Moreover, the study of the management of risk, which is essentially an offshoot of portfolio theory, has developed immensely, influencing both the content and the dynamics of the science of economics.

> Portfolio theory is widely used, which implies that in practice it appears to "work" quite well. The main reason for this is that portfolio theory gives specific, quantitative answers to portfolio management questions.

Introducing a risk-free asset

Portfolio analysis becomes more complete if an asset that yields a specific level of return with certainty is included in the portfolio of risky assets. Such an asset could be, for example, an interest-bearing Treasury bill or a Certificate of Deposit. In the light of the experience of the eurozone sovereign debt crisis in the late 2000s, there are no completely risk-free securities. Thus, more generally, the risk-free asset could be an asset that bears minimum risk in a specific capital market. A further assumption in this analysis is that the borrowing rate is equal to the lending rate. Although quite simplistic, this assumption does not alter generalizability of results and simplifies calculations.

The introduction of a risk-free asset changes optimal investment choices, which are now depicted by the **capital market line**, the line that crosses the y-axis at the risk-free rate r_f and is tangent to the efficient frontier (Figure A.2). The point of tangency of the capital market and the efficient frontier is the **market portfolio** (point M). The market portfolio includes all risky assets that trade in the capital market. It, therefore, extends beyond the boundaries of the stock market. In reality, however, the market portfolio does not exist. There is no way for an investor to construct a portfolio that includes all capital goods in the economy. Thus, to the extent that the capital market is efficient, the market portfolio is proxied by buying and including in a portfolio all the shares that trade in the stock market.

In this context, portfolio choice depends on investor preferences. The specific preferences of each investor determine the portfolio (point of the capital market line) that suits them best. The practical importance of the capital market line is enormous. The capital market line lies to the left of all points of the efficient frontier

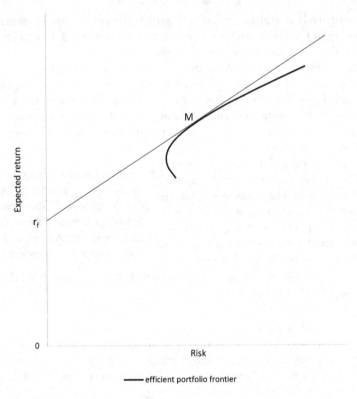

Figure A.2 The capital market line

with the exception of the point of tangency, which represents the market portfolio. Given that a line can be defined by the coordinates of two points it goes through, the capital market line is fully defined by the risk-free asset and the market portfolio. Each point (portfolio) on the capital market line can be defined as a linear combination of the risk-free asset and the market portfolio. In investment terms, a linear combination implies investing a proportion w in the market portfolio and $1 - w$ in the risk-free asset. The points on the capital market line that are located to the left of the market portfolio have $w < 1$. The further to the left in the capital market line the portfolio, the greater the proportion of the risk-free asset. Correspondingly, the further to the right of the capital market line, the greater the proportion of the market portfolio. The points on the capital market line that lie to the right of the market portfolio imply a negative position in the risk-free asset. In this case, the investor borrows in order to invest more than 100% of their total wealth in the market portfolio ($w > 1$).

The fact that the capital market line lies to the left of the efficient frontier means that portfolios that lie on the capital market line are preferable to all other portfolios on the efficient frontier, because they involve higher expected return for a given level of risk (or, to put it differently, they involve lower risk for a given level of expected return). In this line of reasoning, the importance of portfolio management by professionals is limited. If all this is true, portfolio managers cannot "beat" a simple portfolio with two components: the market portfolio and the risk-free asset. Any investor may construct their own portfolio, selecting a proportion w to invest in the risk-free asset, and the remaining amount in the market portfolio.[14] This presupposes that the basic assumptions of portfolio theory apply, particularly the efficient markets hypothesis. However, portfolio managers and speculators do have a role to play in the event that the market is not efficient or in order to contribute to required correction to help the market remain efficient. Moreover, even in the context of market efficiency, portfolio managers can help identify the market portfolio and risk-free asset combination that suits the preferences of each different investor.

> Portfolios that lie on the capital market line are preferable to all other portfolios on the efficient frontier, because they involve higher expected return for a given level of risk.

MONEY AND CREDIT

Money is a **promise to pay** and, therefore, it is based on credit (trust) between individuals and organizations that articulate and accept promises to pay. A deposit in a bank account is also money and constitutes a promise on the part of the bank to pay the amount in the account to the depositor. A loan – which creates a deposit in the borrower's bank account – is a promise to pay the lender. A deposit of a commercial bank to the central bank is a promise of the central bank to pay the amount of the deposit to the commercial bank. A paper note is a promise of the central banker to pay the bearer an amount equal to that stated on the paper note. The resources of a central bank usually include foreign exchange, bonds, gold, bills, and other promises to pay. As the central bank's resources include promises to pay of other economic agents, such the government, the flow of promises is circular, further stressing the emergence of money through social agreements, rather than "objective" value. Thus, it turns out that the possibility of the central bank to create money is limited: the value of assets – government bonds and bills, among others – decreases as the state cannot collect taxes to meet its obligations and its ability to collect taxes depends on the performance of the business sector and the public sector of the real economy.

> Money is a promise to pay and, therefore, it is based on credit (trust) between individuals and organizations that articulate and accept promises to pay.

Because money is based on a set of promises, it is a social institution that denotes the network of behaviors, rules, and individuals who make and receive promises to pay. Understanding money means understanding reliability. In turn, reliability is a concept with varying content from place to place, from season to season, from society to society. In the case of a promise to pay, reliability implies **creditworthiness**, which in turn determines the amount of money in circulation in the economy, thereby affecting the course of an economy towards growth and prosperity. For example, decline in the credibility of a government to fulfill its own payment promises makes investors in capital markets reluctant to lend it, leading to intergovernmental or supranational support mechanisms that provide finance at more favorable interest rates, but imposing conditions on the structure of the economy. Being based on credit (trust), money serves as a **medium of exchange**, a **store of value**, and a **measure of value** or unit of accounting (Figure A.3).

As a medium of exchange, money is the key means for the exchange of goods: in a grocery store, we give up money to get food in return, we give money to the doctors in exchange for their medical services, we give up money in the jewelry shop to buy a piece of jewelry, etc. If money were not a medium of exchange, to buy a piece of jewelry, we would have to exchange another product with the jeweler: for example, a writer would offer the jeweler copies of his new book, hoping that these would be useful reads for the jeweler or to other customers of the jeweler. Clearly, this mode of exchange – called **barter** or **barter economy** – is quite restrictive for trade and, therefore, production and economic development. In the context of exchange, money also functions as a means of measuring value: we say that a piece of jewelry is worth €150, a doctor's diagnosis €50, a chicken roll €12. Measurement of value is essential for evaluation of a purchase or sale, an investment, or a political decision. The introduction of money as a commonly accepted measure of value immensely facilitates comparison between alternatives and, therefore, it constitutes a very important determinant of economic growth and development.[15] Money functions as a medium of exchange and measure of value, because it is also a means of storing value: a loaf of bread that costs €1 today will not have the same value in a week's time. By contrast, one euro will still buy the same quantity bread in a week's time, provided that the price of bread remains stable: inflation restricts the function of money as a store of value.

In financial theory, in addition to coins and paper notes, any security generated with the prospect of being converted into money within one year, such as demand deposits, three-month time deposits, Treasury bills, etc. is considered to be **money**.

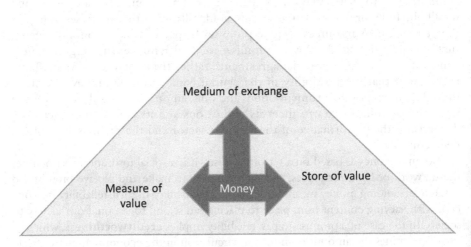

Figure A.3 The functions of money

In contrast, **capital** is defined as any security that is generated with the prospect of being converted into money in a period longer than a year, such as shares, bonds, etc.

Both money and capital are exchanged in respective **money and capital markets**. They include, but are not limited to, bank lending and stock exchanges. In general, money and capital markets are divided in primary markets, where transactions between suppliers and recipients of finance are conducted, and secondary markets, where transactions between investors are conducted. Money and capital markets have the basic characteristics of any market, namely they are exchange networks defined by individuals, they have written and unwritten rules, procedures, and infrastructure. In the stock market, for example, securities owned by listed companies are being exchanged. In fact, markets do not always have a physical presence or specific geographical location, but may be electronic networks, as in the case of foreign exchange markets.

> Any security generated with the prospect of being converted into money within one year, such as demand deposits, three-month time deposits, Treasury bills, etc. are considered to be money.

> Money and capital markets are exchange networks defined by individuals, they have written and unwritten rules, procedures, and infrastructure.

BANKS AND OTHER FINANCIAL COMPANIES

Banks are key mechanisms in the creation and circulation of money. They are companies that mainly accept deposits, grant loans, and offer payment services.[16] Interest payments constitute both a source of revenue from granting loans, as well as an expense when paid on deposits. Obviously, for a bank to be profitable, the interest rate paid on deposits must be lower than the interest rate charged on loans.

In the process of lending, banks seek to increase their interest revenue by lowering the borrowers' default risk (known as credit risk), minimize the cost of services provided, ensure convertibility of receivables into cash in order to deal with emergencies, and/or seize opportunities (government bonds are easily converted to cash, while mortgages are harder to sell). Depositors are in fact lenders of the bank supplying cash in anticipation of receiving interest income. As lenders, depositors have similar priorities, namely to increase their income from interest, to minimize the costs associated with ownership of a deposit (such as bank commissions), and be sure that the bank will safeguard their deposits and will allow them to withdraw their money promptly whenever they need it. Correspondingly, borrowers need funding for a specific period of time that fits their purposes and seek to incur as little interest as possible.

Outside banks, financial companies include a wide range of non-depository organizations, such as **mutual funds**, **leasing companies**, **insurance companies**, **pension funds**, etc. Frequently, the boundaries between banks and non-depository organizations are indistinguishable, with different types of intermediation companies belonging to the same group of companies. In addition, the emergence of **financial**

technology companies (fintech), which offer banking, investment, and insurance services over the internet, redefines the traditional classification of financial services. The range of services provided by financial companies is very broad and its full description goes beyond the scope of this appendix.

Banks and other financial companies form a "promise to pay" network, which is necessary for the daily operation of both the economy as a whole and each economic unit separately. The role of banks in the economy is neither static nor given. It has a content and significance that are determined by the broader economic and political conditions of a specific place and time period. This underlines, among other things, the importance of the regulatory framework of the financial system, which is a function of specific choices regarding paths to economic growth or major economic failures, such as the recent global crisis, but determines the dynamics of the financial system.

The importance of banks in the economy

Because deposits are promises to pay on the part of the bank to depositors and loans are promises to pay on the part of borrowers to banks, the banks are central nodes in the grid of promises to pay that determine money and capital flows in the economy (Figure A.4).

Banks are key mechanisms of money creation in modern economies through the granting of loans.[17] Granting a loan does not imply a reduction of the savings of one depositor (in order to grant the loan to another depositor). Granting a loan, the bank creates a deposit for the borrower at the same time. Thus, the bank raises income from promises to (re)pay loans, in order to be able to meet the requirements of its depositors and other lenders. This process is particularly challenging because: a) the size of loans tends to be different from the size of savings (savers usually deposit small amounts, compared to the amounts needed in the case or business loans or mortgages); b) the maturity of the loans tends to be different than the maturity of deposits (some types of loans are granted for many years, while deposits can be withdrawn from the bank in a much shorter time period); c) the default risk on loans is far greater than that incurred by depositors in the case of a bank account.

> Banks are key mechanisms of money creation in modern economies through the granting of loans.

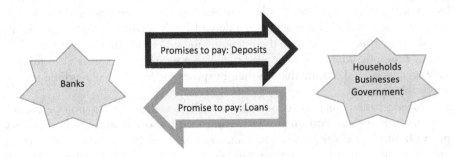

Figure A.4 Banks and promises to pay

As hubs of credit, banks address such challenges more effectively compared to individual creditors. In fact, this is their greatest contribution to the economy. Bank lending is not the only road; there are also lending agreements between individuals and legal entities outside the banking system. However, in these cases of lending, inherent problems associated with credit are clearly bigger. If one wishes to borrow an amount of money from a fellow citizen, one needs to search much more intensely (compared to borrowing from a bank) in order to find someone who would have the capital needed, would be willing to wait to be repaid for as long as needed until cash flows are accrued to the borrower, and would be willing to take the risk implied by the uncertainty of the borrower's future income and, consequently, the borrower's ability to repay. Also, the borrower's personal financial situation and solvency would be rather unknown to an individual creditor, thus exacerbating problems of asymmetric information and adverse selection. Addressing all these difficulties would require extremely high transaction costs, which would be difficult for an individual creditor to take on. The result would be much less credit available in the economy and on much worse terms. Thus, eventually economic activity would be severely restricted.

These needs are satisfied through operation of commercial banks: they have the resources, the knowledge, the regulatory framework, and above all the public confidence needed to manage financial liabilities and receivables with different maturity, size, and risk, to control liquidity in the real economy and see that money and capital are allocated to efficient uses. This feature enables depositors to use banks as both property custodian mechanisms and a way to earn interest income. It also gives borrowers access to capital needed to set up and pursue economic activities.

All this implies that banks play a key role in the operation of modern economies. Of course, the fact that banks are necessary does not guarantee their sound operation. Financial stability of the economy and the contribution of capital markets to economic development constitute, in a way, public goods, and, as mentioned in the first chapter of this book, markets occasionally fail to produce public goods in sufficient quantities. Thus, both the regulatory framework and the structure of the banking sector need to be designed in such a way to minimize systemic failure, such as the global financial crisis of the late 2000s, and safeguard the role of banks in the process of economic development.

The central bank

Central banks are financial organizations that are responsible for the conduct of monetary policy in a certain country or in a group of countries. Monetary policy determines the level of the supply of money in the economy.

> Central banks are financial organizations that are responsible for the conduct of monetary policy in a certain country or in a group of countries.

Thus, the central bank issues coins and paper notes, and safeguards liquidity in the commercial banking sector, determining the ability of commercial banks to provide credit to the real economy. This role is particularly important in times of crisis, where the central bank is the **lender of the last resort** for commercial banks. In addition, the central bank is the bank of the state, keeping all bank accounts of the government, as well as foreign exchange and gold reserves.

In particular, **monetary policy** is mainly pursued through determination of the interest rate at which the central bank lends commercial banks. This interest rate in turn determines the interest rate at which commercial banks supply finance to the economy and, consequently, the money supply.[18] In addition, the central bank regulates the money supply through purchases and sales of government securities in the money and capital markets. Selling government securities, the central bank draws cash from the market, restricting the supply of money (contractionary monetary policy). Conversely, buying government securities, the central bank injects liquidity in the market, increasing the money supply (expansionary monetary policy).

Monetary policy goals include attainment of stability of the average general price level. Particularly in the eurozone, the mandate of the European Central Bank (ECB) is to maintain an average level of inflation in the eurozone economies that does not exceed 2% per annum. **Price stability** protects incomes from a reduction in purchasing power induced by unanticipated inflation and contributes to economic stability in general. In addition, central banks pursue exchange rate stability, protecting the economy from wide fluctuations in the exchange rate of the local currency in international foreign exchange markets. Central bank goals are part of the fundamental goal of any economic policy, which is economic development. In addition to economic growth, economic development is about overall improvements in the standards of living in the economy. The pursuit of monetary stability by the central bank is ultimately justified solely to the extent that it supports economic development.

Although central banks pursue policies that affect directly the well-being of all citizens in a country, central bankers are largely independent of governments. For example, in the case of the eurozone, the president of the ECB is appointed by the European Council for a seven-year term, following consultation with the Council of Finance Ministers (ECOFIN) and the European Parliament. The term and appointment of the president are not affected by European elections or national elections. Central bank **independence** safeguards the stability of monetary policy, but also raises a question about the democratic legitimacy of monetary policy. Elections enable citizens to vote the government out if they are not satisfied with the specific fiscal policy pursued (taxes, salaries, pensions). In the case of the ECB, European citizens do not have this opportunity in the event that they are not satisfied with liquidity in the market, the level prices, or the exchange rate. Essentially, the architecture of monetary policy institutions is the outcome of weighing the need for monetary stability against the need for monetary policy accountability to affected citizens.

CAPITAL AND MONEY MARKET FAILURE

The economic, social, and political conditions that shape the financial system affect the overall assessment of the role of banks in welfare, as well as the purpose and orientation of the regulatory framework of money and capital markets in general and bank regulation in particular. The financial system is a resource allocation mechanism and, consequently, it constitutes an orientation mechanism for production and consumption. A business that gets a loan is responsible for allocating the funds it borrowed to the production of output. Similarly, a government that sells bonds to commercial banks is responsible for allocating funds to the provision of public goods, such as national defense and public education, as needed.

> The financial system is a resource allocation mechanism and, consequently, it constitutes an orientation mechanism for production and consumption.

Thus, evaluation of capital and money markets is based on their impact on the allocation of resources to production and, ultimately, to welfare. Evaluation of the financial system is political because welfare analysis is political:

> Capital markets often fail, in the sense that their outcomes do not augment the well-being of all members of society.

the contribution of money and capital markets to welfare is directly dependent upon the meaning assigned to welfare. For example, there is a plethora of studies ascertaining that development of organized capital contributes to boosting global economic growth, as access to money and capital is essential for expansion of production.[19] In contrast, growth and deregulation of the financial sector determine the transformation of global capitalism towards neoliberalism and are considered key factors underlying the global financial crisis of the late 2000s.[20] Other research concludes that the impact of organized capital markets on welfare is determined by the quality of local institutions, productivity, the degree of financial sector expansion, and the local level of economic growth, thus varying widely from one area to another.[21,22] In practice, capital markets often fail, in the sense that their outcomes do not augment the well-being of all members of society. The global financial crisis of the late 2000s and the ensuing sovereign debt crisis in the eurozone constitute a typical example in this regard.

As stated earlier, the financial system is a grid of promises to pay. Thus, a financial crisis comes forth when public confidence that payments will materialize collapses. A crisis is characterized by lack of trust that the bank will repay deposits on demand, that borrowers will pay off their debts promptly, that insurance companies will pay pensions as promised to those insured, or that businesses will pay their creditors promptly. Ultimately, the public ceases to trust that the state will be capable of offering all the capital required to meet a significant proportion of the promises to pay delivered by banks and businesses. Sometimes, as in the case of the Greek public debt crisis, the direction of escalation of a crisis is reversed. Lack of trust that the government is capable of fulfilling its own promises to pay precedes and causes a crisis, leading to collapse in confidence that banks, businesses, or individuals will be capable of meeting their obligations.[23] Since money is primarily a promise to pay, collapse of trust in materializing promises means that money ceases to perform its basic functions as a store of value, measure of value, and medium of exchange. This way, a financial crisis becomes a fully blown economic crisis, transforming the structure and dynamics of the real economy.

Causes of confidence are highly complex, vary from economy to economy and from one point in time to another, just like capitalism takes different forms in different economies and eras.[24] However, with regard to the financial crisis of the late 2000s, the structure of credit escaped the required dynamics and went beyond the control of the real economy. The responsibility for this development lies primarily with the companies that are responsible for the flow of money into the economy (the central bank and commercial banks), the supervisory and regulatory authorities (the role of the central bank is very important in this case too), political institutions that determine the regulatory framework of the financial system, and, ultimately, all investors, businesses, and citizens, whose financial choices may reproduce or transform the economy.

NOTES

1   Jensen and Meckling (1976).

2   Own capital denotes capital contributed by the owners of the firm. External capital is capital raised from the lenders of the firm. The sum of own and external capital gives total capital of the firm.

3   See Andrikopoulos (2015).

4   Chung et al. (2013).

5   See Myers and Majluf (1984) and Abel (2018).

6   Myers and Majluf (1984).

7   Baker and Wurgler (2002).

8   Graham et al. (2015), DeAngelo and Roll (2015).

9   See, for example, Baker and Wurgler (2004), DeAngelo et al. (2006), Brav et al. (2005), Baker et al. (2016).

10   On the different types of risk, see Brealey, Myers, and Allen (2014).

11   For portfolio theory and investment analysis, see Elton et al. (2014).

12   Portfolio theory is based on the work of Markowitz (1952, 1959).

13   The main assumptions of portfolio theory are:

 ♦ Investors make decisions solely on the basis of two criteria: expected return and risk.

 ♦ Investors undertake higher risk if higher return is expected.

 ♦ Security returns are fully described by the expected value and the standard deviations of returns.

 ♦ The standard deviation of returns reflects the risk borne by investors.

 ♦ Investors are well informed and able to make all the necessary calculations for the construction of their portfolios.

 ♦ There are no transaction costs.

 ♦ Investors can be long or short on a security. A long position usually denotes that the investor is a security owner or depositor. A short position denotes that the investor is a borrower. A long position implies that the investor has bought a security, while a short position denotes that the investor has borrowed a security to sell it and buy it back after a few days to return it to its owner (short sale). In short sales, the investor expects to repurchase the security at a lower price than originally sold at.

14   Investing in the market portfolio is fairly straightforward for individual investors, as most banks offer investment products that track stock market indexes.

15   The term "economic growth" denotes an increase in the output produced by the economy. The term "economic development" includes improvements in the standard of living and prosperity in the economy.

16   Casu et al. (2015).

17   For an introduction to the money creation process, see McLeary et al. (2014).

18   On the money creation process by central banks, see the presentation of Naqvi and Southgate (2013).

19   For example, Arestis et al. (2015), Bruhn and Love (2014), Han and Shen (2015), Rapp and Udoieva (2018).

20   See, for example, Lucarelli (2012), Mahmud (2013).

21   Shen and Lee (2006), Henderson et al. (2013), Rewilak (2013), Arcand et al. (2015), Broner and Ventura (2016).

22   In the absence of financial markets, the functions of financial intermediaries would need to be incorporated in business productive activities and hierarchical structures (e.g., in the absence of banks, total credit extended by a certain company would go through its own financial department). Ford Credit and GM Bank constitute typical examples.

23   On the bi-directional relationship between sovereign debt crises and financial crises, see indicatively Reinhart and Rogoff (2011).

24   For an introductory survey on varieties of capitalism, see Becker (2009).

REFERENCES

Abel, A.B., 2018. Optimal debt and profitability in the trade-off theory. *Journal of Finance*, 73(1), 95–143. https://doi.org/10.1111/jofi.12590.

Andrikopoulos, A., 2015. Truth and financial economics: A review and assessment. *International Review of Financial Analysis*, 39, 186–195. https://doi.org/10.1016/j.irfa.2014.12.003.

Arcand, J.L., Berkes, E., and Panizza, U., 2015. Too much finance? *Journal of Economic Growth*, 20(2), 105–148. https://doi.org/10.1007/s10887-015-9115-2.

Arestis, A., Chortareas, G., and Magkonis, G., 2015. The financial development and growth nexus: A meta-analysis. *Journal of Economic Surveys*, 29(3), 549–565. https://doi.org/10.1111/joes.12086.

Baker, M., and Wurgler, J., 2002. Market timing and capital structure. *Journal of Finance*, 57(1), 1–32. https://doi.org/10.1111/1540-6261.00414.

Baker, M., and Wurgler, J., 2004. A catering theory of dividends. *Journal of Finance*, 59(3), 1125–1165. https://doi.org/10.1111/j.1540-6261.2004.00658.x.

Baker, M., Mendel, B., and Wurgler, J., 2016. Dividends as reference points: A behavioral signaling approach. *Review of Financial Studies*, 29(3), 697–738. https://doi.org/10.1093/rfs/hhv058.

Becker, U., 2009. *Open varieties of capitalism: Continuity, change and performances*. New York: Palgrave Macmillan.

Brav, A., Graham, J.R., Harvey, C.R., and Michaely, R., 2005. Payout policy in the 21st century. *Journal of Financial Economics*, 77(3), 483–527. https://doi.org/10.1016/j.jfineco.2004.07.004.

Brealey, R., Myers, S., and Allen, F., 2014. *Principles of corporate finance*. 11th Edition. New York: McGraw-Hill.

Broner, F., and Ventura, J., 2016. Rethinking the effects of financial globalization. *Quarterly Journal of Economics*, 131(3), 1497–1542. https://doi.org/10.1093/qje/qjw010.

Bruhn, M., and Love, I., 2014. The real impact of improved access to finance: Evidence from Mexico. *Journal of Finance*, 69(3), 1347–1376. https://doi.org/10.1111/jofi.12091.

Casu, B., Girardone, C., and Molyneux, A., 2015. *Introduction to banking*. 2nd Edition. Harlow: Pearson.

Chung, Y.A., Na, H.S., and Smith, R., 2013. How important is capital structure policy to firm survival? *Journal of Corporate Finance*, 22, 83–103. https://doi.org/10.1016/j.jcorpfin.2013.04.002.

DeAngelo, H., DeAngelo, L., and Stulz, R.M., 2006. Dividend policy and the earned/contributed capital mix: A test of the life-cycle theory. *Journal of Financial Economics*, 81(2), 227–254. https://doi.org/10.1016/j.jfineco.2005.07.005.

DeAngelo, H., and Roll, R., 2015. How stable are corporate capital structures? *Journal of Finance*, 70(1), 373–418. https://doi.org/10.1111/jofi.12163.

Elton, E.J., Gruber, M.J., Brown, S.J., and Goetzmann, W.N., 2014. *Modern portfolio theory and investment analysis*. 9th Edition. Hoboken, NJ: Wiley.

Graham, J.R., Leary, M.T., and Roberts, M.R., 2015. A century of capital structure: The leveraging of corporate America. *Journal of Financial Economics*, 118(3), 658–683.

Han, J., and Shen, Y., 2015. Financial development and total factor productivity: Evidence from China. *Emerging Markets Finance and Trade*, 51, S261–S274. https://doi.org/10.1080/1540496X.2014.998928.

Henderson, D.J., Papageorgiou, C., and Parameter, C.F., 2013. Who benefits from financial development? New methods, new evidence. *European Economic Review*, 63, 47–67. https://doi.org/10.1016/j.euroecorev.2013.05.007.

Jensen, M.C., and Meckling, W.H., 1976. Theory of the firm: Managerial behavior, agency costs and ownership structure. *Journal of Financial Economics*, 3(4), 305–360. https://doi.org/10.1016/0304-405X(76)90026-X.

Knight, F., 1921. *Risk, uncertainty and profit*. Boston and New York: Houghton Mifflin Company.

Lucarelli, B., 2012. Financialization and global imbalances: Prelude to crisis. *Review of Radical Political Economics*, 44(4), 429–447. https://doi.org/10.1177%2F0486613411434385.

Mahmud, T., 2013. Debt and discipline: Neoliberal political economy and the working classes. *Kentucky Law Journal*, 101(1), Article 4.

Markowitz, H., 1952. Portfolio selection. *Journal of Finance*, 7(1), 77–91. https://doi.org/10.1111/j.1540-6261.1952.tb01525.x.

Markowitz, H., 1959. *Portfolio selection: Efficient diversification of investments*. New York: Wiley.

McLeary, M., Radia, A., and Thomas, R., 2014. Money creation in the modern economy. *Bank of England Quarterly Bulletin Q1*, 54(1), 14–27.

Myers, S.C., and Majluf, N.S., 1984. Corporate financing and investment decisions when firms have information that investors do not have. *Journal of Financial Economics*, 13(2), 187–221.

Naqvi, M., and Southgate, J., 2013. Banknotes, local currencies and central bank objectives. *Bank of England Quarterly Bulletin Q4*, 1–9.

Rapp, M.S., and Udoieva, I.A., 2018. What matters in the finance-growth nexus of advanced economies? Evidence from OECD countries. *Applied Economics*, 50(6), 676–690. https://doi.org/10.1080/00036846.2017.1337867.

Reinhart, C.M., and Rogoff, K.S., 2011. From financial crash to debt crisis. *American Economic Review*, 101(5), 1676–1706. https://doi.org/10.1257/aer.101.5.1676.

Rewilak, J., 2013. Finance is good for the poor but it depends on where you live. *Journal of Banking and Finance*, 37(5), 1451–1459.

Shen, C.-H., and Lee, C.C., 2006. Same financial development, yet different economic growth – Why? *Journal of Money, Credit and Banking*, 38(7), 1907–1944.

Index

Printed in the United States
by Baker & Taylor Publisher Services